Advance Praise for
Rescue the Problem Project

"Whether you are trying to prevent, identify, or recover a failing project, this book shows you how to analyze the interaction between people, process, and technology. *Rescue the Problem Project* is an insightful, comprehensive guide for recovering failing projects. The discussion of project methodologies offers a realistic look at the application of competing processes and highlights their strengths and weaknesses."

– Jackie Barretta, Senior Vice President and CIO, Con-way, Inc.

"Mr. Williams is a 25-year veteran in high-tech project recovery whose work we've seen first hand. Who better to address the acute business problem of high-tech project failure than someone who has been diagnosing and fixing this issue for years? Mr. Williams confronts this very real need head-on. Rather than [being] an overly technical or theoretical how-to book, *Rescue the Problem Project* takes a very practical approach to the issue that doesn't gloss over what is often the key driver of success: people. Through the use of multiple case studies, the application of Mr. Williams' expertise becomes very tangible for any organization."

– Dan McMillan, Vice President, Insurance Services Group, Standard Insurance Company

"In today's business climate, where change is constant and time to market is measured in days, *Rescue the Problem Project* should be compulsory reading for anyone managing projects from the newly minted project manager to program veterans. Todd has successfully distilled complex concepts into actions that are easily understood and executable at any stage of your project."

– Martin Hanssmann, President and CEO, AltaStream Consulting (Former VP Sales, Brooks Automation, Boston, MA)

"Rescue the Problem Project addresses what everyone on the team, from the CEO to the individual contributor, needs to know about recovering projects. This includes understanding the root causes to each problem that pulled the project into the red. Furthermore, it suggests actions to guide corporate change and create an agile and aggressive company."

– Dick Albani, Vice President (retired), TRW, Inc.

Rescue the Problem Project

A Complete Guide to Identifying, Preventing,
and Recovering from Project Failure

Todd C. Williams, PMP

Foreword by
Tom Kendrick

HARPERCOLLINS
LEADERSHIP

AN IMPRINT OF HARPERCOLLINS

Rescue the Problem Project

© 2011 Todd C. Williams

Published by HarperCollins Leadership, an imprint of HarperCollins Focus LLC.

Any internet addresses, phone numbers, or company or product information printed in this book are offered as a resource and are not intended in any way to be or to imply an endorsement by HarperCollins Leadership, nor does HarperCollins Leadership vouch for the existence, content, or services of these sites, phone numbers, companies, or products beyond the life of this book.

Bulk discounts available. For details visit:
www.harpercollinsleadership.com/bulkquotes
Email: customercare@harpercollins.com

ISBN 978-0-8144-3941-8

In memory of

my Dad,
William W. Williams,

and my son,
Jesse C. Williams.

Contents

Contents

Acknowledgments

Special thanks to the people who worked so hard in the preparation of this book. Barbara Chernow, Sandoval McNair, Bob Nirkind, and Bonnie Owen have continually put up with my passive voice, omission of words, and late night calls. You have been wonderful. Thanks to Cliff Gray, Tom Kendrick, and Dan McMillan for their precious time in reviewing proposals, individual chapters, and early drafts, along with their suggestions on the applicability of the material to their world.

There are also the people who have listened to me banter about this subject *ad nauseam*. They need credit for telling me when an idea was half-baked or I needed to be quiet and let someone else talk. This starts with Lori Comstock, Josef Pfister, Greg Sievers, and Tess Stewart, but must also include all the attendees of the PMI® Vancouver and Northwest Roundtables. All of you helped solidify my ideas and inspire me to write this book.

Acknowledgements would be incomplete without thanking the people I worked with while correcting too many problems on too many projects. This list includes Robert Gunderson, Paul Howe, Geoff Unland, Ted Urbanowicz, Kurt Wieneke, and many more. Without these people, I would be lacking the knowledge I have today. Thank you.

Thanks to Tammi, my beloved wife, for her encouragement while undertaking this project; to my children, Dannielle, Jesse, and Garrett, for excusing dad while he was hopping around the world every time someone asked for help; and most recently, to my granddaughter Kennedy, who vied with various editors for my attention. Lastly, an extra thought to Jesse, my oldest son, who would have been proud of this accomplishment.

Foreword

"When you are in a hole. . . ."

Most projects start well, and with perfectly good intentions. Before too long, however, many stray from this path, and the project team finds itself overwhelmed with too much to do, too little progress, and criticism from all directions. A standard response to this is to increase the pressure: "Work harder! Work faster! What are you—stupid?" This strategy rarely succeeds and often makes a bad situation even worse.

When a project is in trouble, increasing the chaos does not help. To restore order, you must first acknowledge that problems exist, and then step back to determine how best to bring the project under control. Todd Williams offers a wealth of proven practices to address this issue in *Rescue the Problem Project*, which outlines a process for recovering failing projects in clear and unambiguous terms. The steps for recovery—recognition, audit, analysis, negotiation, and reexecution—are applicable to troubled projects of nearly any type. The book provides ample guidance to assist you in tailoring the process to your specific needs.

Recovering failing projects requires help. Todd extensively addresses the support you will need, and he offers useful advice on how to secure it. You need help from the team that is presently engaged because its members know what is happening (and more often than not, what to do to fix it). You need help from management, customers, and other project stakeholders. You will probably also need help from outside the project to bring in the fresh perspective that recovery nearly always requires. You need all of this help because restoring a failing project to health inevitably depends on change. If you lack sufficient support, resistance to change will ultimately thwart all your recovery efforts. A project in motion tends to remain in motion, even when it is moving in the wrong direction.

Determining what to change begins with a realization that *red status* is a subjective, not an objective, assessment. When seeking a path forward from the current unacceptable situation, you need to thoroughly evaluate the status quo. This includes fully understanding the project's constraints, including assessing which are truly immovable and which are negotiable. You also must validate anew project requirements, remaining workflow, estimates, and resource needs. In seeking alternatives for recovery, you need this information to determine which options for the project are likely to be most acceptable and successful. *Rescue the Problem Project* offers plentiful advice for diagnosing these aspects of your ailing project.

Albert Einstein, as quoted in Chapter 17, said, "A new type of thinking is essential if mankind is to survive and move toward higher levels." Todd thoroughly addresses the usefulness of a fresh perspective in the recovery of failing projects. Effective recovery generally depends on thinking "outside the box" or, at a minimum, introducing a bit of fresh air into the mix. Changes such as this can be sensitive and political, though. You will find the tactics described here to be practical and designed to generate minimum angst.

Ultimately, of course, it is best to avoid having projects slide into yellow and then into red status. *Rescue the Problem Project* concludes with sound advice for keeping your projects within bounds. In fact, the processes included throughout this book provide excellent advice for setting up robust, successful projects. The ideas also provide effective guidance for dealing with the issues and variances while they remain small. It is much easier and less contentious to change course when you first notice that you are heading toward a cliff than after you have driven over it.

In an ideal world, using good project management skill coupled with common sense should render project recovery unnecessary. But we know that is not how things always go. Should you have a project that is wandering into the red zone, here you will find effective guidance to help you bring it back on track.

Tom Kendrick

San Carlos, CA

Introduction

"There are a great many doors open;
but a door must be of a man's size or it is not meant for him."

—Henry Ward Beecher,
Congregational Clergyman,
Henry Ward Beecher: His Life and Work

People say it is tenacity that makes me good at recovering projects. Some say it is my attention to detail; others just think I have a penchant for headaches, heartburn, and working long hours. I doubt there is one reason. As for myself, be it clocks or cars, printers or projects, I like figuring out how things work and, if broken, fixing them. After working on a variety of "red projects"—projects in shambles needing someone to put them back together—I developed a process for fixing them that also educates people on how to avoid these problems in the first place.

Of all the goals I went after in life, recovering projects was not one. Instead, recovering red projects came after me. Bosses or cohorts would call about a project in serious need of attention—it was behind schedule, losing money, confronted by an unhappy customer, or experiencing some combination of all three. Many times the conversation simply started with, "How current is your passport?" Soon I was on an airplane. Upon arrival, I would go through contracts and deliverables, talking to everyone on the project to try to understand what was working, what was missing, and what should be happening. I would put together a plan of action and sell it to management. I never really thought of it as a forte or specialization; red projects were the norm, and they needed fixing.

In the early years of my career, I had no authority to make changes. Rather, I worked through others to get the plans implemented. I started by working with bosses, superiors, and managers, getting them to sell the ideas to the people who would need to implement them. I became very good at writing copious and thorough emails that would eventually be cut and pasted into someone else's email to provide the direction needed. It was irrelevant. The project was getting fixed, and I was excited to see the plans work.

Eventually, people on the project figured out where the ideas came from and would ask me directly for advice. Soon after this discovery, I would attend management meetings and no longer needed to work through their superiors. This made it easier for them, since they looked better to their bosses; it made it easier for me, since I avoided having to deal with inaccurately relayed plans. The process, however, was awkward and created animosity. It would have worked much better if I had been given the authority to conduct the recovery.

Often, others accompanied me. At times, a group of us, a SWAT team of sorts, was dropped into a project to assess and fix the problems. Many times, we stayed on the project through to completion.

I learned to make effective use of the team as a tool. I would get the team aligned and have them drive the project's management. Befriending the key project team members enabled us to take over the project and get it moving in the right direction. Management would eventually follow.

At first, this was a little hard to do and always felt covert. Although it added a sporty and clandestine spirit to the recovery, it was an inappropriate way to run an organization. I have shied away from this, but the team-building techniques required to accomplish this are invaluable assets. A tight and dedicated team, with near gang-member mentality, is one of the most powerful and efficient groups you will find.

From this came a very important lesson—good teams with bad management can be successful. They need to know the deficiencies in the project's management and determine ways to cope with them. This became rule number one in recovering projects—the team knows what needs to be done. Finding the right people and exploiting their knowledge will get you to an answer very quickly.

Soon I realized the second lesson—mediocre teams with the right inspiration and leadership can do great things. They are only mediocre because of the way they are treated. Looking at the individuals and leveraging their strengths, instead of using them to fill a slot, is essential. When people have the wrong skills or training to do a task, they will most likely fail.

To keep in touch with the team and make it stronger, I had to be seen as a peer. I was their superior only on paper. Unlike many other project managers, I stayed in touch with the project's day-to-day activities. I refused to remain in an office or cubicle or to court the executives. I was involved with the requirements, architecture, coding, and testing of the product. I would even help write functional specifications and test scripts.

The goal with managers was to keep them apprised; appreciation would come with delivery. Executives like seeing tasks completed, but they tend to forget about the project once it begins running well. This is good, in my opinion; the last thing I want is the CEO visiting my desk on a daily basis. I learned to overcome the disadvantages created by my lack of visibility.

To this day, my mode of operation is to get into the project; talk to the people involved; learn what is wrong; create a recovery plan; negotiate the details with the project sponsor, executive management, or the steering committee; and then disappear into the project, spending as little time as needed with senior management. Immersion in the project is by far the best way to fix it.

This led to the third lesson—stay immersed in the team. By doing this I can see and feel the project move. There is no need for status reports because I am there. I understand all sides of an issue and can direct the team. I know the project's details and intricacies at all times. The downside is that summarization can be difficult. I am often asked, "Can't you just give a yes or no answer?" My reply is "No. . . Oh, I guess I can. Oops, maybe not." People usually laugh. They may be frustrated with the verbosity, but they know I am providing well-researched opinions. If people want details, they get them quickly and completely. They rarely second guess my understanding of a project.

This resulted in the fourth lesson—objective data is your friend. Most people know this as data is power. It is only powerful, however, if held close. Shared data is friendly and powerful. When faced with an issue or unanticipated question, fact-based decisions are the key to going in the right direction and being trusted to do the right thing.

Armed with these four lessons:

1. The answers are in the team.
2. A strong team can surmount most problems.
3. Stay involved with the team.
4. Objective data is your friend, providing the key way out of any situation.

I join a project and work to fix its ills.

The Recovery Process

Rescue the Problem Project is for anyone trying to find the missing link in managing a project, regardless of whether it is in trouble. The project manager, customer, project sponsor, executive management, steering committee member, or individual contributor all have something to learn here. Although this book teaches how to recover a failing project, failure's harsh lessons bring knowledge. The book is full of lessons to keep a project on track. The focus is to show what to do for a project that has gotten into serious trouble; trouble that is at the point of impasse where the team cannot come to consensus on the issues facing it. At this stage of the project, everyone is defensive; finger pointing and laying blame is the norm. The project has stalled.

These lessons teach a number of techniques to become a better manager and transform you into a leader. When recovering a project, solid teams are required. With red projects, teams are often beat up and demoralized. Therefore, the recovery manager must allocate a significant amount of time for rebuilding the team and regaining the respect of its members.

As outlined in Chapter 1, and discussed in detail in each section, this book will lead you through a series of steps that make up the recovery process once there is a realization of a problem. These steps are:

0. Realization of a problem: Management must realize there is a problem to solve before the process can be established.
1. Audit the project: Objectively determine the problems on the project.
2. Analyze the data: Determine the root causes for the problems and develop a solution.
3. Negotiate the solution: Meditate an acceptable solution between the supplier and customer.
4. Execute the new plan: Implement the corrective actions to the problems, and run the project.

Critical to success is management's realization that a problem exists. This is step zero in the process (see Figure 1-2 on pg. 9). It is a prerequisite to all other steps. It enables you to build the outline of any process. For example, before planning a trip to the grocery store, you must realize that you need food. Then, you can plan the steps of the trip. Without this step, the problems and subsequent corrective action plan lack upper management's endorsement, and the recovery will fail from a lack of its support. Chapter 2 discusses this.

It is worth pointing out the four integrally numbered steps of this process are a negotiation process:

Audit the project – Acquire data about the subject. Determine the customer's goals based on what is truly valuable in the product—the items critical to quality.

Analyze the data – Determine the options to meet the request. Look at the data accrued and determine the options available to solve the problems. Highlight the proposed solution's advantages.

Negotiate the solution – Propose the options. Barter around the recommended solution to address concerns voiced by the customer and management. Achieve the highest value for all stakeholders.

Execute the new plan – Close the deal. Document and implement the agreed on solution.

Chapter 14, which focuses on the negotiation process' proposal and bartering step, discusses these. That being said, this book only covers the aspects of negotiation relevant to project recovery. You should spend some time with a good book on negotiation. Appendix 2 recommends two such books.

The Case Studies

The text includes detailed descriptions of the work required and numerous case studies. Every project has something unique, so tracking what works or is unsuccessful in correcting issues is the best education for recovering the next project.

The case studies are based primarily on manufacturing and information technology projects. They illustrate the types of behavior to watch for and what helped or hindered the recovery; underscore a point; and demonstrate techniques used to approach some aspect of the project. Although some characteristics are distinct to these projects, namely the technology issues, most of the techniques can be applied to other disciplines. They come from 25 years of experience as a project manager and architect. They are for products developed internally or by third parties.

The projects cover a breadth of styles, including large-scale system integration of manufacturing systems, equipment integration, Web-based collaboration tools, thick clients with automated Internet updates, and business systems integration. They were located along the Pacific Rim, throughout North America, and in the Middle East; the teams were dispersed in as many as five countries, three continents, and countless time zones. Some of these projects were captive, in-house, time-and-materials projects, while others were outsourced fixed-priced contracts.

Most projects completed successfully after realigning the objectives and teams to ensure all parties received value from the deliverable. Based on the initial audit's recommendation, cancellation was the only logical option for the rest.

A few of the problems repeated across projects. Table I-1 summarizes the more common problems encountered. Unfortunately, the resolutions had little in common.

Table I-1: Major Failure Reasons

Problem Area	Type of Problem
Team	Communication
	Attitude and motivation
	Skill set
	Interrelationships
Process	Change management and scope issues
	Documentation
	Estimation and scheduling
	Risk management
Customer	Incomplete understanding of product
	Lack of project management
	Difficult, trying to get something outside of scope

There is a disclaimer on the case studies. Most people like seeing their names in print, but not every place. The exceptions include the police blotter, most newspaper headlines, and this book. Therefore, the case studies are written with discretion. General descriptions, in all but a few cases, obfuscate the source client, project, and, for that matter, person. Still, if you participated on one of these projects, you may take exception to some of the details. In trying to conceal the client, nonpertinent information has been altered—maybe gender or product type. In addition, some of these situations happened almost identically on multiple projects, so please resist jumping to conclusions. Missing an accurate synopsis of one project may frustrate you. If the project were yours, however, the alteration would surely be appreciated.

How to Use This Book

Rescue the Problem Project is not another how-to book on project management. It assumes that you are familiar with project best practices as defined by the Project Management Institute's (PMI®) PMBOK® or the UK's Office of Government Commerce PRINCE2™. This book is for people who need an understanding of the special needs of a project in serious trouble. Numerous other books will provide templates on how to run a project. One worth mentioning is *Project Rescue: Avoiding a*

Project Management Disaster by Sanjiv Purba and Joseph Zucchero. It provides significant background in basic project management. Its primary thrust is process.

As with any rule, there are exceptions. Even though this book shies away from remedial topics, three chapters (Chapter 7, "Determining and Initiating Remedial Action," Chapter 19, "Properly Dealing with Risk," and Chapter 20, "Implementing Effective Change Management") describe some common-sense project management skills. These are the most ignored and frequent causes of methodology failures in projects. Therefore, a little process education is appropriate. Implement the guidance in Chapters 7 and 20 as soon as possible after the audit—far in advance of getting the full recovery plan approved.

To use the book as a desktop reference, it will be helpful to see the parallels in the sections on auditing and analyzing. Problems on red projects are intertwined and more difficult to solve. Read the entire book first. If you are looking to solve a problem using the techniques described in the auditing and analyzing sections, there is not a one-to-one correlation. Table I-2 maps a how the audit chapters align with the analysis chapters.

Table I-2: Chapter Relationships

Audit	Analyze
Chapter 3 - Assessing the Human Role in Project Failure	Chapter 7 - Determining and Initiating Remedial Action
	Chapter 8 - Building an Extended Project Team
Chapter 4 - Auditing Scope on a Red Project	Chapter 11 - How Agile Methodology Can Assist in a Recovery
	Chapter 13 - Comparing the Relative Value of Methodologies for Project Recovery
	Chapter 20 - Implementing Effective Change Management
Chapter 5 - Determining Timeline Constraints	Chapter 10 - Assessing How Methodology Affects the Project
	Chapter 11 - How Agile Methodology Can Assist in a Recovery
	Chapter 12 - How Critical Chain Methodology Can Assist in a Recovery
Chapter 6 - Examining Technology's Effect on the Project	Chapter 9 - Considering Options for Realigning Technology

Some projects will only need a subset of the investigation outlined in this book. If the scope is well under control, then there is no need to spend copious amounts of time on it. You need to apply discretion on the extent of the application.

To create a reasonably sized book, some subjects are described further on the book's Web site. This includes additional case studies, information on auditing complex project structures, project management style, and templates. The appendix contains a partial list of this material.

By the end of *Rescue the Problem Project*, you will have a thorough understanding of the recovery process and, in theory, have the information needed to move forward in taming an errant beast. As with everything in life, knowledge holds little to the wisdom experience brings. Therefore, start slowly.

Understanding the Process and Realizing a Problem Exists

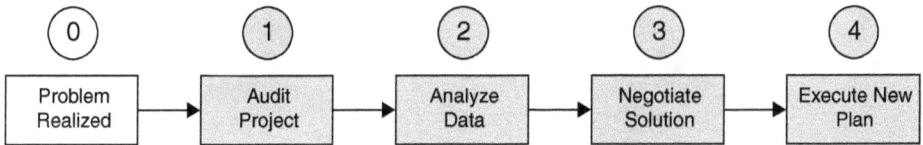

0	1	2	3	4
Problem Realized	Audit Project	Analyze Data	Negotiate Solution	Execute New Plan

A project has a problem that needs corrective action. The team is aware of the trouble and is frustrated. The members have tried to describe the issues and their negative implications to senior management, but their concerns have gone unheard. This problem will continue until management acknowledges it.

Before a project can become a candidate for recovery, senior management must:

- Recognize that the project is in trouble.
- Make a commitment to fixing it.
- Establish recovery guidelines.
- Assign a recovery manager.

Unless management commits to these four steps, the project will continue to flounder and failure is inevitable.

This section introduces the fundamentals of the recovery process. It explains the terms needed to describe and discuss troubled projects, outlines the steering committee's responsibilities, and defines the qualifications a recovery manager needs to succeed. The actions described in this section lay the foundation for a successful recovery.

1

The Basics of the Recovery Process

"Red: any of a group of colors that may vary in lightness and saturation and whose hue resembles that of blood."

—*The American Heritage Dictionary*

Projects do not self-destruct—they need help. The people on and around the project provide that assistance. Neither do projects get into trouble overnight. It takes time, and usually the failure starts shortly after someone thinks, "It would really be cool if we could . . ." From that point forward, the project's future is destined for success or failure. In other words, a project's fate is sealed from the time of its first concept, long before it is actually considered a project.

Rather than the dreams or required innovation they are based on, projects fail because of the way they are managed. For example, projects that develop highly innovative products need a structure to accommodate unknowns, rapid change in the concept, and all the other challenges of new product development. Projects based on mundane repetitive activities need the rigor of a process and the awareness that, despite superficial appearances, no project is simple. Both complex and simple projects—and all those in between—need a proper foundation. Without one, any project will end up red.

As with all effective communication, the first step is a mutual understanding of common goals. Unless you define such basic terms as *success* and *failure*, a red project cannot be saved. It is even a good idea to define the term *project*, whose meaning varies depending on the user's point of reference.

The Context of a Project

The Project Management Institute's (PMI®) and the UK's Office of Government Commerce's (OGC) definitions of a *project* are equivalent. These important definitions are referenced throughout this book.

PMI's® A Guide to the *Project Management Body of Knowledge*, Fourth Edition (PMBOK® Guide), defines a project as

> "a temporary endeavor undertaken to create a unique product, service, or result."[1]

According to OGC's PRINCE2™, a project is

> "a temporary organization that is created for the purpose of delivering one or more business products according to an agreed Business Case."[2]

Even if we accept these definitions, the term *project* is relative based on the charters of the groups participating in an endeavor. All projects are actually two projects—the customer's and the supplier's. And, depending on the structure required to build the product, there may be numerous other project perspectives; for example, a subcontractor selected to work on some part of the project. Figure 1-1 illustrates the varying perspectives that are possible for a project.

The criteria used to define project's success or failure is derived from the perspectives of the various participants. The *customer* and the *supplier* teams may all work for the same company, but each group has specific responsibilities and goals. One team cannot realistically be expected to fulfill the responsibilities of another team that did not meet its goals, except when the failure of one team causes failure in the other. In such a case, there must be substantial support if the rescue effort is to be successful, as well as significant reward (value) for the rescuing team.

From the customer's perspective, the project is successful when it meets its delivery, budget, and value goals, regardless of the supplier's trials and tribulations. On the other hand, if, say, the customer specifies the product incorrectly or misidentifies the desired market, the project is a failure.

From the supplier's perspective, regardless of the project team's overall performance, a project is a failure if it is significantly over budget. However, a customer's product marketing failure does not translate into failure for the supplier. As shown in Figure 1-1, a subcontractor has its own perspectives on a project. Therefore, each team's point of view sets the relative definition of *success, failure, red,* and other terms.

Figure 1-1: Perspectives on a Project

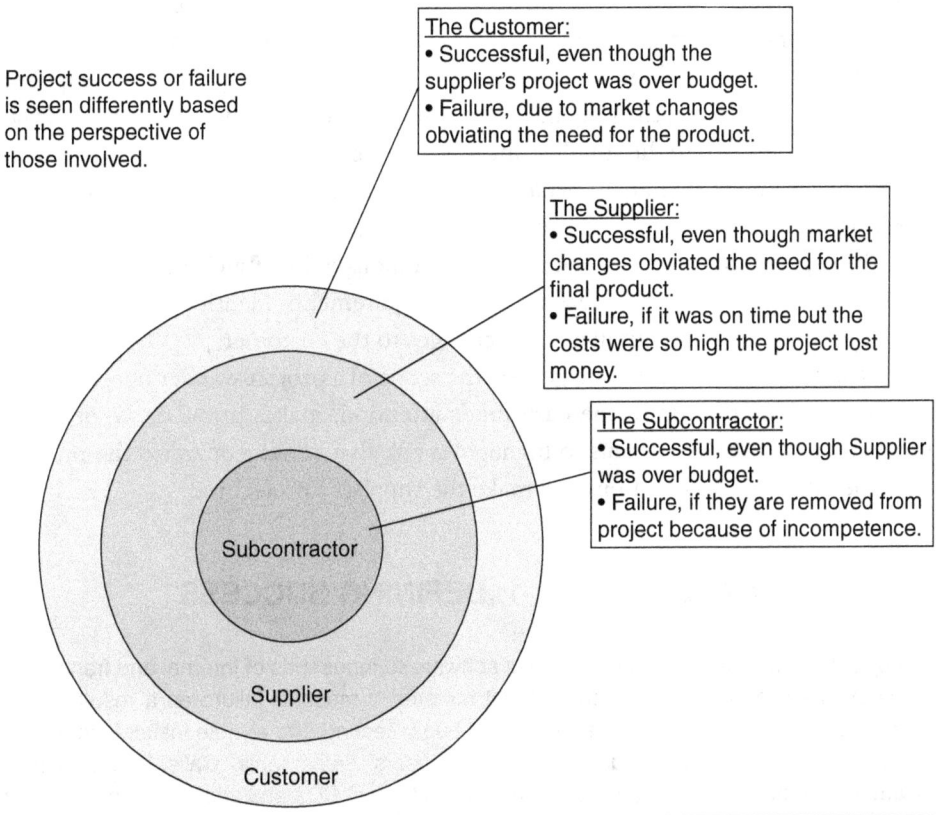

Project success or failure
is seen differently based
on the perspective of
those involved.

The Customer:
• Successful, even though the
supplier's project was over budget.
• Failure, due to market changes
obviating the need for the product.

The Supplier:
• Successful, even though market
changes obviated the need for the
final product.
• Failure, if it was on time but the
costs were so high the project lost
money.

The Subcontractor:
• Successful, even though Supplier
was over budget.
• Failure, if they are removed from
project because of incompetence.

Subcontractor

Supplier

Customer

Understanding Project Success

The definition of project *success* is:

- The project delivers value to all parties in the project.
- The project maintains the scope, schedule, and cost established by the original definition, as well as any before-the-fact change orders.

Delivering value to all parties means that both the customer and supplier get *what they need;* the project's original definition is irrelevant in determining whether this has happened. For instance, it makes no sense to deliver the original design if it fails to meet the customer's needs. The definition of product value changes in tandem with overall business conditions; the project must adapt to those changes in a proactive manner. The frequency of change is an unreasonable gauge for judging whether a project is in trouble; improperly managed change always threatens the success of a project.

As for the second point, the scope, timeline, and budget that evolve over the course of a project may differ greatly from the original definitions, leaving the customer feeling that the project is less than successful. However, if the project managers manage change (identifying and initiating changes proactively) and the supplier delivers on its promises, the project is successful from the supplier's standpoint. The customer, as opposed to the supplier, must be held accountable for the poor planning and inadequate assessment of its needs. The project is fulfilling the customer's business needs; its subject matter experts must define the goal.

The supplier does own a small part of the responsibility in such a case. Generally, the supplier should be able to detect a drift in requirements, identify changes that are inappropriate, and point out ill-advised changes to the customer.

If the supplier's project manager lets the scope of a project wander uncontrolled, fails to call discrepancies to the customer's attention, makes promises he or she is incapable of delivering, or fails to highlight a risk that could jeopardize the project, then the effects of these actions can make the supplier's project red.

CASE STUDY 1-1: DEFINING SUCCESS

A project that was delivering vehicle sales software to thousands of internal and franchised sales units across North America had just suffered a massive failure as a result of two problems. First, the product had a number of bugs; second, the remote install feature had failed, thereby disabling hundreds of remote users' sales tools. Calls for assistance swamped the help desk, and it was taking weeks to mail CDs and assist novice computer users in manually installing the product. The team was under extreme pressure to release a bug fix.

The bug fixes were going to be distributed over the Internet. They required using the same tools that failed in the prior deployment, but hopefully all the issues had been resolved. When the team, severely demoralized and nervous, asked how to measure the success of the deployment, I responded with the following criteria:

- Rapid and professional handling of anticipated issues.
- Identification of all risk in the deployment.
- Having working mitigation plans for potential problems.

The deployment was successful, exercising only a few mitigation plans, all of which worked. In other words, the problems were anticipated and properly mitigated.

What Is a Red Project?

The designation of a project as *red* derives from the commonly used green-yellow-red color system. The organization defines a set of project attributes that are monitored (say scope, budget, schedule, quality, and resources) and assigns a formula to indicate the degree of control. Next, the appropriate color designation thresholds are defined: green, for okay; yellow when the project has minor issues; and red for a project that is in trouble. For instance, management might decide that if the period-to-date actual cost is less than 10 percent different from its projected value, then the budget is green; everything is okay. However, if the actual is between 10 and 15 percent off, it is considered yellow. More than 15 percent off, it is red. Additional shop-defined conditions may further state that if two or more monitored factors are red (say, time and resources), then the project is red.

In other words, a project is red when unanticipated and uncontrolled actions cause senior management to determine that it is performing insufficiently, based on agreed parameters. Being red is a subjective quality of a project, an unanticipated variance from the project's current definition based on each organization's rules. As discussed, the project's perspective constrains the extent to which this designation will affect each participating group. The supplier's portion of the project can be red, while the customer's project is under control, or vice versa. From the supplier's point of view, as long as the agreed-on parameters are met, a project is not red.

What Is Project Failure?

A project is a *failure* when its product is unsuccessful in providing value to all the parties. From the customer's standpoint, the product the project is building provides the value; from the supplier's side, it is most likely the revenue. If a project is supposed to deliver on a certain date, no sooner and no later, finishing early will have as negative a result as being late. To ignore an issue and let it continue unabated will result in failure.

As long as change requests account for any changes in schedule and budget, the ability to accept numerous requests, even if they significantly alter the project's scope, indicates a healthy change management process. Numerous changes may, however, be a death knell for the customer's project. Too many changes will drive up costs and delay the project, even if these attributes were incorrect from the beginning.

What Is Project Recovery?

When a project has been *recovered*, new plans and processes have addressed the issues that caused its red status. The project has been through a corrective action process; its current parameters fall within newly planned limits, and all parties (customer and suppliers) are amenable to the project's proposed outcome. The scope may be different, the timeline may be elongated, or the project may even be canceled.

Canceling a project may seem like a failure, but for a project to be successful, it must provide value to all parties. The best value is to minimize the project's overall negative impact on all parties in terms of both time and money. If the only option is to proceed with a scaled-down project, one that delivers late, or one that costs significantly more, the result may be worse than canceling the project. It may be more prudent to invest the time and resources on an alternate endeavor or to reconstitute the project in the future using a different team and revised parameters.

When recovering a project, there is also the option of doing nothing. Doing nothing based on ignorance will most likely result in failure. However, performing an audit or analysis of a project and then making a decision to make no changes is an action—a conscious decision to let the problems resolve themselves. This is a valid choice. The best example of this is when a project is incorrectly declared to be in trouble; for example, a set of people (say, other managers or a group of politicians) may claim a project is in trouble for their own reasons. An example of this, which resulted from a lack of understanding the project's risk, is discussed in Chapter 19.

The Recovery Process

Red projects need recovery. Something must change. Time has been lost and money spent; one or both are over established limits. The recovery plan (a deliverable of the recovery process) is necessarily different from the original project plan. In fact, the recovered project's product or service may bear little resemblance to the initial concept. Because of these changes, the project sponsor and executive management need to agree to and approve the changes; however, arriving at an amenable solution will require negotiation. Therefore, to design a successful *recovery process*, the best approach is to adapt the four general steps of a negotiation process (see Figure 1-2). As part of the resulting process, a recovery manager formulates a recovery plan and mediates step 3, the actual negotiation.

Before recovering a project, the project sponsor, executive management, or steering committee must realize that the project has a problem and needs new direction. Without this understanding and commitment to change, recovery is impossible.

A qualified recovery manager, rather than management, needs to invest time in the project and determine what is actually wrong. When management steps in to help, the recovery effort is likely to be part time and consists of asking for reports or meetings. It does little to find root problems. To properly analyze and fix the project requires a different approach. It needs well-planned corrective actions and a true recovery process, not point fixes. The realization process' deliverables are funding, a dedicated recovery manager, and guidelines for the recovery.

Once the executives understand a problem's impact, they must set the recovery's parameters by providing recovery guidelines for an acceptable outcome. This process begins with the realization step in the core recovery process—step zero in Figure 1-2.

After accepting that the project has problems, recovery proceeds in four steps—audit the project, analyze the data, negotiate the solution, and execute the new plan. In general, it is best to follow these steps in order, but remedial processes may be implemented in the analysis phase.

The first step in the recovery process is an *audit* to assess the project and understand the issues it has encountered. The audit is a raw and, therefore, objective data-gathering procedure. The recovery manager systematically gathers all the information about the project for analysis.

The second step is to *analyze* this information to formulate a corrective action and recovery plan based on root-cause analysis of the issues plaguing the project. In this step, the information is collated, combined, and analyzed for trends, patterns, and problems. As the problems are solved, the errant project becomes a normal project that is easier to manage. This is a distinguishing feature of my approach; other approaches often omit root-cause analysis or leave it for the end of the process.

Although determining root causes up front takes more time and requires making tough decisions early, in the end it requires less management and increases the odds of a successful recovery. If root-cause analysis is left to the end of the process, it may never occur. Executives can decide to cut the process, along with other retrospective analyses, because of a lack of interest or as a cost-saving measure. By this point, managers feel that the project has already cost too much, and they just want the project behind them.

Figure 1-2: First Correction Steps

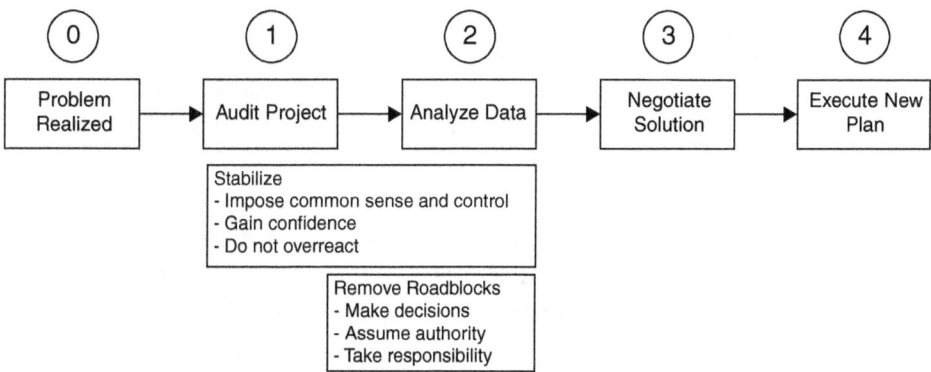

In contrast, when all root causes are uncovered, the recovery manager can best determine and document the corrective actions needed to fix those issues. In addition, he or she assembles the recovery plan, with multiple alternatives, to complete the newly redefined project. The plan's goal is to fix the issues at their root and then, after arriving at a compromise on the new scope, schedule, and budget, to deliver the product.

CASE STUDY 1-2: THE PROBLEM'S EXTENT

A red project never has one problem causing its ills. Following is a representative list of issues that threatened a $1.2 million project to deliver sales tools to a sales and marketing organization:

- Scope creep
- Maintenance included in the project
- End user undefined
- Project sponsor undefined
- Executive management failing to monitor the project
- Releasing all functionality in one release
- Product maintenance group missing
- Failure to delegate authority to the people needing it
- Trying to do too much with the skill set available
- Inability to make decisions

Only three of the issues above are root causes:

- End user undefined
- Inappropriate executive management involvement
- Product maintenance group missing

The recovery plan is necessarily different from the existing project plan. Something must change, as time has been lost and money spent; one or the other is over budget. Stakeholders need to approve any changes. Therefore, the third step is to *negotiate the solution*—to propose and barter an acceptable resolution. Although most people consider this step the entire negotiation process, it is actually the shortest part of a complete process. In this step, the plan that most closely fits the recovery guidelines is proposed, and the recovery manager tailors the solution to meet the stakeholders' desires.

It is poor practice to incorporate "gates" into this series of steps—that is, to require the completion of one step prior to starting the next. Such an approach adds unnecessary overhead and jeopardizes the recovery's success. Throughout this book, there are multiple references to actions where strict step sequence should be preserved; for some steps, "ASAP" may be too slow. For example, Figure 1-2 presents some remedial actions that can be taken to address obvious failures. These actions may include such simple steps as implementing change management or improving communication processes.

One cannot ignore that the project is ongoing while the recovery process is proceeding. It takes time to get to a resolution, but it is also imprudent to continue spending money on a failing project. Therefore, there are two options:

1. Stop the project
2. Slow the bleeding

The second is the preferred option for three primary reasons:

1. To properly diagnose a system, it must be running. Stopping the project also stops the errant behavior and makes it difficult to find problems and their root causes.
2. Waiting until after the recovery plan acceptance to implement all the changes increases the risk to the project by increasing the number of changes that must happen simultaneously. Remedial changes can take place while the recovery team is still auditing and analyzing.
3. Implementing remedial fixes exercises the system in a new way by both changing and tightening processes. These activities will uncover other issues to address and often point to some root causes.

These considerations justify overlapping the recovery process steps. Although some situations may benefit from stopping a project following either the audit or the analysis, these are rare. A better approach is to slow the bleeding by implementing remedial fixes. Also, exercising the system while the audit, analysis, and negotiation are under way will uncover other issues.

Roles in the Extended Project Structure

The roles in a project vary greatly from organization to organization, even among standards organizations. What follows are typical roles on the extended project team. Figure 1-3 illustrates their logical relationships, beginning with the steering committee.

- The *steering committee* is comprised of managers and executives from the supplier and the customer who guide the project. They provide high-level guidance and are the final level of escalation for project issues. Outsourced projects often use this concept. This group should recommend bringing in the recovery manager and set the guidelines for the recovery. In the absence of a steering committee, the project sponsor and someone from executive management may perform this function.

The team is then divided into two main groups that include other role categories:

- *Customer:* The group paying for and receiving the project's product or service. The customer may be within or outside the supplier's company. Roles on the customer side include the project sponsor, the customer's project team, and the end users.
- *Supplier or contractor:* The group paid to manage and provide the project's product or service. This group, which includes executive management, the

Figure 1-3: Extended Project Team

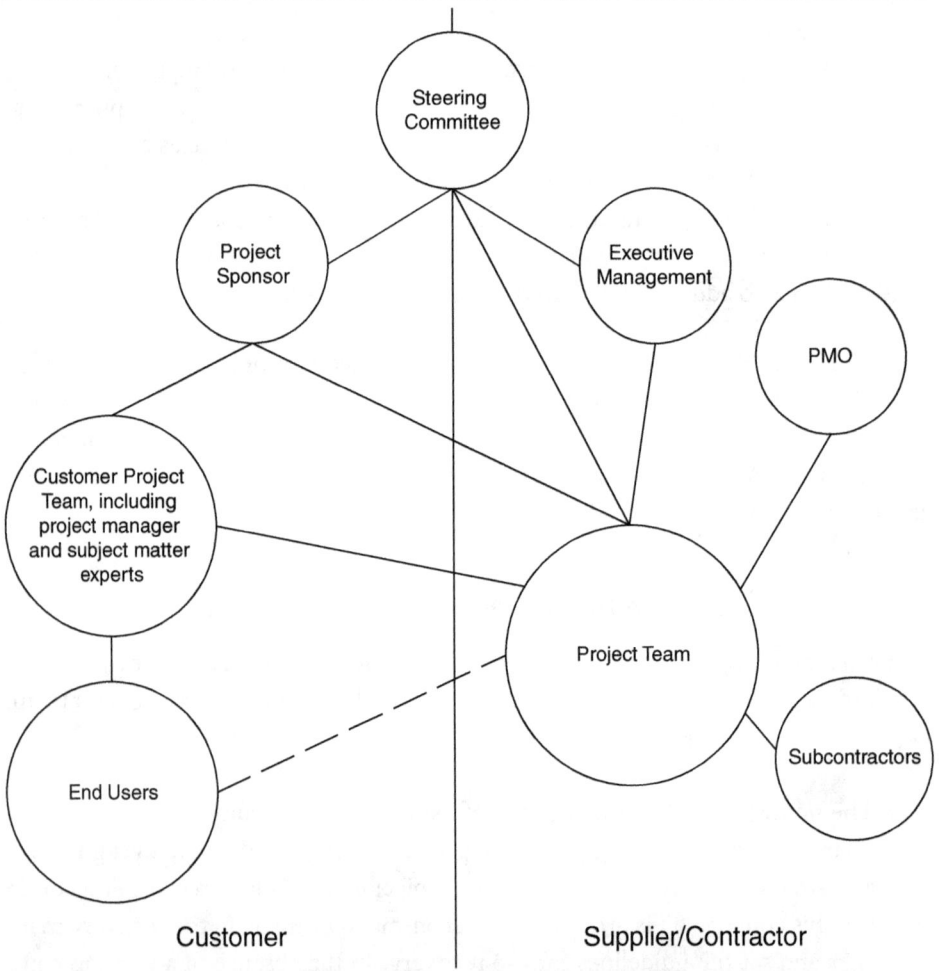

Project Management Office (PMO), the project team, and any subcontractors, may belong to the same company as the customer (that is, it is another business unit).

Other roles include:

- *Executive management:* The set of managers for the team who are paid to provide the product or service. A subset of the executive management group should sit on the steering committee.
- *Project sponsor:* The primary representative for the customer. The project sponsor approves payment for the product or service. He or she is the person from the customer's organization who is responsible for the project delivery and who has authority over all aspects of the customer's side of the project. This person is the final escalation point for project issues before sending them to the steering committee.
- *Project* or *Program Management Office (PMO):* A governance body providing project management and process guidance. In some organizations, this group may assist in staging projects to level the workload. Members may also orchestrate resource assignment. Many industries do not include this function in extended project teams.
- *Customer project team:* For most projects, the customer has a parallel project team that performs an accompanying set of tasks, including requirements definition, training, and testing. Team members can include the customer's project manager, subject matter experts (SMEs), analysts, trainers, and other talents as needed.
- *End users:* Most often, the customer's project team is different from the product's or service's end users. The project team should have access to this group of people. If end users are missing from the team, note this as a project risk.
- *Project team:* The group of people funded to build the product or service and the supporting infrastructure. The project manager directly manages this group, which is separate from the customer's project team, although, customers may be included.
- *Subcontractor:* An outside company usually brought in by the supplier (the prime contractor) to provide part of the solution.

Projects may have a larger or smaller number of groups, but the functions outlined above must be present in some form for the project to have proper direction.

Chapter Takeaway

- A successful project delivers the product or service the customer requested within the established schedule and budget after processing all before-the-fact change requests. All parties who participate in the project must receive value from the project.

- *Red* is a subjective term that indicates a project is failing—that is, it is outside the acceptable limits defined by the organization.

- A failing project is experiencing uncontrolled changes in scope, schedule, or budget, or is on track to deliver a product or service that does not provide value to the customer or supplier.

- Recovering an errant project requires bringing it within new parameters and addressing the root causes of the problems.

- Before starting a recovery process, the project sponsor and executive management must acknowledge that a problem exists, commit to fixing it, provide guidelines for the recovery, and assign the recovery manager.

- The recovery process is similar to a negotiation process. It is a four-step procedure that occurs only when the problem has been recognized and acknowledged. The four steps are auditing the project, analyzing the data, negotiating a solution, and implementing the recovery plan.

- The project should remain running while being recovered so the problems can be seen firsthand.

CHAPTER

2

Management's Responsibility in Identifying the Problem

"All problems become smaller if you don't dodge them but confront them."

—Admiral William F. Halsey, U.S. Navy Fleet Admiral, World War II

All afflictions, from everyday ailments to addictions, have one thing in common—if people choose to ignore them, they remain untreated. Therefore, before you start any process you must admit there is a problem. Without admitting a problem exists and committing to resolve it, the problem will continue. It may morph and manifest itself in a new way, but it still exists.

The same is true for red projects. Before recovering any project, the proper authority, ideally the steering committee, must declare the project in trouble and commit to fixing it. This sounds obvious, but achieving this state is difficult. Pride, ego, emotion, denial, and inertia intrude. Project managers think they can correct the problems themselves or their management approaches the issues by creating new tasks, processes, spreadsheets, and reports. Eventually, the customer becomes aware of the situation and goes to the executive management or the steering committee demanding action. The latter step is the only effective one, as it escalates the problem to the people who can make a difference—executives able to make the decision to fund someone to audit the project.

Declaring a Project Red

Because the customer has escalated the issue, the project becomes red without any official metrics, charts, or reports. Even if people on the team have warned executives, management is still surprised. Of course, escalation can also occur without the customer reacting. The astute project manager who sees the project is out of control can report that condition, but this is rare and usually indicates the situation is even worse than the reports indicate. The result is that the steering committee must declare the project is red.

For this action to have meaning, however, it must result in the steering committee providing direction and funding for project recovery. The single most valuable action that executives can take is to approve funding to bring in a qualified person to recover the project; the people involved in the project are already too deep in the forest to distance themselves enough to see the problem issues.

CASE STUDY 2-1: BEING RED THROUGH RUMOR

A semiconductor manufacturing automation project had been running for multiple years. Progress seemed slow, but the project and program manager assured the steering committee that it was on track for completion in three months. Executive management requested I join the project as a test manager, so that a new set of eyes could provide a perspective on the project's internal workings.

Numerous issues made the delivery date impossible to hit. The situation was inconsistent with the rosy picture presented to management. Team communication had broken down, the customer was unable to get answers, and specifications failed to line up. Acting as a mole on the project, I reported the problems to upper management, whose members were too removed to see how dire the situation had become.

The project's management knew communication problems existed within the team, but it was trying to hide the discord to save people's jobs. Nonetheless, shortly after my report, the project was declared red, thereby initiating corrective action.

Had the project management team admitted the problem sooner, corrective action could have begun much earlier. In the end, many people were terminated because the cost overruns put a huge strain on the company.

The steering committee provides recovery guidelines that detail the bounds within which the recovery manager is required to work. These guidelines define the recovery's direction and propose a suitable solution. They may include timeframes, budgets, or other constraints, or they may be vaguer, such as the instruction "to bring the project down to size where it is delivering only the product's essential functionality." Regardless, the bounds must be set. Without guidelines, the recovery manager is directionless.

After declaring a project red, the steering committee needs to assign someone to audit and repair it. This is the first test, as management is probably part of the problem. Unless someone is assigned to the recovery, the problems will persist. Similarly, if there is too much personal investment in the project to encourage action, its recovery will stall. Still, over time, this is self-correcting. On a project, time is money, and eventually someone will get tired of paying. A boss, or even stockholders, will eventually issue a directive to hire someone to make the assessment that will result in the project's correction or its cancellation.

Assigning a recovery manager to audit or recover the project gives implicit authority to the recovery manager to do whatever is necessary to get the project under control and, then, propose a corrective action plan. This may include the right to make decisions, realign staff, negotiate alternatives, and reopen issues that may have been closed without proper due diligence. More succinctly, it is the authority to root out the project's ills and fix them.

There is another important aspect to calling the project red—the acknowledgement that action is required. The project will need to change because it is late, over budget, or both. To correct its problems will necessitate some combination of a later delivery date, higher cost, and less scope. By declaring the project red, management gives tacit approval to the severe action that is required.

Assigning a recovery manager, especially if from outside the team, sends a message to the team that this is a serious issue, and it needs to heed the direction being given.

Traits of a Good Recovery Manager

Selecting the right recovery manager is critical. Avoid choosing someone currently involved with the project, as people involved in the project are too close to see the issues and may be perceived as biased by the stakeholders. At a minimum, the person doing the audit should be someone outside the extended project and unassociated with the product. An objective view is critical to a proper audit and reducing any preconceptions of a solution. The ideal candidate is a seasoned, objective project manager who is external to the supplier and customer, has recovery experience, and a strong technical background (for the conversations with the technical team). Compare this with hiring a financial auditor. No one would ever recommend engaging someone internal or with no experience, as it would create too high a chance of someone not believing the audit results.

CASE STUDY 2-2:
LOYALTY QUIZ FOR THE RECOVERY MANAGER

Too often, the hiring organization wants the recovery manager's allegiance. However, the recovery manager must remain independent. This may create difficulties if the recovery manager finds problems attributable to the organization funding his or her position.

For example, an IT department was doing a very poor job of delivering a sales tool to the business unit on an internal project. The director of IT asked me where my loyalties were: "Are you more loyal to IT or the business unit?" I replied, "Neither. My loyalty is to the project."

This should also be true for a project manager. If a project manager becomes biased about specific parts of the project, thereby failing to maintain a fair and equitable relationship between the supplier and customer, the project will get in trouble.

Effective leadership is required in project recovery. Recoveries need leaders, not just managers. The recovery manager must work with the project sponsor, executive management, project team, and other stakeholders to determine what is wrong, negotiate a solution, and take corrective action. At first, the recovery manager's job is management and control. However, this quickly turns to leadership when defining and implementing changes. Such leadership is probably missing from the project, so its addition will be greatly welcomed.

Attributes for leaders include being supportive of the team, and accountable for the team's actions, stepping in to break a stalemate, clarifying the ambiguity in the project, being objective, and addressing problems with concise, clear decisions. The recovery manager must turn the team from the past, step over blame, and push the project toward a new beginning, thereby creating hope and excitement. Of these, two traits are the most important—decision making and accountability.

Projects become red because they faltered under the guidance and supervision of the existing steering committee, project sponsor, executive management, and PMO. This group of executives has failed to identify and correct problems before the project fell into serious trouble. While none of these groups is responsible for the project's proper execution—that is the project manager's responsibility—they have responsibility for monitoring and guidance. They were either unsuccessful at seeing the problems in time to correct the situation or are contributing to their development. The project manager should be accountable for all that has gone on, but the project's management should have checks and balances to minimize the chances of failure. The extended project's entire organizational structure may be at fault.

CASE STUDY 2-3: GETTING PEOPLE ON THE SAME PAGE

At times, the two teams may be so far apart that the recovery manager needs to sit in the middle and renegotiate the project and the relationship. One such project involved a vendor that was designing and implementing a custom manufacturing automation system for an electronics manufacturing company. Although delivery was supposed to be imminent, the audit showed that the system was far from complete. The relationship between project members had become acidic, with both making claims about deliverables that had no basis in the contractual documents. The only solution was to seat them around a table to go through the contract and come up with a mutually agreed upon set of deliverables. Had the project managers been familiar with the contract deliverables, these answers would have been readily available. Relations would have been fact-based and unemotional.

Above all, recovery managers need to be honest brokers—objectivity is paramount. They cannot have allegiance to either side of the project. Unfortunately, their loyalty often leans to the side of the project approving the timecards. This is the reason the steering committee, a mixture of suppliers and customers whose focus is a successful project, should be responsible for bringing in the recovery manager.

Recovery managers must honestly assess both the supplier's and customer's interests. This requires an objective assessment of the problems and conflicts, with recommendations for fair and equitable resolutions. Fact-based nonpartisan decisions will win the project participants' respect and enlist cooperation.

To achieve this, recovery managers become mediators in a negotiation process. This is a difficult task. Being human, they form opinions quickly. People like to please others, and being objective in a highly partisan environment is a challenging goal. Recovery managers, however, need to be neutral in developing the recovery plan. Otherwise, the solution will be unacceptable to a large portion of the stakeholders and the recovery manager's job will become virtually impossible.

Too often, the organization paying for the recovery wants the recovery manager's allegiance. This might seem reasonable, but partisan recovery managers will be unable to achieve concessions from the group when issues arise. This will lead to more difficulties in trying to implement a solution and execute the new plan.

In some cases, allegiance indicates that someone else is running the recovery and that the recovery manager is merely a messenger for the shadow manager. This set-up eliminates the recovery manager's ability to resolve issues quickly, if at all. He or she becomes the sales clerk running back to the actual manager to settle the price. This neutralizes the recovery manager and makes him or her irrelevant to driving the project and making critical decisions. In additional, the decision maker's distant nature means that the decisions will be incomplete and the recovery will fail.

Friction always arises when people have separate agendas. These may include pushing for a specific solution, trying to promote a product or service, or working to promote themselves. An honest broker must meet these situations openly by asking the steering committee for direction and then following that instruction. In fact, this should be an agenda item in meetings. A stated direction to use a product or service is not a hidden agenda. If the team is unaware of the direction, then perception, however inaccurate, becomes reality. People who fail to follow the direction should be removed from the project.

The Relationship of the Candidate Recovery Manager to the Project

In most red situations, stakeholders will not trust the project manager to fix the project. The stigma surrounding him or her undermines any trust. This frequently culminates with the customer demanding a new project manager. A number of options are available. Most commonly:

- Assign an internal resource unassociated with the project or product.
- Hire a new resource.
- Contract with a recovery specialist.

Table 2-1 summarizes the advantages and disadvantages of these options.

The first option is to replace or supplement the project manager with a different internal resource. Although this is rarely a good option, it is usually the least expensive method of solving the problem. Before taking this approach, the organization must:

- Understand why management failed to apply this resource to the project earlier to avoid current problems.
- Ensure that the person is objective. Projects fail over time and are the topic of conversation and gossip, so finding objective individuals inside the organization is difficult.
- Validate that the person has project recovery experience.
- Ensure that the problem was the project manager as opposed to an organization issue (methodology, process, procedure, executive management, etc.) that an internal replacement will unable to fix.

A second option is to hire a new project manager. This is a good approach if all the conditions warrant it. The key is that the candidate must have project recovery experience. Therefore, the organization should have a goal of specializing in project recovery, be in the process of acquiring other projects requiring due diligence, or have a large number of projects running into problems. In addition to fixing the

Table 2-1: Options for a Recovery Manager

Option	Advantages	Disadvantages
Replace the project manager with a different internal resource.	Removes the potential problems with a given individual. Usually the least expensive option.	Assumes the entire problem is with one person as opposed to the organization or methodology. The required skills are probably missing from the organization.
Hire a new project manager to replace the existing one.	Removes the potential problems with a given individual and brings in new methodologies, fresh ideas, or more experience to the project.	Assumes the entire problem is with one person as opposed to the organization or methodology. Need for specialized skills in red project recovery may be short term and only exist for one project.
Replace the project manager with a contract resource.	Removes the potential problems with a given individual. Brings in new methodologies, fresh ideas, and more experience. Unbiased view of the project's management. If the project is short term, it can be very cost effective. The consultant can mentor others to retain the knowledge.	The project management knowledge potentially leaves when the person leaves.

project at hand, this person can become part of project reviews and mentoring. Without some additional driving factor, this is not a viable option, especially if the person hired has a career goal of recovering projects.

The third, and recommended, option is to replace the project manager with a contract resource. Contract resources are available with the specialized skills, recovery experience, and other attributes required for fixing red projects—characteristics rarely required on an ongoing basis. The organization needs the skills only temporarily to identify and fix a specific set of problems or implement processes or methodologies to prevent their reoccurrence, and train the organization on these processes. If only one project needs this resource, a temporary person can perform these tasks cost effectively.

The following parameters minimize the investment and maximize retention of the recovery process knowledge:

- Minimize the consultant's tenure, thereby decreasing the financial impact.
- Require mentoring of an employee in the corrective action process.
- Train the staff on these techniques to preserve the investment.

When red projects are rare and the conditions creating the problems have little or no chance of recurring, hiring a consultant to recover and run the project is the best option. A consultant with a clear statement of work (see below) can focus on solving the problems with the project, thereby reducing the overall cost. To retain any applicable knowledge, a shadow project manager should be assigned for mentoring.

The Benefits of Involving a Third Party

Hiring a consultant to run a recovery has a number of advantages. The most obvious is that this approach brings in a set of skills missing from the organization. These skills could be in managing risk, managing change, working with remote teams, handling demoralized teams, rectifying problems in the management chain, or managing the customer. However, often the biggest advantage is that the person is new to the group and brings a fresh set of ideas to the project. Table 2-2 enumerates some of the benefits of hiring a consultant.

There are also less tangible benefits. It is common for consultants to get the ear of executives simply by virtue of the fact that they are from outside. Ideas they propose may be similar to those offered by the project team in the past, but management listens to them without significant questions. This is the result of the psychology of having a consultant make the statement, as well as the benefit derived from the honeymoon period that accompanies any new relationship.

Table 2-2: Benefits in Hiring a Consultant

Need	Benefit
Objective view	Someone from the outside has an objective view and no history with the company, people, or project.
New management style	Can assess the customer, team, and executives to suggest or implement new management techniques and processes.
Large project experience	A different resource can implement new approaches (e.g., phasing the project) to better handle the scope. Can implement processes and train team members on different methods of handling the project.
Methodology expertise	The resource has experience with agile, critical chain, lean, or other methodologies.
Control of frequent change	Will analyze change logs for the number of changes in the project requirements. Implement a change management process, restart the project at the design phase implementing processes for gathering the requirements properly, or accommodate change.
Short-term specialized needs	Can manage the project in the most cost-effective manner, minimizing the investment in training and infrastructure changes.
Mentoring and training	Identify the areas of the organization needing improvement, train individuals, or implement processes to build the group.
Headcount or scope reduction	Perform hatchet-man functions, reducing headcount or scope to stabilize the project. A temporary resource minimizes residual animosity.

Regardless of the reason, management tends to adopt consultants' suggestions more quickly.

Another advantage is that consultants have no history with the team—there is nothing preconceived about the project or the people. They can be objective and review the staff and the processes without the bias of familiarity with people's personalities and previous actions.

Team members also tend to be more open with a consultant than with other team members. They open up to an outsider because they feel their comments are less likely to be judged or biased. Team members with a history of being quiet can become vocal, as they now feel their views will be heard. As a result, a consultant can uncover issues hidden to others in the organization.

Many projects require that difficult decisions be made and executed. This might include reducing scope, restructuring resources, or terminating team members. Often these actions result in lingering animosity. By using a consultant with a relatively short tenure, many of these negative feelings leave with that person. This can help diffuse some contentious situations.

In the negotiation step, the recovery manager mediates the solution for both sides. If this person is an outside party, neither the customer nor the supplier should perceive any bias. The recovery manager can propose a solution without the perception that he or she is trying to gain some tactical advantage or get the upper hand. There is no possibility of contention caused by a group proposing a one-sided solution. The negotiation is fair and even.

Moreover, selecting the right consultant can bring an entirely new set of ideas and skills to the organization. These include prior red project experience, objectivity, new processes, new procedures, and attention to detail.

Creating the Assignment's Statement of Work

Identifying the need for an individual, outside consultant, or employee is a big step toward fixing the problem. Everyone—the team, management, and the customer—needs to understand the reason for the selection. To ensure that the organization understands the reasons, the steering committee should create a mission statement for the recovery that defines the recovery guidelines for the engagement, the reasons a recovery manager is required, and the expected results.

If an external resource is used, clearly articulate the reasons. They may include that the organization lacks the expertise for managing this style project, lacks the skills for recovering red projects, needs experience with new methodologies (critical chain, agile, lean, etc.), needs skills in meeting the ever-changing customer's demands, or needs an objective resource. Whatever the reasons, make them public.

Executive management and the project sponsor (or their counterparts on the steering committee) must agree to solve the problems with the project, regardless of the group responsible for the failure. They need to understand that these changes will require their assistance and may affect them directly. By informing management of both organizations that changes will be required and that the recovery manager will define and implement those changes will greatly expedite the process of getting the project back on track.

To make this clear to everyone, the steering committee should create a statement of work (SOW) for the project recovery that identifies:

- The parties responsible for approving the recovery plan.
- The responsible party for overseeing implementation of the recovery plan.
- The engagement's extent—which phases are part of the assignment and any conditions (e.g., review of audit findings before going into analysis).
- The deliverables from the engagement, frequency of reports, and their recipients.
- The recovery guidelines.
- The recovery manager's reporting structure (which should be someone on the steering committee).

Ideally, the engagement will cover all four steps of the recovery process. However, some situations require a more conservative approach, and the scope will be limited to the audit so that management can reassess its options after seeing what is wrong with the project. The statement of work should list any conditions and stipulations regarding the length of the engagement.

Defining the Responsibilities by Phase in the SOW

The Audit Phase

The first step must be a project audit, and the SOW should enumerate the following tasks for the recovery manager to perform:

- Analyze the methods, processes, and procedures.
- Review staff, stakeholder, and customer roles.
- Determine the root causes of all problems.
- Perform the work independent of others in the organization to provide an unbiased and candid assessment of the project.
- Review all aspects of the project, including the customer and the executive management team.

The audit identifies the focus of the next steps for recovery. The deliverable should be a report that includes:

- Items contributing to the project's failure.
- Identification of the root causes of the problem.
- Areas where more study is required to determine the root cause.
- Actions required prior to proceeding with the project.

The audit can be the only step in the recovery process. After its completion, management has objective data to use in determining how to proceed. The key decision is whether to continue or cancel the project. This decision is based on whether:

- There is a business justification to fix the project.
- More funds will be needed to complete the project.
- Recovery manager should continue by analyzing the project and implementing the solution (possibly changing the SOW).
- Other consultants should bid on the analysis and implementation phase.

The Analysis Phase

The analysis phase of the recovery process looks at all the failures and:

- Validates the root causes.
- Formulates recovery plans, including alternate options.
- Initiates rudimentary project improvements.

The deliverable is a recovery plan that includes the:

- Corrective actions, plans, processes, and procedures to be implemented.
- Level-of-effort estimates for developing a budget for the recovery.
- Execute phase SOW.

The Negotiation Phase

This phase is the recovery plan's formal submission and reconciliation with various parties. The deliverables are:

- Corrective actions to address the root causes of problems.
- A recovery plan defining how to execute the project.
- Assumptions that were made when developing the corrective actions and recovery plan.
- A risk register of the risks (see Chapter 7).
- The new scope of work.
- A tentative schedule for the corrective actions and new project plan.
- A revised budget for the corrective actions and new project plan.

The Execute Phase

For the execute phase, the SOW should clearly state whether the recovery manager will implement the recovery plan and manage the project. If this is the case, the recovery manager should prepare a separate statement of work specifically for the implementation. This is an analysis phase deliverable, and it is extremely valuable to all parties because it clearly defines the responsibilities of the recovery manager, executive management, and the project sponsor. It also provides measurable criteria to judge the recovery manager's effectiveness, identifies the success criteria, and defines the authority he or she will have while implementing the changes. The SOW should state:

- How running the project will differ from the recovery engagement.
- What the expected results are from the recovery manager.

If the recovery manager will implement the plan, this statement of work should include additional items to help retain knowledge in the organization, including:

- Mentoring a project manager in the recovery process.
- Training other project managers to prevent recurrence.
- Documenting the processes and procedures implemented.

To expedite the recovery and reduce confusion, some simple ground rules should be set before the recovery manager commences work. The organization must be ready to provide:

- The authority to execute the recommendations.
- A resource to mentor, even if only part time.

Giving the recovery manager the authority to execute decisions sets the process up for success. Granting authority does not mean that the recovery manager has a blank check to do whatever he or she wants. The intent is to remove obstructions, such as managers reopening decisions at every step. For instance, assume there is a need for a new change management process requiring organization changes that quality assurance will administer. Once the recovery plan is approved, the corporate quality assurance manager must support the action rather than having veto rights to stop the plan. The recovery manager has the authority to assign tasks, reorganize staff, implement new processes, and take any other previously agreed on actions to execute the plan.

There is a lot to learn in a recovery process. One of the most important techniques is root cause analysis to keep problems from recurring. The knowledge gained is applicable in many future situations, as well as in finishing off the project. For this reason, the statement of work should include mentoring and training an internal project manager to take over the project's day-to-day operation. This retains the knowledge in the organization and reduces the dependence on the consultant. The result is a reduction in the short-term and long-term costs.

Establishing the Recovery Manager's Authority

The level of authority given to the recovery manager is paramount. The recovery manager needs to know how much authority he or she has before the engagement begins so that when boundaries are crossed the recovery manager knows how thin the ice is. Recovery managers regularly have to assume authority, often on the first day. A common problem is that management has neglected to empower the team to make decisions. This may be real or perceived, but at times, the simplest decision can get the project moving.

Pay special attention when crossing these boundaries. Regardless of whether the recovery manager is implementing the recovery plan, it is more a case of *when*, rather than *if*, he or she assumes authority. By asking the recovery manager to fix the project, there must be trust, and with that comes a significant degree of authority. It should be used wisely and the recovery manager must know when to ask for permission, when to inform superiors of a decision made, and when to ask for forgiveness.

Since the auditing function needs minimal authority, the recovery manager may get authority after the audit. This needs to be spelled out in the statement of work so that the authority is available when needed. For an audit, the recovery manager will require unfettered access to the team, management, and the customer, all of whom must understand they need to be available when needed. In essence, the recovery manager has the authority to get on anyone's calendar.

If that person continues through the analysis and negotiation phases of the recovery process or, even further, through the implementation phase, then the authority must increase. Implementation requires the authority to implement decisions, reallocate resources, purchase capital equipment, negotiate everything from schedules to scope with the customer, or request a budget increase, and management must supply this authority to make these actions happen.

Accepting the Role as a Recovery Manager

Recovering a red project is exciting, challenging, and fast paced. It is also rewarding, since a huge amount of trust is placed in the recovery manager. A visit or phone call from a boss, trusted friend, or potential client is what will bring the potential candidate into the fold of a project that has gone red. The person making the call understands that he or she needs help in understanding and resolving the project's issues, and trusts the candidate can help. The call itself shows only a portion of the trust in that candidate.

This can cloud one's judgment on whether to accept the assignment. However, the conditions on the assignment must allow for success. The potential recovery manager needs to know the requirements and have the skill set to perform the job. Understanding the ground rules and recovery guidelines for fixing the project is critical. Request a statement of work, as described above; generate one if it has not been created.

In addition, the following questions should be answered to determine the viable options for the recovery:

- Is shutting down the project an option?
- May the scope of the project be changed?
- How late can the delivery be?
- May the recovery manager replace resources with deficient skills?
- Will the recovery manager be able to pick the people for the project?
- What are the monetary bounds?
- Are there restrictions on how it is completed? (For instance, are there contractual obligations to use a given technology, can the project be phased, or is there a drop-dead date for the project?)

The assignment's parameters must be understood from the start.

Further, clarification as to how the recovery manager is supposed to function is essential. There needs to be a clear set of expectations. If this is a short-term assignment to perform the audit and analysis so that a recovery plan can be developed, then the intensity is high, and it should be treated like a sprint. If the assignment also includes managing the new recovery plan, then this is a marathon and must be run at a sustainable pace.

Creating an Outline of the Recovery

After getting a project overview, reviewing the statement of work, and confirming the recovery constraints, the recovery manager must provide a plan for developing the recovery plan. The project sponsor and executive management need to know when they can expect to see it. If they expect more details at this point, their expectations are unrealistic, and this should be explained. What is acceptable is a brief outline of the process for recovering the project, which should quell their curiosity and give them confidence the job will be completed.

Chapter Takeaway

- The first step required in any recovery is that executive management, the project sponsor, or steering committee realize the project is in trouble and needs help.

- Selection of a recovery manager is critical. The required traits include being an honest broker experienced in red project recovery, who is trusted by all parties and is independent of both the supplier and customer.

- Third party consultants are excellent candidates for recovery managers. Base the selection on all the traits needed in a recovery manager, especially experience.

- Create a statement of work for the recovery manager. It should include:

  - The parties responsible for approving the recovery plan.

  - The responsible party to oversee implementing the recovery plan.

  - The engagement's extent—which phases are part of the assignment and any conditions (such as a review of audit findings before going into analysis).

  - The deliverables from the engagement, frequency of reports, and their recipients.

  - The recovery guidelines.

  - The recovery manager's reporting structure (which should be someone on the steering committee).

- Potential recovery managers should ensure that the recovery process is well defined and has a statement of work.

- The recovery manager requires authority and trust to do the job.

II

Auditing the Project

Understanding the Issues

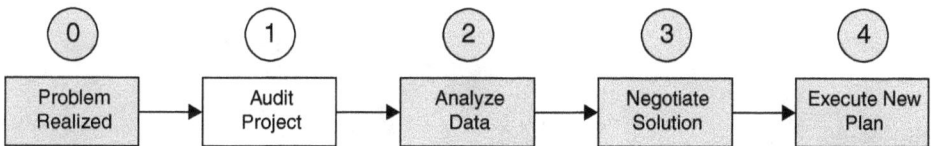

0		1		2		3		4
Problem Realized	→	Audit Project	→	Analyze Data	→	Negotiate Solution	→	Execute New Plan

The steering committee, project sponsor, and executive management realize there is a problem to solve and have taken action. The project now has their support, clear direction, and a recovery manager. They have defined the assignment and the ground rules for success. The recovery process's first step, the audit, may proceed.

This section will cover investigating the symptoms of what went wrong and will touch on some corrective actions. After methodically investigating the people, scope, timeline, and technology involved in the project, the recovery manager will be able to identify the problems—and perhaps even some root causes. The audit will identify who is supposed to be doing what work. More importantly, it will be evident who or what is functioning improperly. The root cause could be a problem with a process, a person, or a group; determining and validating the root cause is the next phase's function (see Part III).

The first step in recovering any project is to identify the failing elements. The history is important in determining root cause, but history cannot change. Searching for blame is counterproductive. Besides, corrective action is only applicable to the current situation.

Interview the extended project team members and understand their view of the project's issues. The act of interviewing the extended project team will improve communication. Other than that, do not implement any other formal processes at this stage of the recovery, although other actions to limit expenses, such as canceling overtime, may be appropriate.

Be sure to read all chapters in this section, even if there is a concern about only one subject. These topics are all interrelated. For instance, missing a clue with personnel may inappropriately lead the auditor to drill down into the technology. Returning to this section for reference, one can select the subject based on the immediate need.

3

Assessing the Human Role in Project Failure

"One must survey his faults and study them,
ere he be able to repeat them."

—Michel de Montaigne,
French Renaissance Author, *Essais*, Book iii

The audit is all about the people. They are the project, and their actions or inactions make or break it. It is a rare occurrence when all the people on a project are doing the right thing and the project still ends up beset with issues. Processes are necessary, but people choose to follow them (or not); people have the required skills (or not); people communicate with others (or not); and people follow direction (or not). It is all about people and whether they have the right qualifications to perform the tasks assigned.

With the right people on a project, it will most likely run okay. Note the two big qualifiers in that sentence: "the right people on a project" and "will most likely run okay." Many factors can get a project in trouble, but the right people will keep the problems under some level of control. As Lesson 2 in the Introduction states: "A strong team can surmount most problems." It can even overcome ineffective management and poor or misapplied processes.

Granted, the best people cannot always make a project successful. Attempting to transform lead into gold is going to fail (unless someone figures out a cheap way to accurately fission a couple of helium atoms out of lead). The people on the project are the ones who should inform stakeholders of the inherent risks; they can look at the project realistically and know when it should be canceled or realigned. An obstinate sponsor who is willing to pour significant money into a project while placing unreasonable constraints on it—for instance, using only material found at the hardware store—can have the best people working on a project and it will still fail. In this case, the person levying the constraints is wrong and is the root problem. If the sponsor understands that the project will require more resources, this will allow the project to succeed, at least theoretically. Was the goal of this project met? Yes. Was it successful? Only to a degree, because the project will be very expensive, will face multiple technical challenges, and have a lengthy time line. Nevertheless, it could run "okay."

People are the critical piece in determining a project's success or failure. They approve the inception, allow scope creep, define the technical solution, and levy constraints. What are the team's dynamics? Who are the sponsors? What are their expectations? What is the leadership's strength? What do these people think is wrong with the project? Does the team have the right skills? What would the team do to fix the project? The answers to these questions lead to more questions and eventually point to the root problems.

One premise of my approach says the answers are in the team—see Lesson 1 in the Introduction. In other words, team members know the problems and their accompanying resolutions; someone just needs to ask them. Therefore, the people involved in a project are the best place to start an audit.

Who Should Be Interviewed?

Before interviewing the team, the recovery manager must know who the members are. On many projects, this is unclear. This was the source of the problem in Case Study 3-3: no one on the project was actually sure who the project's end users were.

The recovery manager must map out the organizational roles and responsibilities in a representation similar to the one in Figure 1-3 (pg. 12). The source for such a map is the people who hired the recovery manager; they will provide their version of the organization's structure, which is mostly likely the correct one. The recovery manager will validate it with the rest of the team and ensure that everyone has the same understanding.

Interviewing the People Involved in the Project

Scope creep, inexperienced teams, poor management, difficult customers, and widely dispersed teams are the most common reasons cited for late or overbudget projects. In nearly all cases, these are symptoms of the overarching illness of poor communication. Thus, the recovery manager needs to start by communicating with everyone on the extended team. He or she must determine the degree of the communication problems and correct any failures. The interview process starts this by encouraging and facilitating frequent two-way communications among team members and is the best approach for gathering information on the project's actual problems.

Interviewing the extended team is the most important step for the recovery manager. It is the way to get to know the team and its troubles. Recovery managers should start this process their first day on the job. Depending on the circumstances surrounding the project, the interviews may start at a variety of places. Ideally, interview people randomly, because this provides a continuous flow of alternating views on the issues.

Scheduling the interviews is a balancing act, though. For example, if the customer is relentlessly making demands on the team, then it is best to start with people on the customer side. Their incessant complaints about how badly the project is progressing, lack of response from the project team, concerns going unheard, incorrect project direction, and so forth, need to stop long enough for the recovery manager to implement a few corrective actions.

However, starting the interview process with the customer has its inherent dangers. Being a new leader and suddenly disappearing to the customer side may make the recovery manager look like he or she is grandstanding rather than working to solve problems and creates unnecessary animosity among members of the team. On the other hand, if the customer continues the assault, there will be no opportunity for the recovery manager to take actions to build the customer's confidence.

CASE STUDY 3-1: THE STOCKHOLM SYNDROME

Shortly after the start of what would prove to be a difficult recovery, I was working remotely from the team at the customer's site. The project manager from the company that hired me entered the office. He declared, "We are concerned that you are experiencing the Stockholm Syndrome." I was unfamiliar with the term, so he explained that it was named after an episode in Stockholm in the 1970s when armed robbers took bank workers captive for five days. The hostages eventually began to identify with and grow sympathetic toward their captors. He explained that this went so far that eventually one of the captives had sex with one of the robbers.

To say the least, I was surprised that uncovering facts about the project would give rise to such an analogy, one that vilified the customer and myself. It revealed the degree of animosity in the project.

By the way, none of the Stockholm hostages had sex with their captors. I have included this exaggerated claim by the project manager to underscore the strong negative emotions that can arise when a project is failing.

Interviewing Techniques

The recovery manager's goal is to gather information. This is Lesson 4: "Objective data is your friend, providing the key out of any situation" (see the Introduction). Knowledge of the data surrounding a project will identify the root causes of problems and provide a basis for building and defending the recovery plan, making it possible to provide quick responses during negotiation. The interviewer's style needs to be tailored to facilitate gleaning this data. The interviewer must be accommodating, friendly, and open; he or she cannot be accusatory or fault-centric, or appear to lead the interviewee.

Begin the interviews with a thin agenda. The following three questions will easily fill a 30-minute meeting:

- What are the issues for this project?
- What would you do to fix it?
- What do you expect of the recovery manager?

Ask the interviewees these questions at the beginning of the meeting. You will likely be amazed by what transpires as the interviewees respond to these three questions. The information will flow, and you will rarely have trouble using all the allotted time. Interviewees provide information on the project manager, project executives, team members, project issues—and sometimes even their family life and good restaurants. It is best to let them ramble. Listen and nudge them gently to stay on task and answer the questions. Most likely, they are feeling unheard and ignored, so hear them out. An interview conducted using this approach will initiate trust building.

CASE STUDY 3-2: THE BEST PERSON FOR THE JOB

One client's Information Technology department was building a Web-based sales tool. Among the project's requirements was integrating a third-party tool to allow online payments—simply a link on an internal Web page. During the interviews, the lead finance analyst went on a tirade. He wanted to remove this feature from the main project because the project was failing. He thought he could manage this one feature's implementation better as a separate project. However, he did not understand the risk this would entail because of the company's inexperience in coordinating with third parties. The analyst's attitude was poisoning the team, since he was expressing these views publicly. Based on his attitude, his involvement was minimized. Another person was assigned the responsibility for working with the third party. Although junior, she was more realistic, cautious, and thorough. Because she was highly respected, placing trust in a junior employee boosted the entire team's morale. The action also showed a new, progressive management style.

There are, of course, more questions to ask. Follow-up questions should be open ended. The only time to use a leading question is if people misunderstand or give answers unrelated to the questions.

Questions requiring answers include:

- How does the team work together?
- How is communication among team members?
- What is the level of urgency on the project?
- Describe the change management process. Who uses it?
- What is the project's scope? Does everyone agree with and understand it?
- What decisions are open on the project?
- What is slowing down problem resolution?
- Which tasks are late? Why?
- What is your role on the project?
- How many hours are you assigned to the project? How often do you need overtime to complete tasks?
- What is impeding your work on the project?
- Which people are over- or underutilized?
- How is the customer engaged in the project?
- What customer deliverables are late?
- What are the customer relationship problems?
- How often are clarifications required on the customer's deliverables? Can you provide some examples?
- How do the subcontractors perform?

Of course, the questions asked will depend on the situation. With a better understanding of the issues, the recovery manager's list will evolve.

CASE STUDY 3-3:
IDENTIFYING THE PROJECT'S CUSTOMER

An in-house project to develop a new Web-based customer maintenance tool was floundering in the scope definition phase—the required features seemed to be increasing faster than the team could capture definitions. During the interviews, it was obvious no one knew who, on the customer side, had responsibility for requirements. Therefore, the regular list of questions was expanded to include the following:
- Who is the project sponsor?
- Who is the system's end user?
- Who will own the system when it is complete (that is, who will end users call to have complaints addressed or bugs fixed)?

The answers varied greatly, but each question elicited two dominant responses. To the first question, the answers were most often Information Technology (separate from the business unit) or Sales. To the second question, it was either the organization's Data Entry unit or the company's customers. To the third question, it was either the organization's Data Entry or Sales unit.

After reviewing the project's history, I determined the original answers to the questions and reset the project to those parameters. The problem was that the Sales and Data Entry groups had different requirements and objectives. The project had been trying to accommodate conflicting goals.

Casually draw out the answers to the questions. Use the answers to provide lead-ins to other questions on the list. Look for opportunities to turn answers into other questions; doing so removes any accusatory tone that might be read into a direct question.

Ensure that the interviewees think about their responses. Challenge them to think independently. One goal of this process is to elicit the underlying basis for why people think the way they do and to avoid the "standard" response among the team—the complaints they bemoan around the water cooler.

For example, the analyst on a project indicates that an engineer lacks the expertise needed to complete a functional specification. One approach might be to counter the statement by suggesting either that another team member work with the engineer to fill in the gaps or that the component the engineer is trying to design is ill-conceived. However, this provides an answer for the problem rather than soliciting information from the interviewee. The goal of the interview is to get the interviewee to suggest solutions to the recovery manager—the answers are in the team (Lesson 1). Analyze the response. The recovery manager should neither agree nor disagree with the answers.

Conduct all interviews in this manner. As this process proceeds, patterns and trends will start to emerge. The recovery manager must consider all of these while formulating a plan of action and avoid jumping to conclusions.

When taking notes on comments about teammates or superiors it is best to repeat the information they have provided. Make sure they are comfortable with the notes. Assure them that their comments are confidential.

Usually, one or two people will adamantly point to a given person as the problem. This may be an expression of their displeasure with the new recovery manager. They may feel they are fully qualified to run the project and should be the one in the driver's seat. Keep their frustration with the project in mind and avoid forming hasty opinions.

CASE STUDY 3-4: YOU NEED TO FIRE. . .

A company had numerous projects running under a Project Management Office. The projects included building a new office to house a data center, moving the existing data center to that office, and implementing a new network and multiple software packages. Almost all of the projects were in trouble, and I was hired to audit the PMO. I had interviewed three or four people on the first day of this new assignment, when a group lead on the infrastructure project told me to fire the helpdesk person on one of the software projects. The lead claimed the helpdesk person was incompetent.

When interviewed, the helpdesk person stated that she had concerns about what the lead had said. I immediately assured her that everyone was evaluated on his or her own merits. She said that the previous project manager had placed her in the job, and she admitted that she was out of her area of expertise. She was trying to learn the job as quickly as possible; unfortunately, management had cut the training budget.

Further investigation uncovered that the lead had violated numerous company policies (for example, buying capital equipment under false pretenses, compromising the firewall so a friend could watch cartoons, and installing pirated software). The helpdesk person was in a position to see many of those violations. The lead was terminated for unethical practices.

The rest of the group, aware of his practices, was pleased to see a level of order come to the group. A large majority of people in the organization viewed the termination as a positive action.

Dealing with People Who Refuse to Talk

A number of team members may be reticent about cooperating with the audit process. People who are participating in a failing project are likely to be frustrated with inadequate leadership and may be blind to the benefits of the interview process. Again, avoid forming hasty opinions that might be biased by the environment. Understand that these individuals may be justified in their reluctance to share and cooperate. Management has ignored them and the project, and they may see the recovery process as more of management's lip service. Explore such situations as best you can, and counter such attitudes with actions. Lead by example. Show the team members you can make a difference, and they will become your strongest supporters.

On occasion, someone's silence tells the entire story. Most people understand that data is power; unfortunately, there are people who use such an understanding maliciously, retaining or dispensing information to create a mystique of their own importance. One interaction tells little; it takes time to make an assessment about an individual. Address repeated behavior like this quickly to minimize its impact.

Interviewing Management

It is important to stress that interviews should include everyone governing a project, from project sponsors, executives, and steering committee members to the supplier's and subcontractor's management.

In these interviews, determine the time line for when the interviewee became aware of the project's problems. The project is in serious trouble, and it took more than a few days to happen, even though management may think it happened overnight. Frederick Brooks, in his book *The Mythical Man-Month* famously wrote, "How does a project get to be a year late? . . . One day at a time."[3] In your interviews with individuals in management positions, determining how they missed the negative progression of events will go a long way in eliciting information about their involvement in the project and its problems. It will also help identify where communication broke down, allowing problems to grow unabated.

If individuals in management attempted corrective action, it is important to capture those actions and to evaluate their degree of success. If, in prior interviews with the team, there were suggestions of problems with a specific manager—say, indecisiveness—then politely probe the issue. In such a case, it is best to focus on specifics: have the claims clarified by the manager and start looking for a pattern.

CASE STUDY 3-5: CUSTOMER NONDELIVERY

On a project integrating equipment into a manufacturing execution system (MES), the customer was responsible for providing the manuals defining the equipment's communication protocol. Without these, the architect would be unable to write the interface specifications. The project was red in part because of the late delivery of the interface specifications. I reported that the problem's source was the customer's failure to deliver the manuals and generated a change request to delay the project, including financial compensation for the time the integration team would be idle. Within two weeks, the customer delivered all equipment manuals.

Unwilling to embarrass the customer's project manager, the supplier's project manager had refused to press the issue. Once the change order, which was worth nearly $100,000, was presented, the customer worked tirelessly to get the required manuals. The embarrassment of being assigned the delay and the huge cost was far worse than it would have been had the supplier pressured the customer for the manuals earlier.

Interviewing Subcontractors

Review each subcontractor's statement of work and contract, and interview as many people on each team as possible. Try to determine if they are being honest. Research their comments and determine if they are trying to blame the client or are trying to be politically correct by avoiding negative comments. An honest relationship is critical.

Determine the status of their deliverables and the reasons any are late. Compare the answers to the specifications in the contract, statement of work, and schedules. Hold the subcontractor accountable.

Research the company and determine if it is in financial trouble. One common issue is that the contract is part of an acquisition. In that case, make sure the new owner has a commitment to the contract's product or service. Assess the subcontractor's risks, and record any in the risk register (see in Chapter 7, "Developing a Thorough Understanding of Project Risk").

Some questions requiring answers are:

- What is the subcontractor's financial status?
- Is the subcontractor's contract part of an acquisition? If so, what is the commitment to the product or service the subcontractor is supplying?
- Does the subcontractor have experience in the customer's business domain?
- Has its business model changed to effect its commitment to this type of work?
- Are any products or services supplied by the subcontractor being removed from its business roadmap?
- What is the support model?
- What are the payment structure and current payments?
- What is the cancellation clause in the contract?
- What are the commercial terms?

CASE STUDY 3-6:
SUBCONTRACTOR ACCOUNTABILITY

A client building a new manufacturing facility and deploying custom-built equipment was having a difficult time with a subcontractor who refused to commit to delivery dates, rarely communicated the status of his deliverables, and delivered items on a random schedule. In the interviews, the subcontractor's account manager was hostile to questioning. He said the questions were irrelevant and refused to answer many of them.

I had already read the statement of work, but my frustration prompted him to read the contract. The payment terms in the contract were for quarterly multi-hundred-thousand-dollar payments until the contract price was paid in full. The contract was devoid of milestone payments. I advised the client to stop payments based on implied breach of contract for nondelivery of product in a timely manner. Eventually the client canceled the subcontractor's contract.

Interviewing the Customer

In every project, the customer has a responsibility to provide some set of deliverables, if nothing more than the requirements for the product. Usually, though, there are numerous other items, which might include signoff, screen designs, testing support, specialized interface specifications, and so forth. Ensure that the project plan properly accounts for these and that the people responsible for their delivery are aware of the commitment.

To manage its responsibilities, the customer must have some form of project team and management structure. Figure 1-3 (pg. 12) shows the structure used for this discussion.

The model for interaction with the customer is critical to the project in order for the project team members to get the information required to do their jobs in a timely fashion. Questions for the customer are much the same as those for the project team, but should also include:

- What issues exist with the project team?
- What are the customer's deliverables?
- Which deliverables have been late and why?
- How are the end users involved?
- What is the relationship between the end users and the customer, the project sponsor, and the project team?

CASE STUDY 3-7: ASSIGNING FAILURE BLAME

One client was using its internal Information Technology department to build a Web-based tool to configure and sell automobiles. The project was plagued with issues, and the PMO hired me to recover the project. IT's executive management and the project team indicated the problem was that the customer, the sales department, was making unreasonable demands.

The customer's executives voiced a significant set of issues; it was clear that they were very displeased with the project and blamed IT's executive management's performance. The result was a complete breakdown in communication. One of my first actions was to interview the steering committee members to hear their grievances. This action met with stern objection from IT executive management, whose members felt that since they were paying for the recovery, I should spend all of my time with the project team to solve the team's problems and develop solutions that were favorable to IT.

I explained that before addressing any issues on the project, the sales department needed to provide a grace period for the audit and analysis. To do that, they needed to feel confident that I would address and fix the issues. They would only feel confident if they understood I had the expertise to do the job and could present a logical plan. With the grace period secured, my attention could turn to the project team.

The issues the sales department voiced were that executive management was unresponsive, had released the product prior to completing proper testing, and refused to treat them like the customer. I confirmed the latter two points directly with IT's executive managers. Their contention was that the sales department was not a customer since they worked for the same company. In addition, for the prior release, they felt product testing was taking too long. They insisted that testing stop and the product be released. This resulted in a truly miserable delivery. They refused to acknowledge that this decision was in error and instead blamed the testing team's inability to meet the schedule.

Although the customer claimed it had made numerous complaints about the project, there was no documentation of that. The previous project management team had refused to keep an action item list; it turned out that it had a separate agenda and resolving issues would have thwarted its goals.

I assured the customer that the issues would be resolved, even though many issues were with the executive management. To start to address this, I needed the customer to give me time and to be patient. My honesty in identifying the sources of the issues and constant communication convinced the customer to grant the time.

I assured the project team that I had bought time from the business unit, allowing breathing room to correct the issues. This was an unexpected relief since the project faced a backlog of badly needed bug fixes from the previous deployment and these bugs were having a severe impact on the business.

After two weeks, I presented an initial recovery plan to the steering committee. It addressed the core issues from the interviews. The key points were:

- Animosity between executive management and the business unit was unbearable. This would need to be the primary focus of the recovery.
- The test environments were inadequate. They were incapable of properly reflecting the end users' environment or executing acceptance test scripts in a timely manner.
- Certain people on the project team were hostile and admittedly unwilling to assist in the project recovery. They would be replaced.
- Executive management failed to understand the need for a product maintenance group; instead, its members used yearly project releases to address product bugs. Frequent bug-fix releases would be required on an ongoing basis.

It is worth noting none of these items relates to an unreasonable customer.

The plan presented in the steering committee meeting addressed the nonpolitical issues. Individual meetings with the customer representatives handled the contentious issues with executive management.

Interviewing End Users

End users are sometimes inaccessible to the project team. It is likely that a project will deal with an end-user representative from the customer's organization, the product development department, a marketing group, or the like. If the end users are directly associated with the project, interview them. Make sure the questions are appropriate for their role. They may be unaware of the project's problems.

Remote Teams, Time Zones, and Work Weeks

Remote teams can pose special problems. Communication is the biggest issue. It takes more time to communicate with someone outside the office, let alone in a different time zone. Assess the available tools (conference calling, videoconferences,

Internet calling, instant messaging, and the like), as well as the possible need for face-to-face meetings; Despite the fact that travel incurs jet lag and introduces obvious budgetary issues, there may need to be more in-person meetings to improve communication and develop a proper team rapport.

CASE STUDY 3-8: A 31-HOUR TIME ZONE DIFFERENCE

When communicating with the Middle East, time zones take on a new meaning. The work week in many countries is Sunday through Thursday. This means that the time that elapses from the start of work on Sunday in the Middle East to the start of work on Monday in North America is actually 31 to 36 hours. Two days of work are complete in the Middle East before the North American team arrives at work.

To resolve the time lag on one project, daily and occasional Sunday night (Mideast time)/Sunday morning (North American time) conference calls were held to maintain a common direction. Holding the meetings at the beginning of the work week splits the four days that were not overlapping evenly. The sequence was two days work in North America, one day working in the Middle East, Sunday meeting, and one day work in the Middle East.

Assessing the Effect of Cultural Differences

On international projects, it is critical to understand cultural differences and change management's style to accommodate it, so spend time learning about a culture you are not familiar with. While adequately addressing this subject is beyond the scope of this book, a couple of examples of such problems may put perspective on the importance of understanding of cultural differences.

Some cultures are very polite and can hardly say the word no. In fact, they will say yes when they mean no; in such cases, the meaning is determined by the context—they agree with the argument as being sound, but they disagree with the statement's direction. This is often referred to as the three yeses—"yes, I agree with you"; "yes, I heard you"; and "yes, it is valid, but the incorrect solution." Following the other side of the conversation closely will help you understand which form of yes is being used. For more on cultural distinctions and how to deal with them, consult the *Kiss, Bow or Shake Hands* series of books (see Recommended Reading).

CASE STUDY 3-9:
CULTURAL REQUIREMENTS IN MEETINGS

On a remote project in a county where haggling over every point is the norm, I was trying to resolve numerous disconnects between specifications. I reviewed one specification and realized a database field had one context for one record type and another context for a different record type, which meant a very poor design. Business rules were being applied to other data in the record to determine the data's meaning. I scheduled a meeting with the customer's project manager and Database Administrator (DBA) to request a change to the structure. The DBA was adamant the design was fine, but I was unwilling to let my client be liable.

The country's culture was to argue rather than discuss. Because I was tired after six weeks of remote work, I suggested completing the discussion after returning from a scheduled trip home. The customer's project manager insisted the meeting continue and pressed for more discussion to resolve the concerns. The meeting was turning into a brawl (horrible when mixed with lack of sleep). I simply refused to have the argument. Instead, the customer's project manager switched to his native language and had a fierce argument with the DBA. At the meeting's completion, the decision was to redesign the database as I originally requested. The culture simply required the argument.

Merchant cultures need to haggle over every point. They expect both sides to concede items in any discussion. Never think of going into one of these meetings with an honest compromise. They will want to haggle and see something forfeited. Know the desired compromise and have plenty of items to concede to get to it. They will equally surrender items to meet in the middle.

Determine the team's language capability; teams using English as a second language (ESL) provide another area for failure. Make sure to use simple English and recruit people for the team fluent in the customer's primary language. Flow charts help bridge part of the communication gap. Never impose rules on using native language; this is offensive.

CASE STUDY 3-10:
USING A COMMON LANGUAGE FOR COMMUNICATION

Most North American teams are monolingual and sensibly rely on the customer's familiarity with English to create a common ground for communication. Unfortunately, on many failed projects, teams adopt rules restricting meetings to English only. Why? Because the monolingual group is insecure about its inability to understand the customer's language and fear the customer's team will have "secret" conversations in the meetings. This is unwise, since people are able to express themselves more easily in their native language. The solution is to let discussion occur in the native language and ask for a summary at the end. Any clarification discussion can be held in English.

Never restrict the group's internal communication; always assume positive intent when the conversation switches to another language.

Assessing the Applicability of Core Processes

The audit must determine whether the core processes to provide the foundation for the project are in place and being followed. Many procedures are required to run a project correctly. Experience shows that deficiencies in four processes (meeting minutes, change management processes, risk registers, and scheduling) constitute the majority of all problems. Simply having the templates or procedures on file is insufficient; the audit must be thorough and ascertain they are actually used. Determine, for instance, whether the team publishes minutes for all meetings, the attendees read and correct the minutes, the action items are captured, logged, tracked, and people are held accountable for resolving them regardless of their title. The audit must analyze risk and mitigation plans to ensure they are current and effective. Each of the processes must be evaluated.

The Outcome of the Interview Process

Listen, glean the issues, build confidence, and determine who should be on the team and whether any people are poisoning the team. The case studies have shown some issues and resolutions.

The obvious question is what happened to allow the project to degenerate to its current state. Why does the new person, the recovery manager, hear the issues as opposed to the existing project manager? It is possible the recovery manager is listening and cares about the project more than the prior management. Many team members give up on a project when, perceived or real, the project manager is too involved in other seemingly more important items. As the project starts to fall apart, communication breaks down further and the downward spiral accelerates.

CASE STUDY 3-11:
ALWAYS COMPLETE THE AUDIT INTERVIEWS

Sometimes, continuing interviews seems nearly pointless. On the first day of a project audit, the project manager was unable to meet at the prearranged time. Instead, he invited me to attend the lead's meeting. This meeting divulged more of the team dynamics than any interview ever would have. The regular participants were the development, requirements, and quality assurance leads. Due to scheduling conflicts, the meeting was a working lunch. The quality assurance manager never showed up. The body language of the project manager's lieutenants was anything but cooperative. The project manager expressed frustration in the lead's inability to get closure on late items. His leads repeatedly asked, "Do we have the authority to limit scope and close the process?" He never provided an answer. It was clear the project manager was neither delegating authority nor making the decisions himself, but was asking his team to close the items. His team, lacking the authority to do their jobs, was rightfully frustrated.

Eventually, I inherited the project and my first step as project manager was to give the leads the authority required to do their jobs. The project showed immediate progress.

This underscores Lesson 4: "Stay involved with the team." Being too absorbed with pleasing management or being imperious shuts down communication and the project manager's ability to feel the project and read the subtleties.

The interview process will divulge a plethora of information about the group and the issues the group is facing. Soon, reoccurring themes will appear to point to the next areas of investigation. Even if the path to recovery seems obvious, continue to interview all the people involved. The recovery manager needs the chance to meet and understand the team. These meetings:

- Build morale.
- Improve communications.
- Allow team members to build a rapport with the new recovery manager.

Look for relationships and trends, but avoid the trap of thinking the commonly mentioned problem is the actual root issue. In Case Study 3-7, the unanimous opinion was the customer was too demanding, unreasonable, and unfair. In actuality, this was false and that attitude was a significant part of the problem. The customer's requests were reasonable, but customer frustration was speaking louder.

There may be an intense desire to show progress and make changes as soon as patterns start appearing. Avoid the temptation of hasty decisions. Progress is critical, but not at the cost of missing the root cause of problems. Quick reaction can be overreaction and add to the project's problems. The goal is to find the source issues and fix them. Addressing symptoms is unsatisfactory.

Solving the problems with the project is nothing magical. Make team members aware of this. Team members provide a vast majority of the data used to solve the problems—Lesson 1. People may have told supervisors numerous times what approach to take. Now, the recovery manager is going to deliver the message and, this time, management will heed the advice.

This is no real mystery. There are many reasons for this behavior. First, management has finally figured out there is a problem with the project. Prior to this epiphany, suggestions to solve problems on a properly functioning project were simply noise. Problems were still within management's level of tolerance. Only when problems reach a critical mass will management decide to acknowledge the issue. This is the Realization step's importance—management's acknowledgment.

Next, since the project is finally on the radar as red, how can management (whose members arguably were inattentive to the project) know who is giving them good advice or just feeding them more finger-pointing accusations? The team, now tainted, needs an objective eye to look at the situation and recommend a solution. (Perceiving the team as tainted is a serious problem needing attention. Chapter 8 discusses this in more detail.)

Lastly, the recovery manager weeds out poor ideas, adds new suggestions, and gives management a holistic set of answers. This comprehensive list addresses all of the project's ills and targets root causes. The team most likely offered independent suggestions, failing to propose a complete set of answers.

Whatever the reason, management failed to listen. There must be sensitivity to this. Management is about to take information similar to what the team has told it, this time from a stranger, and act on it. Hard feelings and animosity will be rife. The recovery manager must explain to the team that they will get credit for helping.

To avoid the appearance of an attack on management's negligence, the recovery manager has to take credit for the plans. Credit is due to the team for its input, cooperation, and buy-in. Point out all the problems with the project, including whether the management team provided the proper oversight and listened to the team. If these issues are present, they must be included in the project's issues. However, unless the recovery manager can find an ally to push it, expect resistance to change.

Chapter Takeaway

- The four lessons learned all relate to working with the team. They are:
  - The answers are in the team.
  - A strong team can surmount most problems.
  - Stay involved with the team.
  - Objective data is your friend, providing the key out of any situation
- Validate or define the working model for the extended team.
- Interview the entire extended team using open-ended questions. Be humble, nonjudgmental, and nonconfrontational.
- Determine deficiencies in the executive management and the customer as well as the project team. Enlist steering committee members or the project sponsor to help resolve issues with the executive management.

4

Auditing Scope on a Red Project

*"The art of leadership is saying no, not yes.
It is very easy to say yes."*

—Tony Blair, former British Prime Minister, *The Mail,* October 2, 1994

Scope creep is the most commonly observed symptom in red projects, even though the root cause may be the people on the project. The recovery manager must compare every aspect of the current scope to the project requirements to determine the problem's pervasiveness. He or she must question team members, customers, and suppliers to discover the root causes. It is important to understand how the requirements were gathered, whether any conflicting views of scope exist, and how the current scope compares to the original. If the scope has changed, the degree and reason for the fluctuation must be documented.

Determining the Efficacy of Change Management

Projects change. Properly managed projects allow for changes in accordance with mutually agreed upon process and guidelines. This includes a formal tracking system for all changes, regardless of monetary value or impact on the schedule. The auditor must add the change orders to the original scope and make sure the aggregate scope matches the work in progress. This confirms that the change management system is working and validates both the project manager's and architect's involvement. If there is a mismatch in scope, study the change management process and change orders to be certain they are properly used and people are implementing only what the approved change order authorizes.

The architect plays the major role, perhaps larger than the project manager, in controlling scope because architects are the primary decision makers on the appropriateness of a change request, and they define the method of implementation. The implementation method significantly impacts the amount of work required and provides insight into the architects' mindset and the organization's perception of his or her role.

In addition, the auditor should assess the customer's degree of sophistication in project management and knowledge of the product or service. Educating a customer new to project management, the product, or both, is time consuming. As customers who are new to a product gradually become more product savvy, they will see limitations in the original design and conceptualize better ways to design the system. As the project proceeds, they try to bend the requirements to meet this new understanding. Educating the customer on project management principles or the product requires a change request to account for the additional effort required.

Most project managers are familiar with inflated customer expectations. These often result from a lack of clarity at the inception of the project (see Chapter 17). Determine the source of the confusion, and document a common understanding of the product. If expectations are in constant flux, examine the supplier's and customer's behavioral patterns to find the source.

CASE STUDY 4-1: UNRESOLVED SCOPE ITEMS

On one large project, the customer and supplier were unable to agree on whether a specific tool's integration was in or out of scope; the statement of work was ambiguous. Neither the customer nor the supplier could provide documentation supporting their case. The customer's expectations were clear; why would it leave out one tool type? The supplier, however, insisted the tool was excluded in an initial definition meeting. The issue was never formally resolved. The customer eventually gave up. The monetary cost of failing to properly set expectations or to document the initial meeting was huge, and the cost in frustration immeasurable.

Auditing the Completeness of the Project Documentation

The first step in auditing the completeness of the project documents is to read all of the project's source artifacts. Depending on the type of project, this includes the request for proposal (RFP), the proposal, the contract, the inception documents, the project charter, and any change orders. Read the specifications to determine how well they match to the contract, charter, and requirements. If there are discrepancies, prepare a reconciliation list. This list consists of the items outlined in the contract, the requirements fulfilling those high-level items, and the features included in each requirement's specification. Map them to one another to make sure current features map back to a source requirement. Do this with a requirements traceability matrix. This document, usually in tabular format, juxtaposes the project's scope as represented in various documents. If the scope is controlled, yet the team thinks it is changing, determine the reasons for this perception.

CASE STUDY 4-2:
WHERE IS THE CHANGE REQUEST LOG?

A project for building a manufacturing facility had suddenly turned yellow, and I was requested to do an audit. I started by reviewing the project manager's documentation to look for clues. When asked for a list of change requests, the project manager verbally listed the requests, but provided no monetary values. To be courteous, I started writing, thinking the list would be small and assuming costs would be on a forthcoming written list. After the fifth or sixth item, I asked for the change request log. The project manager replied there was no formal list because this was an informal process established by him and the customer's project manager. He assured me that the change orders' net result would have no financial impact, since he was trading scope out for anything added. When the list was complete, I asked for all the offsets—what was removed from scope to cover the items added—and their monetary values. The answers were vague.

The project manager later explained that they had refrained from generating a list since the customer's management would reject any change requests. The two project managers, knowing this would result in an unusable system, developed an informal workaround rather than resolving the core problem.

After generating the change request log, I found a strong bias in the customer's favor constituting a significant amount of scope creep. In addition, it showed multiple outstanding change requests that would take significant time to evaluate, adding even more work to an already overburdened team.

Because I had little authority on the project, I escalated the issue and asked that a formal process be established. The changes already processed were continued, but few new changes were approved because of their impact on the customer's budget.

When reading contracts, charters, or inception documents, use three colors of sticky notes or highlighters—one for "What," another for "When," and a third for "Who." Flag each line of the document referring to any of these categories. Add comments on any issues or contradictions needing clarification. When complete, extract these items into a separate worksheet. In this format, it is easier to compare documents to ensure they cover the items defined in the source documents and to detect when new scope appears. Create a set of columns for each document and compare the features declared in each back to the source documents. Spreadsheets are great tools for this. Refer to Case Study 4-7 for an example.

Make sure all the scope elements are defined. Although this task appears simple, undefined items are often found months into a project. Contentious items are a frequent source of undefined scope. These are quick to identify in interviews because they are a source of angst. Vaguely defined items in the contract, differing memories about the project's proposal stage, and items removed in negotiation can also become areas of contention.

Unquantifiable terms are keywords for finding these items. Examples of words too vague to have in any contract or charter include *some, many, large, small, simple,* and *complex.* When the documents were written, the intent of these words may have been clear, but once the project starts, the project manager needs to define them in quantitative terms. Unfortunately, customer and supplier teams have very different definitions of these terms—a simple user interface can do complex transactions. The recovery manager must define all contentious items.

CASE STUDY 4-3:
QUALITATIVE WORD USAGE: SIMPLE AND COMPLEX

Following are lines from two separate contracts, one in a software project and another in a business process reengineering project. They illustrate the importance of clarifying terms as soon as possible on a project.
  1. "The vendor will build 18 simple user interfaces."
  2. "Complex client policies will be considered out of scope."

Addressing these items before work starts on the project ensures the team is working on the correct scope. Allowing the team to work on other parts of the project removes the project manager's advantage for achieving quick and concise resolution of the contract vagaries.

In both cases, numerous meetings were required to resolve the terms' usage. In the former, it was addressed but never resolved, forever nagging the project; in the latter, it was successfully resolved in a couple of weeks by a prudent customer.

New items will be noticeable, as they appear to come out of nowhere. In fact, their source is often differing expectations. The project needs to be driven back to the contractually agreed deliverables (the contract plus any approved change orders). This can affect either party, but most often affects the customer more than the supplier. The customer will need to give up the added scope, and the supplier needs to define the ambiguous items in an equitable manner. The recovery manager's neutrality is crucial; he or she must enforce the contract equally for both parties. This means correcting any previous bias. Inevitably, the group incurring most of this change will judge it as unfair. The recovery manager needs to make sure everyone understands the decision is based on the contract as opposed to being part of a compromise.

Differing expectations about the project delivery arise when the proposal document includes features that are absent from documents produced later in the bid process. Often, proposed features are removed in the contract or charter to make the project fit with other financial or resource constraints. Procurement or program offices commonly change features to meet a given commercial goal. Customers and project managers overlooking these changes require project management education. They need to read the final contract or project charter to understand the actual scope.

Salespeople can unknowingly, often with all good intent, increase scope by continuing to promise features for a project. Salespeople never say no, so the recovery manager needs to intervene. All meetings with the customer should include the recovery manager, especially if a suspicion exists that the account manager or sales representative is inadvertently influencing the scope, even when the person is following the change management process. Evaluating change orders for proposed features can steal significant time from critical resources, thereby causing delays.

Scope Creep Induced by the Project Team

Internal scope creep occurs when the team causes scope to increase; this is the most difficult form of scope creep to identify and contain. It has three main sources:

- Team-suggested enhancements.
- Expanding the design to include additional features available in the technology.
- Implementing overly complex technology.

Internal scope creep is often innocent. The action is overt, and the resulting increase in scope is unintentional. The technical team members consider this performing detailed design rather than causing scope creep.

Enhancements suggested by the team are another form of internal scope creep in which architects, the requirements team, or developers working with the customer suggest adding features to the product. While done with the best of intentions, this shows innocent disregard for the effects it may have on the project as a whole.

The people making these suggestions classify them as implementation details. They feel this justifies the action being outside the governance of a scope management process. For example, assume a new data entry system allows users to cancel their work at any time before the data are committed to the database. The designer working on the implementation asks if there should be a confirmation when the cancellation is requested (e.g., "Are you sure you want to lose your work?"). While capturing the details of what this entails, the team member proposes printing the data entered so the end user has all the data in one report. This will make it easier to reenter. While this is a noble and valuable offer, the request is more than a simple print function. It requires report design (always emotional because of layout preferences), unit testing, system test modifications, training enhancements, and additional maintenance. In addition, one needs to determine if all users have a printer and, if there is personal identifying information such as addresses, phone numbers, and tax identification numbers, whether printing will compromise security. In other words, this simple suggestion adds significant scope to the project, which, when completed, could be unusable.

This form of scope creep can be uncovered by attending definition meetings and customer demonstrations. Listening for phrases like "Would it be beneficial if . . ." will point to where scope is increasing one suggestion at a time. It is also valuable to review edits in test plans or training material. Continually educate and coach the team on how to prevent this type of scope creep.

For some in-house projects, internal scope creep is rampant. Team members feel that delivering more to the customer is best for the company. They are trying to do what is right for the customer, but are unaware of the impact. If this is a standard mode of operation for the organization, then restricting team-induced scope changes will meet with strong resistance. Cultural changes are the hardest to correct since management may be unaware of the impact. The interview process may not always pick this up.

Scope creep is rarely attributed to architectural and technology tasks, although the connection is common. For instance, assume a project goal is to enhance an existing in-house product. The previous version was coded using one set of tools and patterns, but the new project offers the option of switching paradigms to a more current form. This decision is usually the architect's, but the decision will profoundly affect the project. Complexity, training (developer, deployment, and support teams), risk, security, refactoring existing systems, deployment, and maintenance work are factors that can drastically increase the project's timeline. The discussion is an emotional one. For many reasons, technical people like working with state-of-the-art technology—they like learning, they want the challenge, and they enjoy the excitement. Thus, scope creep due to technology differences is difficult to uncover. The team prefers the newer technology, while the project's management and customer may prefer the lower cost and less risky older technology. Some architects refuse to address the issue directly with the project's management. They feel it is their decision alone to make. Thus, the recovery manager needs to listen very carefully to discover this source of creep. Educational requests are sure signs of new technology. Investigate the reasons for classes and validate if they were specified at the project's inception.

CASE STUDY 4-4:
ALIGNING WITH MANAGEMENT: FINDING RELIGION

Trying to get the team to follow management's wishes can be difficult. Steering committees have a much broader view of the company's strategic plan than do project participants. It is the project team's responsibility to provide objective information to management on the short- and long-term costs of possible options. Based on this information, the steering committee will make a decision that the team members need to respect. They need to have faith that the decision is right for the company. I call this "finding religion." If the project team follows a different path in the implementation, scope creep is internal to the project and has no dependence on the customer.

A project I had previously recovered was in phase two of its recovery. It consisted primarily of the prior team's supplier and customer members. It was obvious the customer's requirements analyst was aggressively addressing the previous issue (customer scope creep). In reading the inception documents, the customer clearly requested an "extremely tactical" solution to fix issues with an existing system. The architect defined a solution moving the system to a different platform and enhancing the prior project's product to provide the functionality. In doing this, multiple tasks were added to the task list. One titled "Refactor Struts to JSF" looked as if it was stepping outside the tactical definition. After dissecting the architect's task list, I determined that the time for updating the base of the prior project's product and moving current functionality to a different platform was more than twice the time of updating the existing older architecture product.

The architect simply felt it was "wrong for the company" to continue with the old architecture. A noble concept, but outside the budget and timeline allotted. The technical team caused significant scope creep by refusing to "believe" in management's direction. A different technical team was assigned to update the older technology, but only after I requested that senior management help resolve this issue.

Another source of internally induced scope creep is making a product extensible—capable of handling future, not yet defined, extensions. Regardless of the product's expected lifetime, extensibility should only be addressed if it is specifically called out as a requirement. This should be brought to the attention of the steering committee; if the committee wants it in the scope, process a change request to add it and capture the extra time and cost. Regardless, require a definition of extensibility and a procedure to test it. If executive management prefers to postpone the cost, it stays out of scope. Building a maintainable system is a best practice and is assumed to be in the project scope. Extensibility, on the other hand, must be part of the requirements; it is not a best practice. This is, once again, difficult for technical teams to understand. Instead of anticipating extensibility, they are faced with the task of going back to refactor the code in the future, enhancing it to handle the situation. It is often more costly in the short run to make a product extensible. If the product is a candidate for replacement, the customer or executive management may want to take the chance and incur the extra cost in the future, if the situation actually arises. It is management's prerogative and the team must follow. It is the project manager's, and now the recovery manager's, job to enforce this. It is likely to be unpopular.

One problem with building for the future is testing. If the contract says the product needs to be extensible, it needs to define what is meant and how to test it. The change request also needs to define these parameters. Extensibility is best achieved through developing well-structured systems and waiting until needed to define enhancements. This is one of the benefits of agile and will be discussed in Chapter 11.

Saying No to Limit Scope Creep

The opening quotation for this chapter sums up the task of saying no: it is difficult. Human nature is to say yes, as it is rewarding to please people. However, trying to maintain a project within achievable limits requires a discerning eye and a practical approach.

CASE STUDY 4-5:
"NO" IS DIFFICULT FOR EVERYONE TO SAY

The inability to say no to increases in scope is pervasive. On a particularly difficult project delivering electronics manufacturing equipment, the recovery team and the customer were unable to reach agreement on whether one particular service associated with equipment delivery was in or out of scope. This item was to integrate an extremely complex piece of equipment into a manufacturing system. It was excluded from the SOW through the qualitative statement, "complex equipment interfaces are out of scope." The issue was escalated for executive management to resolve with the customer. Unfortunately, the executive had great difficulty telling the customer it would not be delivered. In every meeting, he would tell the customer the issue was contentious and that something "would be worked out." After each meeting, he would insist he closed the issue. Neither the customer nor the recovery team could understand how it was resolved. The recovery team had to defer all discussion back to the executive. All other deliverables were built for the project and the excluded item was commercially resolved years later.

The Recovery and Project Managers

The project manager must assiduously stick to limiting scope and convince the team to do the same. If the project's prior management failed to do this, the recovery manager must implement processes to do so immediately after the audit. This can be quite a struggle if team members have been browbeaten into feeling they are the problem. It is worse when it is a captive in-house project, since everyone is working for the same company and the feeling is, "what is good for the customer is good for the company." This attitude must be corrected and brought into perspective. Everyone (project team, customer, executive management, etc.) must strictly adhere to the defined scope to achieve the success the customer and executives originally conceived for the portfolio—a far greater issue than the project at hand. The case studies in Chapter 6 provide clear examples of this.

Ultimately, the recovery manager needs to be the curmudgeon, who refuses to expand the scope for the sake of completing the project. A project in trouble needs scope contraction rather than expansion. If scope continues to grow, someone will cancel the project. It is a question of whether the customer wants a product with a modest set of features or no product at all.

At times, the recovery manager needs to refuse change requests. As defined in Chapter 1, success is building a product of value for the customer. This may require significant change order processing. However, the recovery manager must be pragmatic and understand a project can stretch to eternity with change requests. The recovery manager and the customer need to understand the reasons behind a high volume of changes. It is usually indicative of a poorly understood product. In this case, the three options are stopping the project until a proper conceptual design is complete, rescoping the project to build a prototype, or changing the methodology to agile.

The Team That Promises Too Much

The team that promises everything is endemic in many projects. No one likes to say no, and it becomes more difficult as the project becomes more stressful. Agreeing with the customer is the comfort food of projects. Thus, this type of internal scope creep can be covert and less innocent than other forms. The customer conditions the reaction. Saying no elicits a response that the project team is unresponsive and the product will be unusable. The team and the customer need to understand that management will cancel the project if scope gets too big, because it will cost too much and take too long.

The team must desist from agreeing, implicitly or explicitly, to any additional work without a change order. The recovery manager needs to ruthlessly detect and address any additional scope commitment. In addition to the requirements traceability matrix, one method is to use the quality assurance team to compare the current product (alpha or beta) to the specifications and the contract. Assess the scope creep based on the difference in the feature sets.

CASE STUDY 4-6:
THE TEAM'S EXPECTATIONS FOR THE PROJECT

A tactical project was supposed to address only immediate problems with an existing buggy and difficult-to-use system. The approved solution was very expensive. In an attempt to justify the cost, the proposal team agreed to develop code that could be used in future systems.

After a short audit, I pointed out:

- The goal of "reusable code" and "immediately fixing issues" were contradictory.
- The cost was significantly higher than the prior year's proposal.
- The reusability of code was neither measurable nor testable.

The customer had expectations that code would be reusable and many discussions, at times heated, failed to resolve the standoff. Since most of the problem was with the project team, I eventually had to escalate the issue to executive management, which reset the customer's and team's expectations by edict. This lowered the project's cost because it removed the requirement for the costly architecture.

Dealing with Demanding Customers

In some cases, the customer demands more features. Perhaps it is the result of promises made prior to the contract, the country's culture, the customer's company policy, the tactics of a shrewd customer project manager, or a junior project manager who thinks it is the customer's right.

In addition, if the technology is new to the customer or the project's product is state of the art, the customer may have an incomplete understanding of the product's possibilities. As the product becomes more tangible, through specifications, test cases, or prototyping, the customer may see new potential and start asking for additional features. Simply evaluating the impact of these change requests will prolong the project and increase costs.

As mentioned earlier, educating the customer in project management and in the project's product is important, but seldom budgeted. Most project managers are aware of the need to constrain scope to achieve the product within time and budget. Customer project managers with little experience will think they are doing their group a great service by trying to get more for the same amount—at least until the project becomes red. Therefore, it is imperative to educate the customer's project manager on scope management. This requires time and perseverance from the recovery manager. It is reasonable to submit a change request for the education, because it highlights the circumstance to the steering committee.

CASE STUDY 4-7: TOOLS FOR REPRESENTING SCOPE CREEP TO MANAGEMENT

It is difficult to represent scope creep to senior management. Foraging through piles of documents written in technical terms is a waste of its time. During interviews on one recovery, the team indicated the project was hastily started—management gave orders to proceed before the customer completed requirements, cost projections, or risk analysis. IT's executive management requested that I audit the project—in part because it was missing milestones.

My first order of business was to determine the project's actual cost and deliverables. Initial estimates indicated the project would be 20 percent over budget at completion. The major issue was one component, Spec-Maker. This component constituted 47 percent of the projected overrun. The remainder included numerous smaller items, each with a low risk mitigation plan to correct their condition. Controlling the cost overrun of Spec-Maker was unresolved.

The team felt the offending component was in trouble because the customer was changing requirements. The lack of product definition prior to project launch was allowing the scope to grow as the project progressed. The customer's sponsor was an active member of the steering committee and success of this component influenced his yearly bonus. The architect had exhausted all means of curtailing changes and being heavy handed with an executive on scope creep would be futile.

The steering committee meeting to review the audit's findings, where this would be discussed, would be intractable, having too many subjects to cover. Trying to focus members on the scope creep issue of a single component would be difficult. Mitigation plans for each item would need to assure the steering committee that a majority of the cost overruns were handled. With that settled, the meeting could focus on Spec-Maker.

To prepare for the meeting, I had to understand how and why there was such a large overrun on this component. The short-term plan was to:

- Find the problems causing the overrun (at this point assumed to be scope creep).
- Develop a plan to fix the problems.
- Convince the steering committee the problems found were the root cause.
- Designate the key steering committee member to help fix the problem.

The team provided the documentation to prove this was classic scope creep. I outlined the following plan:

- There were too many documents to construct a simple but coherent thread. References would be limited to only three key documents. Otherwise, the convolution in describing the drift would detract from the goal.
- The presentation format would have to show expansion without any need to read the design documents.
- The executive owner was detail oriented, so variations in scope would need to be accurate and well documented. Cross-references to source documents would help with quick and accurate rebuttal to the executive's comments.
- Added or changed requirements would be highlighted using colors. (No one was color blind.)

The three primary versions of the definition document evolved over the prior nine-month timeframe. I extracted the requirements and entered them into a spreadsheet. Working with the design team to determine the requirements' evolution, we summarized the work required to do each one.

Because of his understanding of the impact to the deliverable, the executive, rather than his lieutenants, was the person to educate and trim back the scope. The problem was to present this without taking the executive through a series of requirements and design documents written for technicians.

The challenge was to formulate a good presentation vehicle. I tested numerous graphical methods on the team and all were inadequate, missing the detail required. I decided on a presentation format derived from a Requirements Traceability Matrix, only using multiple versions of the same document versus different documents from the project's life cycle:

- Each column in a table would represent a document version.
- Each requirement in each document would have three data elements presented: the requirement, a document page reference, and a red/green indicator to show if it was the same as the version on the left (green) or different/new (red).
- Any added or changed wording in the requirement was highlighted in red; deleted text was struck through, and colored red.
- Each functional area and its requirements would be grouped in sections.

This method resulted in a table providing:
- Easy-to-analyze details.
- A summary of the features by functional area.
- A visual tool to show growth in the component's scope, even from a distance.

When printed for the presentation to the steering committee, the table was two feet wide and four feet tall, obviously too large to include here. The stark color contrast created a bold visual. Even though the text was unreadable, unless one was within a foot or two of the document, it was easy for the attendees to see large blocks of added requirements where none existed in previous documents and the increasing flood of red over green, emphasizing the additions. To see the actual spreadsheet, please visit the book's website (see Appendix).

To maintain focus and ensure all subjects were covered, I created the following agenda for the meeting:
- Present the project's cost issues.
- Present the recovery plan for the 53 percent of the cost overrun unrelated to Spec-Maker.
- Gain acceptance of the plans covered to this point.
- Graphically present the requirements drift of Spec-Maker and the associated cost.
- Present a recovery plan for Spec-Maker.

The presentation's impact was immediate and positive. As expected, the executive challenged the accusation of scope expansion, but the embedded cross-references provided a quick, strong defense. The steering committee remained focused and discussion on the areas under control was minimal. The desired result, a subsequent meeting to drive the scope back to the original document, was held later that day.

Lesson 4 revisited—"Objective data is your friend, providing the key out of any situation." Data is important, but presenting data in a concise fashion for executives is an art. Graphics help. The old adage is very true: a picture is worth a thousand words.

Chapter Takeaway

- The baseline scope is the contractual scope plus any approved change orders, nothing more.
- Scope creep is the most common symptom of a red project.
- To find scope creep, compare the contract, statement of work, project charter, and change orders with the current scope defined in functional specifications or test specifications.
- Use a requirements traceability matrix to illustrate scope creep.
- Internally induced scope creep (scope creep by the project team) can be difficult to uncover. Sources include:
  - Adding technical requirements unnecessary or contrary to the project's intent.
  - Making the product extensible.
  - Refactoring code.
  - Adding usability features.
- Contentious issues can remain open and be potential sources of scope creep. Their source can be:
  - Expectations from proposals or the inception phase.
  - Vaguely worded items in the statement of work.
- The customer can increase scope from:
  - Incorrect expectations.
  - New requirements as the product becomes tangible.
  - Changing business needs.
  - The desire to get more out of the project.

5

Determining Timeline Constraints

"You may delay, but time will not."

—Benjamin Franklin, American Statesman,
Poor Richard's Almanack

The project is red. The two factors that raise a red flag to management are cost and timeline. The two are inextricably intertwined. As the timeline extends, there is a commensurate increase in cost; similarly, as cost goes up (usually from increased scope), the timeline lengthens. The recovery manager must look at each attribute separately and determine the root problems.

Confirming the Project's Triple Constraints

Customers define triple constraints to convey the relative importance of schedule, budget, and scope. Many factors can change the triple constraints, including any negotiation between the customer and the supplier during the contract award, the processing of change requests, and the recovery process. Be cognizant of these changes and ensure that the team is aware of them. As the relative importance of the triple constraints is based on a number of assumptions specific to each business situation, changes in assumptions can change the relative importance of the constraints.

Validate the existing constraints with the sponsor to determine the timeline's relative importance. The customer's perception of importance is affected by lateness, cost overruns, and ballooning scope. Although the customer is responsible for defining the triple constraints, it is also valuable to ask the executive management to provide its ranking of these factors. This will highlight any differences between management and the customer. For in-house projects, this can have a major effect on the recovery's direction—a superior shared by the customer and the supplier (i.e., the CEO or steering committee) may be driving each group in a different direction.

Although this step is frequently overlooked, remember to document the assumptions on the triple constraints. Scope may be the most important constraint, especially if the assumption is that the customer has trimmed project features to a minimum or that enough time was allowed for schedule overruns with little impact on the business. This assumption may now be invalid, as scope may no longer be the most important constraint, particularly if the customer realizes that developing the features is no longer worth the cost.

Of the triple constraints, the team has the most control over scope and budget. The timeline presents different challenges, as time cannot be stopped. Time simply happens. Work can stop on the project and reassigning people to other projects can bring the burn rate close to zero, but the clock will continue to tick. An absolute deadline cannot be reset.

Projects with time problems are abundant. The impact may relate to tax cycles, school sessions, elections, census data, and government regulations, to name a few. Missing the deadline may postpone the project's usefulness by years, rather than weeks or months. Consider what would happen if one of the multiple U.S. personal tax programs used by millions of people was delayed until March, when taxes are due on April 15. The impact would be devastating to the business. In these cases, the cost of a delay is so large that everything else is subordinate to the release date. Canceling the project is not an option, as that would be tantamount to closing the doors on the business.

Validating the Schedule's Derivation

Since the timeline could be the entire problem, determine the parameters used to build the original schedule and then validate that no changes have been made. Three major methods are used to build a schedule:

1. *Backward pass:* Start with the end date and build the schedule backward to arrive at the start date.
2. *Forward pass:* Begin with a projected start date and add tasks to determine the end date.
3. *Squeeze method:* Set an end date and change durations and dependencies until the project fits in the time allowed.

The first two are sensible ways to build a schedule. However, all too often, the third option is used. This option builds an unrealistic schedule. Assuming task time estimates are correct, the only way to squeeze projects reliably into a timeline is to change the methodology, remove scope, or both. Simply making it fit is a common problem with a project manager who wants to please management. When a project must be squeezed to make a date, the primary triple constraint is obvious—the schedule is the most important constraint and scope, budget, or both must suffer. Since, contrary to popular belief, money does not solve everything, begin by cutting scope until the project meets the required end date.

Schedule high-risk items as early as possible. Frontloading risk provides reaction time. If, on the other hand, the project manager frontloaded the schedule with easier tasks to give the appearance of quick execution, the riskier items and problems surface closer to the end of the schedule. This could negate assumptions and result in rework of previously completed tasks.

For example, a new product is envisioned that exposes a legacy application to a new set of users. The application encapsulates limited features with simple business rules. The project will provide viewing and modification functions. Instead of providing these features all at once, it makes more sense to implement the reporting and viewing features first and concomitantly develop a proof of concept for the transactional system. A later phase can release the maintenance features. This will help solidify the query mechanism to the backend application prior to implementing the transactional processing functions for data entry. The proof of concept starts to uncover the unknowns in the transactional area. This method gets functionality to the users earlier than in the monolithic approach, providing value sooner, an earlier return on investment (ROI), and reduced risk.

The rule of pulling risk forward does not mean increasing project risk by deploying the transactional functions first. Developing the low-risk query functions first is the logical way to build the system, pushing the more complex transactional functions after it. Putting the proof of concept into the first phase brings the risk forward, thereby allowing reaction time. One goal in the recovery's audit phase is to find where risk can be brought forward and to get people to think about this concept before developing the corrective action.

CASE STUDY 5-1: BIG-BANG DEPLOYMENT ISSUES

Many customers are enamored of the concept of deploying their product all at once—a big-bang deployment. There is a good reason for this. Deployments require effort—effort to test, deploy, train, create new standard operating procedures (SOPs), and market. The approach, though, has significant inherent risk. The coordination efforts are exponentially worse in a single-phase project than in a multiphase project. In a monolithic deployment, issues found in a base design or assumptions determined to be false after deployment, can be a monumental feat to correct. However, finding these same issues in a smaller first phase of a project will be easier to fix, with little or no impact on the end user.

Although some costs double with multiple deployments, not all will. Testing is less complex—the effort will be greater, but not doubled. Training will have set-up costs replicated, but the material will be different. Analyze each component of cost to determine the overall impact.

Numerous methods can be used to show customers the benefits of multiphase deliveries. On a project that was building and delivering a set of sales tools, the customer was persuaded to phase the delivery, as the salespeople would have less to learn with each deployment. As a result, the project ran smoother and was also easier to manage, as fewer people were involved.

On another project, where the company's customers were updating their employee records, the marketing department used multiple deployments to create more sales opportunities with the customer. The multiple deployments resulted in more contact with the customer while promoting the roadmap. This increased annual sales.

Phasing also provides more flexibility in reprioritizing requirements. After seeing the first set of features deployed on a handheld meter's prototype, the customer feedback resulted in reprioritization of the importance of other features. This is one of the many advantages of agile development.

Issues to Investigate on Estimation Methods

Study the method of determining the task's resource, dependency, and duration estimates. Common mistakes in creating a schedule are:

- Managers determining task effort and resource requirements. They are too far from the actual work to understand its complexity.
- Estimates surrounding new technology are too short since the team members are unaware of the issues they will encounter in the implementation—the devil is in the details.
- The project manager or team is unclear on the estimation process.
- The team is using a mixture of durations and efforts to generate the schedule.
- The effect on the task's duration when adding resources is misunderstood— nine women cannot make a baby in a month.
- Overoptimistic resource allocation, neglecting inter- and intraproject conflict, vacations, training, and holidays.
- Overbooking resources by neglecting to level the resource loading.
- Assuming all resources can perform a given task with the same efficiency.
- Making tasks fit a given delivery date.

Managers should educate their teams to use the same estimation process. This will provide a modicum of consistency in the results. By creating a common method, the recovery manager will have a better understanding of how changes will influence tasks.

CASE STUDY 5-2:
VACATIONS IN THE MONTH OF AUGUST

A common faux pas in creating schedules is ignoring cultural differences in vacation and holiday schedules. Thus, projects outside Europe often schedule European resources to work throughout the summer. However, many European countries take the month of August as a holiday. This same issue is true in other cultures when it comes to holidays and work weeks. Take, for instance, the work slowdown in the United States between Thanksgiving and Christmas. Even the length of the work week may be different. Neglecting to account for this in a schedule can be disastrous.

For example, a project to start a new manufacturing facility in September had a major supplier based in France. Unfortunately, the project manager did not realize the supplier would not have staff available in August for equipment qualification. The supplier, on the other hand, thought that everyone was aware of the European holiday tradition. The project was delayed almost eight weeks due to problems in rescheduling other vendors.

Reviewing the estimation and schedule building process will identify other constraints and dependencies. Document any additional relationships found and communicate them to management. Derive and report the impact to date and the projected project delay.

When building a schedule most managers ask people how long it will take them to complete a given task with some degree of certainty—"How long *will* it take you to complete this task?" The respondents base their answers on experience performing this, or a similar, task in the past. This determines the duration of work, rather than effort. The estimates include the time spent doing other nontask-related duties. To achieve a degree of certainty, respondents give a number that, experiments show, have approximately an 80 percent certainty. This means 80 percent of the time the task *should* be completed early. If each task has the same certainty of completion, this inserts a significant amount of padding into the schedule. Understanding how the estimates were created determines where people have padded the schedule or omitted critical portions of work or risk. The problems with excessively padding the schedule are discussed in Chapter 12.

Critical resources can also create a scheduling problem. These resources have unique capabilities in the project or company. If they are used heavily in the schedule, or worse, in other projects, their scarcity may generate significant risk.

Investigate augmenting these resources with others inside or outside the company. Assess their effect on the schedule and ask them for a mitigation plan.

Determine each requirement's actual delivery date—the date when it must be delivered. Just because the initial proposal provides a date does not mean all the features need to be delivered at that time. Changing the deliverables' sequencing may be imperative to implementing a successful recovery plan. Many customers request the delivery of all functionality at one time—the big-bang approach. This concept effectively increases the scope for a given time period. If it is possible to phase the project, then scope for each phase is much smaller and more manageable. Negotiating a phased delivery will be covered in Chapter 14, but the data needs to be accrued in the audit phase to understand the possible options. Spend time drilling into the need for each feature in the initial delivery. Often, differences of opinion may be found between different business groups, and this will provide fresh ideas of how phasing might work.

Understanding How Team Progress Is Reported

How people report their progress on a task can be misleading. Understand how information regarding status is collected. When capturing the status of a task, the manager should ask about the effort required to complete the task rather than the percentage completed. It is very difficult for someone to estimate if a task is 30 percent or 60 percent complete, so they may answer by comparing the time they have spent to the total time or the subtasks they have completed to all subtasks. Neither is accurate and is usually just a guess. Instead, individuals should report the amount of time they will need to complete the task. This alone can explain an apparent stall in a project. If tasks are stuck at 80 percent, individuals may be completing work on items missed in the original estimates, mitigating risk, or gold plating the deliverable. Asking for a list of subtasks to complete the current task will expose this problem.

While accruing data about task completion, take the opportunity to look for gold plating of the deliverable. Gold plating is adding qualities, features, and functions that are nice, but have low priority. Although this issue is often attributed to developers and engineers, other team members can gold plate the project.

Some examples are:

- Ensuring documents are in a common font or style when they are already readable.
- Adding nonspecified print functions when screen prints would suffice.
- Providing too much detail to a schedule (i.e., to the hour).
- Adding redundant inspections.
- Designing automated features that are more easily done manually.

Gold plating is often harder to detect with architects and developers because they tend to want to handle all possible situations. This issue was addressed in Chapter 4, "Scope Creep Induced by the Project Team," but bears repeating because it consumes significant time. Adding "little" features that would be nice to have (i.e., autocompletion of field values, additional light, etc.) or reusing previously built components may be proposed with the best of intentions, but require time to incorporate, test, and train, and often introduce issues unrelated to the base requirements.

One way to find gold plating is to keep track of subtasks. In the early stages, as the task is being understood, the list of subtasks may grow. However, as the task nears completion, the list should remain constant. If it does not, find out why. If the list stays the same and time drags on, review the resource's work. Subtasks may be being added covertly. When looking at remaining subtasks, an astute task manager can determine if gold plating is present.

Although quality is paramount, quality, like the word project, is relative to the person. To use a Six Sigma term, some features are not critical to quality. The phrase critical to quality refers to items of value in the product. Because quality is judged by the value of features, working on items of little value to the customer wastes time and money. The critical-to-quality concept ensures the project is focusing on the elements with the greatest value. A feature done perfectly is useless if it has no value to the customer. The entire time spent on its development, testing, and training is wasted. For instance, some people spend hours reformatting documents ensuring they are attractive or use a common font or style. Although this may improve readability of the documents, it does not provide value to the product. It is not something an architect or engineer should spend time on. If these attributes really are needed, hire a document coordinator to perform these tasks more quickly and cost effectively. However, if the document is an advertising piece (in other words, the product), then font selection and consistency could be very important—it is critical to quality.

Striving for perfection is another action that will destroy a schedule. Too often quality and perfection are confused. Making the perfect system is akin to gold plating. Beware of the perfectionist. The product will never be perfect, documents will never read eloquently, systems can always run faster, and colors can always be better. Make sure the goals are defined and achievable in the allotted time.

If work seems to drag on after completion, inhibiting people from starting their next task, make sure people's task completion dates are actually the date they will stop working on the task. Some people give a date to hand off the deliverable instead of a date on which they will be finished with their work. It may be a date someone else can start using the output. Tasks ranging from final editing and testing to approvals can stretch out the work the resource has to do after handing the product to the next person. The task appears complete on the schedule, but the resource continues to invest time, preventing him or her from performing other tasks. Determine the effort expended after a task is declared complete, and either stop the behavior or build the time into the schedule.

Often, to meet a deadline, quality will be sacrificed. The task will be declared complete and a successor task will start, but work will continue on cleaning up the prior deliverable. This unfortunate situation hits the timeline doubly hard, as poor quality results in time devoted to reworking the product and the subsequent products using it. In addition, this increases frustration, creates loss of confidence, and can result in a deterioration of team interaction. Interviews usually discover low quality, but the frustration may be directed at a resource instead of at the pressure to make a delivery date.

If milestones are being missed, determine if the responsibility falls to one or two individuals or to the entire team. If only a small set of critical resources is involved, then find ways to assist them. Is it possible to offload preparation or wrap-up work? Is input data to the task the right format, complete, and to a quality to expedite the resource's work? If the entire team is missing milestones, then examine the original assumptions around the schedule. This is a sign the schedule is being forced into a time-box to appease management.

Overtime is a definite indication the schedule has issues, even if the project is relatively on track. Overtime will destroy a budget and ruin morale. Understand why people are being asked to work overtime. Extra hours can bring the schedule in, but can burn out a team. If time is spent reworking or making up for unplanned events, it has an even greater effect. The norm for the project should be a standard work shift.

Unplanned events also show a poor planning process. Although this sounds obvious, people regularly overlook it. The team will insist that planning went well, but unforeseen and unanticipated issues arose that caused schedules to slip. This is usually a poorly understood or ill-defined project. Be it lack of experience with the product, poor assessment of risk, or inappropriate mitigation plans, some form of replanning is required.

As referred to earlier, resource allocation and loading is important. Although rarely done, resources should be dedicated to the project and, at a minimum, to the task. Multitasking individuals among projects or other efforts can create unseen scheduling conflicts. During interviews, find the people allocated to multiple projects and determine if they are overloaded. For each of them, create and enforce priorities that reflect the relative importance of other projects. This should start prior to getting approval on the recovery plan. This is a wonderful area in which to take control and potentially reduce the frustration of resources that are being pulled in multiple directions. If this project has a lower priority, then the tasks may be fully justified in being late. Ensure management understands the conflict.

As discussed in Part III, set realistic expectations for schedules early in the recovery process. Timelines cannot be developed until there is a complete understanding of what is wrong with the project. At this point, the recovery manager can only set expectations around the degree of schedule trouble. Most importantly, a plan is needed to develop a schedule. Present those plans early and keep them updated. Although schedules may slide, it instills mistrust to let this happen without notification.

Finally, be aware of the organization's culture. The norm may be late delivery. Identify and note this as an issue since significant effort outside the project manager's purview will be required to countermand the practice.

Chapter Takeaway

- Determine the actual milestone requirements and understand their business impact.
- Review the estimates for the schedule:
  - Everyone should be educated on and using the same process.
  - Estimates should be realistic, instead of guesses or heavily padded, and made with full understanding of the tasks.
- Determine who the critical resources are.
- Review the schedule's resource loading and ascertain if overloaded individuals actually are overloaded.
- Determine if tasks have room for gold plating and whether it is being done.
- If task completion dates are regularly missed, determine if this is a problem or if other tasks are completed ahead of schedule to compensate.
- Ensure tasks that are reported complete are actually complete.
- Understand the reason for any overtime.
- Document if resources are used on multiple projects, the project's relative priority, and how the project manager is notified when the resource is used.

CHAPTER

6

Examining Technology's Effect on the Project

"Technology. . . is a queer thing. It brings you great gifts
with one hand, and it stabs you in the back with the other."

—C. P. Snow, English Physicist and Novelist,
The Two Cultures

Nearly every project today has a technical component, be it a word processor or a microprocessor, that creates unusual challenges. Technology's impact is the project's most difficult area to assess because recovery managers generally lack current technical knowledge, the technical teams prefer working on new technology, and there are variations in the proposed product's lifecycle. Determining the correct balance of technological elements required to meet the project's goals is an art.

The Importance of Technical Expertise in the Audit

If the project has a technical component, the recovery manager should have a strong technical background so that he or she can talk with the technical team on its own level, gaining trust as someone who understands the challenges. This must be coupled with an independent critical eye questioning the direction. Many aspects of technology development can contribute or even cause trouble on a project. A recovery manager grounded in accepted best practices as well as the latest in technological advances, tools, and methodologies is invaluable in determining where problems may manifest themselves.

The organization's architectural group should assist the recovery manager in analyzing the technical direction in the context of the contract or charter. It is crucial that the implementation remain focused on the project's goals. Architectural groups cannot let the organization's goals bias their view of a signed contract. That would lead to scope expansion. If there is no architectural group, as with many subcontracted projects, an unbiased party may be difficult to find, since the architects from the customer or supplier will be looked upon as prejudiced to financial goals of their employers. The three options are:

- Bring in an outside party.
- Find two architects (one from each team) who can objectively evaluate the solution.
- Have the recovery manager perform the evaluation.

Understanding the Technology Goals of the Project

Start by determining the project's technology goals. The triple constraints sometimes fail to reflect this. In most cases, the customer should be neutral about the technology. The primary concern should be the product's features and whether the resulting system meets the customer's short-term, long-term, and maintenance needs. Therefore, the technology used for the solution's implementation is specified behind the scenes, reflecting the engineering team's desires rather than the project's goals. This can cause a division in the project, as the technical team pushes technology (scope) where the customer's triple constraints may be schedule, budget, or a different set of scope.

It is possible that the customer will require a certain technology. There are a number of reasons this could be a valid requirement. The audit must assess the technology's impact and ensure it is part of the requirements.

CASE STUDY 6-1: WHEN TECHNOLOGY IS AN INTEGRAL PART OF THE PROJECT

At times, a project requires something new. A large software integration project was such a case. A client was starting a new line of business that required capturing data that its current systems were incapable of storing.

In addition, the client was plagued with multiple poorly integrated systems necessitating redundant data entry. A separate initiative was in progress to use a new product to store the common data and to use a messaging architecture to integrate all business systems.

The new line of business was an ideal application of this new technology. However, the technology's impact on this project, due to bugs, lack of understanding of the new product, and overreaching promises from the vendor, required numerous shortcuts in the implementation. This violated the new technology's strategic nature. Compromises were required in the implementation to deliver the project on time (it was truly time constrained). The compromises had to be rectified in a subsequent project.

Products new to the team (regardless of whether they are state-of-the-art) pose risk to the project because the team is unaware of the implementation's details and inherent issues. This could result in:

- Increased implementation time as the design team understands the impact of a decision.
- Increased time to build as the product is being understood.
- Design rework, if the people trying to build the product determine a design decision is incorrect or if the product functions improperly.
- Replacing the technology or changes in scope if it is determined that the requirements cannot be fulfilled.

The first three of these of these can be addressed in the audit as quantifiable risk. Interviewing the team can determine the degree of familiarity with the technology and establish reasonable estimates for learning curves and rework. The last issue can only be noted as an unquantifiable risk, since the degree of the impact and the uncertainty of what area it will effect make it very difficult to account for in advance.

Understanding Architects' Biases

Many architects, with the best of intentions, attempt to build a more robust solution than is required. For instance, they add features to the design to accommodate future expansion. Some of this is sensible, but unless time and money are budgeted for it, it must be avoided.

Justification lies in the fact that workarounds and quick fixes are never replaced. Shortcuts stick around forever, and money is rarely budgeted for proper solutions. Nearly anyone can name multiple situations where a quick fix is implemented and never replaced. People become frustrated because these solutions are difficult to maintain, the ones who built it have left the company, and maintenance becomes nearly impossible. However, the fact of the matter is, if this caused real pain for management, it would make funds available to replace the workarounds. Management has other more burning issues to address. Determine if there is an edict to follow a technically compromised direction from management and work with the architects and developers to align them to this direction. The technicians must "find religion" (see Case Study 4-4, pg. 55) and believe management is doing the right thing.

Gold plating, the behavior of overbuilding the solution, can be overt or covert, and the audit should document and report its occurrence. Senior management will probably need to help adjust the behavior. Overt gold plating is easy to address, but covert action can be difficult to rectify. As discussed in Part III, dealing with covert actions will require more effort.

CASE STUDY 6-2: CONFLICT OF INTEREST WHEN DEFINING THE SOLUTION

I was asked to run a software upgrade project that had been through the inception process. It looked to be an extremely simple project, but it had a business constraint that required completion in six months. The existing product, which the project would replace, was poorly designed and bug laden. The customer was told numerous times that the underlying technology, a programming language, was defective and was the reason for the product's lack of such features as prepopulation of screens. The architectural team refused to look at upgrading the existing product by fixing the numerous bugs and adding the prepopulation function. As it turned out, the architect for the project was the architect and proponent for another product. He wanted to incorporate the existing functionality and new features into this other product. This was significant scope creep. In addition, the architect reported to the product's owner instead of a neutral architecture group. Although the solution he was proposing was technically better, it required nearly twice the work. His justification was that it was the right thing for the company and that management was unaware of the consequences of its decision. He had yet to "find religion."

Assessing Technology's Effects on the Team's Behavior

As hinted at in the previous section, technology has a huge effect on behavior. Most people enjoy working with something new and different. It adds interest to the workday, since it is fun to learn something new. In high-tech fields, this opportunity presents itself every day. Technology is advancing at a rapid pace. Shortly after a product is deployed, newer versions of tools, paradigms, and languages are available. Architects, engineers, and developers find the continuing education about new tools and techniques, problem solving, and exposure to new problems exciting. With this comes the concern that they must keep up with technology trends or diminish their net worth. Worse yet, they fear becoming obsolete.

These conditions create an atmosphere in which technologists need to adopt new technologies to ensure they are up to date on the latest skills. This creates a conflict of interest in the project. Project managers want their teams to be happy; technologists want to work with new technology. However, technology costs money—to purchase, for training, to debug, and to handle myriad associated risks. For these reasons, management may disagree with the technologists on the role technology should play in the project.

Architects, engineers, and developers are pleased seeing a sharp-looking, feature-filled, bug-free product in front of their customer. They get accolades for its ease of use and the benefits. This input is an automatic feedback system to reinforce the promotion of new technology, adding yet more features, tweaking the component just a little more, adding just a couple of more hours to make it just that much better. The environment rewards the technologists for this behavior. They enjoy being the hero, and the customer applauds the behavior. The entire culture is set up for promoting an increase in scope, adding more features, and using the technology to its fullest, regardless of the added time, cost, and risk.

New and untested products can further pique the technical team members' interest because they add excitement to the project, increase their knowledge, and improve their résumés. Because of this, estimates for the tool's or product's use are subconsciously optimistic. In their zeal to use the new technology, team members may have bought into the sales pitch without understanding the risks involved. Often teams will look at a potential tool and feel it will be the answer to all the project's problems—a silver bullet. This is usually a fatal mistake, as the new technology is sure to have as many, or more, issues to resolve because of its lack of maturity. Seasoned project managers commonly decry that the tool they have now is the devil they know, while the new tool is the devil to be met and reckoned with.

The recovery manager has to look at the project's requirements, break through the technologist's behavior, find the right compromise for the project, and sell that to the team. If it cannot be sold, it must be an edict.

Assessing the Team's Capability with the Technology

The recovery manager needs to determine the team's skill set with respect to the technology used. Whether it is old or new, COBOL or Java, lathe-and-plaster or carbon fiber composites, the team must understand more than the technology; it must also understand the business rules and processes. This is most evident in older systems. As time goes on, legacy systems get older, the people working on these systems retire, or, in an attempt to keep themselves marketable, move on to newer opportunities. The tribal knowledge of the system disappears.

With special technology comes another issue—the indispensable person. The indispensable person is the only person on the project knowing the technology. The numerous issues arising from this include:

- Increased risk if the person leaves the project.
- Creating bottlenecked tasks by relying on one person's skills.
- Animosity in the group because of this person's arrogance or feeling of superiority.

Identify these individuals and develop plans to minimize any adverse effects they may have on the team.

Evaluating Make-Buy Options

With the adoption of new products, the recovery manager should ask questions to determine the fundamental requirement and the approach's applicability. The questioning should determine if:

- The implementation is actually part of a strategic effort.
- Common-off-the-shelf (COTS) products have similar functionality.
- External resources might do the work more efficiently.

Integrating a third-party product presents its own challenges. The requirements need to be relatively flexible to allow a smooth integration. Rarely will the third-party product contain the ideal features. If critical requirements remain unfulfilled, the recovery manager has the option of requesting that the vendor customize the product, adding the features with a custom-built solution, or modifying the requirement. The first option should be to change the requirement. If the requirement cannot be modified, then significant resources, time, and money may be needed to accommodate it.

Chapter Takeaway

- Technology has a strong impact on any project, even more so in high-tech projects.
- The audit requires a technology knowledgeable recovery manager or assistance from an unbiased architect.
- Only in rare cases should a customer be concerned with technology. If so, the statement of work should list it as a requirement.
- There are no silver bullets. New technology poses more risk than existing technology as the team is inexperienced with the new technology.

- The desire to implement a technology can cause conflicts in the project's triple constraints.
- The recovery manager will need to strike a compromise between the technical team's desire for new and more advanced technology and management's time, budget, and business constraints.
- In technology-challenged groups, look for common off-the-shelf solutions.
- Document all of resource concerns and mitigation plans.

III

Analyzing the Data

Planning for Project Recovery

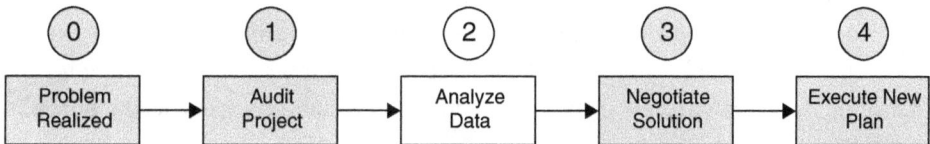

0		1		2		3		4
Problem Realized	→	Audit Project	→	Analyze Data	→	Negotiate Solution	→	Execute New Plan

The first step in the recovery process was to interview project team members to learn their perspectives on the issues troubling the project. It also provided clues to finding the root causes of those problems. Before proceeding further, two things must be done. First, reevaluate the audit's assumptions and, second, if the guidelines request it, deliver the audit report.

The first four chapters of this section discuss two major activities: analyzing the data and building a recovery plan. These activities include a further analysis of the data and the development and testing of potential plans for project recovery. The purpose is to convert pieces of data about what went wrong into a successful approach to the way the project will run in the future.

The recovery plan consists of a recommended project charter, corrective actions, and project plan. Together, they define how to bring the project back from red. The recommendation will be to:

- Cancel the project.
- Do nothing.

- Implement a set of corrective actions and a new project plan to complete a newly defined deliverable.

The recovery plan will define the areas to fix and recommend changes in the project and product to achieve the desired result.

With the audit complete, the recovery manager should implement limited constraints around the team to improve communication and to get scope, technology, and timeline under control. Even in this early phase, some obvious procedural problems will become evident. Implementing rudimentary processes and procedures will slow the bleeding.

As part of the go-forward plan, it is critical to look at the methodology used in the project. Processes are important to any project, failing or successful. Many times, poorly defined or missing processes are the problem with a project. Groups of processes constitute the methodology. Therefore, the methodology is critical to the project's success.

Ensuring the methodology is the right fit for the type of project is time well spent. Construction, facilities, hardware deployments, and software upgrades need to be well defined prior to implementation. Innovative products, however, need a highly adaptable process to allow discovery when building something for the first time. In other words, organizations with a portfolio of projects need a portfolio of processes.

The last four chapters of this section discuss the advantages of three methodologies in solving issues. They provide the basic knowledge for implementing aspects of phased, agile, and critical chain methodologies to solve specific project ills. Recovery is the bias of this presentation and therefore requires a good understanding of limited aspects of these tools. Recommended Reading offers in-depth resources.

7

Determining and Initiating Remedial Action

"The shortest answer is doing."

—Lord Edward Herbert, British Soldier and Diplomat,
The Autobiography of Edward, Lord Herbert of Cherbury

With the audit's completion, there is a thorough understanding of what is wrong with the project. Many of the issues have been assigned preliminary root causes. Now is the time to validate the findings and formulate the corrective action plan.

Before proceeding, though, the recovery manager should:

- Reevaluate decisions made and actions taken.
- Start to take some remedial action to correct basic issues.
- Implement the missing best practices.

To do this, the recovery manager must step out of the nonjudgmental role and take charge.

The Audit Report

If the recovery guidelines require an audit report, develop it now. The audit report needs to identify what went wrong and what needs to happen before continuing with the project. This will not include all the corrective actions and the new project plans, as they are developed during this phase. The report should have enough data to tell the steering committee the order of magnitude of the work needed to move the project forward. Chapter 14 discusses preparing for these types of meetings. Even though the need for negotiation is missing, all other aspects are the same.

Determining Whether to Continue or Cancel the Project

Regardless of the requirement for an audit report, it is logical to review the appropriateness of actions taken and decisions made. The recommendation is to keep the project running and implement rudimentary corrective actions prior to the major ones.

Now that you are armed with more data on how specific issues are affecting the project, conduct a sanity check to validate if the project should continue. If slowing the bleeding will deplete resources from other healthy projects or return negative value to the organization, then the project should be suspended or canceled.

The project cannot wait until the recovery manager finishes analyzing the data, building a recovery plan, and getting approval before implementing further changes. Therefore, start taking action early; it will provide valuable data on how the team responds to change. With the knowledge gained from the audit, many options should be obvious. Some will be noncontroversial and easy to implement.

Another advantage to implementing highly visible rudimentary fixes is to ensure anxious executives that action is being taken, thereby giving the recovery manager time to determine the root causes of the project's problems. It is rarely the case that one problem has caused all this grief or that all root causes will be discovered during the audit. Therefore, the recovery manager should resist jumping to conclusions.

Transitioning from the Auditor's Role to Taking Charge

After the audit is complete, the recovery manager needs to take obvious and indisputable charge of the project. Taking control too early will compromise collecting objective data because acting too much like a boss will bias the data gathered. To start the recovery process, the recovery manager first accepts responsibility for identifying and fixing all problems on the project. This should be a humble act, without accolades about prior successes or assigning blame for current conditions. What is required are honest acceptance and a plan for addressing the issues. Time will bring credit to the recovery manager, as the project's successful completion will speak loudly. The team needs to know the recovery manager will take the heat for all problems and any issues caused by team members. The team needs to understand the importance of reporting all issues promptly and with as much warning as possible. Reprimands should be private and fair. Blame will rarely, if ever, be assigned, as this is usually counterproductive. Only assign blame if the company culture demands it.

The stakeholders also need to understand that the recovery manager is in charge. Implement a strict policy that all communication goes through the recovery manager. No one from outside the team should go to the team members without the recovery manager's knowledge and approval. Why? Because scope creep and communication are the two biggest problems. Therefore, funneling all communications through the recovery manager will quickly show where the problems are and will let the recovery manager resolve them directly.

Restricting communications will meet with a lot of resistance, but it is required in the initial phases of recovery. Executive management and the customer will try to bypass this policy by going directly to team members with changes. The recovery manager needs to shut down these channels and unconditionally support the team.

A common concern is that people work well together and more layers of management will further slow progress. Assure people that this communication policy is a transient requirement to bring the recovery manager into the communication loop. When critics say this is too dictatorial, remind them that the project is failing and drastic actions are required. Unfortunately, for them, successful projects are not democratic institutions.

Red projects have numerous open issues, and someone needs to assume responsibility for them. Therefore, the recovery manager should take all open action items and determine how to resolve them. Assign people to work on them without assigning blame for why they are open. This is easier than it sounds. Many issues are smaller than purported simply because the team is in trouble and small issues get overblown. The project's paralyzed state inhibits many decisions. The data mined in the audit is a big benefit in providing direction for attacking the problems. Some issues can be resolved on this data alone. Solve as many issues as possible with the data available. Even if some of the decisions are less than ideal, the project will at least begin moving forward. Just be ready to act on new data and update the decision.

If the recovery manager cannot resolve the action items with data from the audit, assign the responsibility to the most qualified people. The assignees must realize this action is to assign accountability to get the tasks done and is not for the placing of blame. This will start changing the team's behavior from defensive to confident.

Most red projects lack decision makers. They are stigmatized by suggestions from too many people and the overwhelming number of critical comments. As a result, people have stopped making decisions for fear of ridicule. The team, on the other hand, is waiting for decisions to clear roadblocks and direct its effort. Decision making will gain trust and inspire people to form a team to help in the recovery.

The recovery manager has to be polite, but firm. This is business in its primal sense, and there is no room for making friends. There needs to be root cause analysis, cold factual decision-making, and corrective actions. This is not necessarily pretty or fun. The application of the actions needs to be just and fair. Favoritism will deteriorate the team and its loyalty to the project and the recovery manager.

CASE STUDY 7-1:
MAKING A DECISION TO GET THE PROJECT MOVING

A large project to develop a new set of data collection hardware had four major components. Definition of two of the components' requirements was complete, and the team wanted to start development. This was possible since these components were distinctly separate from the others and the interface requirements were complete. The PMO, however, had a methodology requiring all steps of a project's phase be complete prior to commencing the next phase, commonly known as a gate process. To get the recovery moving, I authorized the team to start building the first units without PMO approval of the definition gate, which was still three weeks away; I would handle the fallout from the decision later. This gained significant trust only after one person decided to complain about my decision to circumvented corporate standards. At the PMO meeting, with most of the leads present, I admitted making the decision to get the project moving after a two-month period of stagnation. The PMO commended the action as a sensible decision that would stop waste. This action solidified the team's trust.

Planning the Right Level of Process for the Project

To run a project efficiently requires many processes. The audit determined which of those were in place. Experience shows that a few processes are commonly missing and are major contributors to project failure. Now, in the analysis phase, implement or amend the missing or ineffective processes. Without this solid foundation, it is impossible to determine the other issues influencing project performance.

The recovery manager must be able to explain why processes were missing or functioning improperly, recommend steps to correct the problems, and provide assurance to the stakeholders that the project will adhere to them in the future. To be sure, it is part of the recovery manager's job to implement and monitor these core processes as quickly as possible.

It is imperative to remove redundant and wasteful processes. This may incur political resistance, but removing wasteful processes will gain significant respect from the team. Eventually even the people who wanted them will understand the reasons.

The fundamental processes to address are meeting minutes, change management processes, risk registers, and schedules. Ultimately, the schedule may be the most important. Surely, this is true for the customer and management, but a useful schedule requires further planning and a solid understanding of scope, risks, and assumptions. Furthermore, management must agree to the changes and will therefore need to wait until a complete recovery plan is developed. A detailed schedule, at this point, is misleading. No schedule at all is better than a misleading schedule. Right now, the most that can be developed is a two- to three-week rolling schedule.

Requiring Meeting Minutes

Meeting minutes are the easiest process to define, since the concept is simple and there is little process involved. Unfortunately, team resistance to performing the task is usually very high and difficult to overcome. Ensuring adherence to this process will require the recovery manager's utmost vigilance.

After developing a meeting minutes' template, identifying a public repository, and educating people on the function, the recovery manager needs to enforce the process and lead by example. Every meeting needs an agenda and minutes—no exception. In addition, the recovery manager needs visibility of every meeting so he or she can validate the process is followed. The recovery manager has to hold the meeting organizer accountable for unpublished minutes.

The resistance comes from a number of areas. Good minutes are difficult to write, no one likes the additional work, and it takes time to see the benefits. However, in two months, when memories have waned, published minutes come to the rescue. It will happen. Few things are more satisfying to the team than to have its work pay off with "According to the minutes. . ."

Some points to keep in mind about minutes:

- All meeting minutes must have action items (with responsibility and due date assigned), a general discussion section, and conclusions.
- The minutes are binding. All meeting attendees need to understand that they have only one week to challenge or amend the minutes.
- Team members should volunteer to take minutes for meetings they attend or organize even though it adds to their workload. Why? First, it is hard to get the customer or management to take minutes on meetings. Second, team members will include items that are meaningful to them and, therefore, to the project team. In contrast, proofreading someone else's minutes is often ineffective and results in many missed items. Further, an administrative assistant is a poor choice unless he or she is intimately aware of the project's subtleties. A common failure of minutes is the omission of the finer points.

- Minutes refresh the meeting in the author's eyes. When project team members write the minutes, the account will better reflect the real meeting results.
- The minutes' general discussion section should summarize all points covered in the meeting—in addition to the conclusions. The minutes serve as a historical record of the objections and rebuttals. It should reference any discussion resulting in an action item, debate prior to a conclusion, and comments leading to the next meeting's agenda.
- They should set the goals for any follow-up meetings.
- All minutes should copy the recovery manager, who must read the minutes to find any indication of divergence from the project plan. This is the place where the recovery manager will stay on top of subtle scope changes by the customer and management.

Note that it is impossible for the recovery manager to change the company's culture on writing minutes, so be persistent. Push to get everyone to follow the rules, but pick battles carefully. The suggested workaround of having someone from the team do the minutes will better serve the purpose, particularly since team members will assign tasks to managers that would otherwise be delegated to people lacking the authority required.

The recovery manager, or assistant, should extract and log all action items and their status from the minutes. Address any item that remains unresolved or with due dates that have been extended more than twice. Work with the responsible individuals and the person or group affected to assess impact. Action items that remain open may actually be unimportant and, after discussion with the parties involved, may be removed from the list. Press the appropriate people to resolve the item, make it a task, or delete it.

If roadblocks or issues arise during the day, add them to the action item list. Determine why they were missed and correct the behavior so they are caught in the future. People will refuse to use an action item log if there is no benefit, so hold people accountable for completing their action items on time.

Implementing a Change Management Process

Implementing a change management process, or following an existing one, is one of the project's thankless jobs. The change management process, however, is critical to the project's success. It is such a prevalent problem that Chapter 20 covers the subject as one of the key methods to prevent projects from getting in trouble. Do this even if the recovery is leaning toward an agile approach (see Chapters 10 and 11); it collects the information needed to support a change in the methodology.

CASE STUDY 7-2:
PROJECT MANAGER INDUCED SCOPE CREEP

On a large factory automation project, scope appeared to be totally out of control. The team kept blaming the project manager. However, the project manager felt he fully understood all the changes' ramifications, including the technical aspects, and therefore neglected to consult the architect before committing to change requests. Many team members mocked his reply to the customer as, "This could be done with an IF statement and a DO loop." Of course, it was more complex.

A rigidly followed change management process averts these issues. Everyone on the team should ask for a change order before altering his or her deliverable.

Prior to attempting the implementation of a change management process, the recovery manager must enlist the support of every person in the escalation path. Members of upper management must understand the process as well as their responsibility. They must understand that if change has gone unchallenged in the past, the implementation of this process is going to meet with resistance. The customer is likely to escalate nearly every change request. If upper management fails to stand behind a majority of the recovery manager's dispositions, the process and the recovery will be defeated. When there is agreement on the process, publish minutes confirming upper management's support and understanding of the process and reiterate the responsibilities of its members.

The process will meet with resistance. The requirement for a change order and the disposition will be met with:

- "We don't need this. It has never been done before."
- "This has to be in scope; the system won't work without it."
- "This is a small change; we don't need all this paperwork."
- "This could never cost that much!"

As change requests, and the effort associated with their implementation, are reviewed, the people who approve them will realize the change's impact: internal cost; external cost (purchase order generation); changes to the project's schedule; and potential effects on individual performance appraisals. The last may provide for some contentious situations.

When people start to challenge change requests, reaffirm upper management's role. Management will need to support the recovery manager and, later, the project manager to ensure that changes properly account for all cost and schedule adjustments. When objections increase on a change request, apprise management of the potential issues and the financial impact. Significant skill and tenacity will be required to maintain management support. Lack of management support may be a significant contributor to the project's trouble. The recovery manager cannot let any change go unaccounted. The precedent of lax change management sets the stage for continual arguments about the process and a high probability for continued failure.

Implementing a change management process may also highlight other issues in the project. If it generates a large number of change requests, it often indicates a poorly understood product. Both the business analyst and the customer need to take responsibility. It can make for a very defensive situation, especially if the customer wants to place all the blame on the project team. The customer will attempt to shift its failures to the business analysts (who, indeed, may bear some of the responsibility), but business analysts rarely know the customer's needs better than the customer, so they rarely deserve all the blame. The customer is surely going to own a majority of the responsibility for a poorly understood product. The recovery manager needs to pay special attention to the accusations and be very objective in assigning responsibility. Regardless, senior management needs to be prepared and ready for the reaction.

Next to communication, scope creep and poor definition are the primary common problems on projects. If either is an issue, change management processes will fail to stop them, but it does provide a mechanism for their management.

Developing a Thorough Understanding of Project Risk

Risk is always an issue because people often fail to understand the risk for their project. The root of this appears to be a disdain for mathematics and a fear of statistics. Chapter 19 focuses on the details of understanding and properly identifying risk, and developing appropriate mitigations and contingencies.

The risk register consists of the description, probability of occurrence, financial and schedule impact, mitigation plans, and its relation to other risks. If a risk register is missing, create one; otherwise, refresh it. The core team needs to be involved and take this task seriously. Note:

- A brainstorming session is the best method to accrue risk elements. Assemble the key team members and ask them to enumerate the risks and assumptions. Accept all the items without question. Make sure they have complete descriptions and everyone understands them. Define the linkage between any risks. Outline mitigation plans for each risk.
- Assumptions are risk. Document all assumptions along with the impact if the assumption is incorrect. Ensure all assumptions on the triple constraints are logged, as these affect the project's foundation.

- If a risk register already exists, compare the results to the list generated. Note all omissions, additions, and any risks that have already happened.
- Remove the risks that have a combination of low probability of occurrence and insignificant impact.
- Place all risks with a probability of occurrence greater than 60 percent in the plan and schedule. Probabilities this high are virtual certainties.

As with nearly any document, prior to publication, make sure key stakeholders are aware of the findings. Report on all risks that have fired, and the success of any mitigation. Although everyone understands that risks will affect the project, few are willing to accept the results, which are additional costs and schedule slides. Recovery managers must hone their diplomatic skills prior to discussing or publishing this list.

The review has immediate benefits for the team. First, the review meeting gets the team together. This provides a great opportunity to reinforce that communication and teamwork is the new order. It highlights the currently burning issues. The team will be quick to point out that some items were unanticipated or out of scope or that their mitigation was inappropriate or failed to be executed. It is possible that problems enumerated here will go a long way in fixing the project.

It also provides awareness so when a risk fires, the team is better prepared to know the probable mitigation plans. Discussing the risk often changes behavior and will reduce the chance of occurrence or lessen its impact.

When reviewing the risk register, it may become apparent that some risk has fired and, though the project compensated for it, scope has changed. Ipso facto, create a change order to note the historical deviation from scope and account for the financial impact.

Risks and their attributes are dynamic. Periodically review, refresh, and publish the list. Discuss any major changes to the list with management and the customer. Adjust and discuss changes to the contingency funds, too.

Tracking Contingency

The risk's financial impact is the contingency fund for the project. Regardless of the organization's policy on contingency funds, the recovery manager should track them. As risks fire or expire, adjust the risk register and the contingency fund. If weighted financial impacts are used, the contingency fund remains unaltered unless new risk is noted. Keep management apprised of the fund's balance. Regardless of whether contingency funds are a formal part of their process, it states their liability. See Chapter 19 for more details.

Creating a Short Horizon Schedule

More data about the project is required to make a detailed schedule. However, enough is known to build a short-horizon schedule. This is a two- to three-week schedule to guide the team through the recovery process and delineate the tasks that members need to focus on to keep the project moving in a productive direction. Some new tasks will be added and existing tasks removed. It will need to be modified regularly, since it is such a short horizon. A detailed schedule can be built after the full analysis is complete.

Chapter Takeaway

- With the audit complete, the recovery manager must:
  - Take charge of the project.
  - Make decisions that will remove roadblocks.
  - Assign responsible parties to all open action items.
  - Implement the rudimentary processes of meeting minutes, change management, and risk tracking.
- Meeting minutes:
  - Improve the organization and control of meetings.
  - Provide a written record of discussion and agreements.
  - Document action items, due dates, and responsible parties.
  - Set goals for subsequent meetings.
- A change management process:
  - Manages scope deviation.
  - Identifies poorly defined components.
  - Retroactively captures scope creep to identify problems with the project.
  - Identifies financial and schedule concerns.
- A risk register:
  - Highlights risk to the extended project team.
  - Enumerates mitigation plans.
  - Identifies existing scope creep and potential schedule modifications.
  - Includes all project assumptions.
  - Is the basis for determining project contingency.
- Create a short-horizon schedule to guide the team though the analysis.

8

Building an Extended Project Team

"Leadership: the art of getting someone else to do something you want done because he wants to do it"

—Dwight D. Eisenhower,
34th President of the United States, Presidential Speech

People are a project's most critical attribute. Without them, a project's chances of success are slim. A group of people, however, is not a team. Projects need teamwork. The audit dealt with understanding the people. Now, the people need to be formed into a team that will drive the project. Developing a team amplifies the power of each individual. A team requires interaction, cooperation, communication, and mutual respect. In analyzing the group, these aspects need to be evaluated and the appropriate corrective action taken.

Dealing with people—who have lives beyond the project—makes this part of the recovery difficult and potentially emotional. Recovery managers cannot let this get in their way. This is business, and action is required. The world has millions of nice people, some working on this project, but even nice people placed in positions where they cannot perform as required become frustrated and must move on. Luckily, many of the actions taken with respect to the team have little to do with the individuals themselves.

The following sections discuss what to look for and how to plan for the right team, the effects of being denied the appropriate resources, and methods to compensate for a deficient team.

Being Realistic About the Team's Ability

The first step is to look at the product's requirements and compare them to the team's ability. If team skills are in question, there are a number of ways to address the deficiency:

- Train individuals in the required skills.
- Reassign individuals to tasks better suited to their skills.
- Acquire new resources with the required skills.
- Remove the deficient resources from the project.

Create a matrix of the people and required project skills. Based on each person's skill set and willingness to perform, make an assignment in the matrix. The people are already frustrated because the project is red; it will only make matters worse to place someone in a position that creates additional frustration.

After completing the matrix, look for under- and overstaffed skill sets and people who are under- and overutilized. For overstaffed blocks, select the best resources to meet the project needs and remove the redundant ones. Determine if underutilized people should have their skills improved with training (allowing them to be used elsewhere in the project) or removed from the project. For the resources missing the needed skills, establish a replacement plan. This will be part of the recovery plan. Start strategizing how to negotiate with the resource manager to acquire people with the right skill set.

To achieve above-average results, the project needs people with above-average skills. To find the right people, begin by gathering data on the people in the resource pool. Find people with the right attitude and skill set. If there are no obvious choices, look outside the pool. Ask people inside the team for potential candidates. If the company has a resource management group, this may violate its rules; fear not, as rules were made to be broken. To underscore the point, include resource replacement as a specific recovery task. This is the reason resource replacement was one of the defining questions on whether the recovery manager candidate should take the job (see Chapter 2, "Accepting the Role as a Recovery Manager"). The inability to replace underperforming resources will cripple the recovery.

CASE STUDY 8-1: REMOVING TEAM MEMBERS CAN HAVE A POSITIVE EFFECT ON THE TEAM

In some circumstances, people may need to be removed from the project. Contrary to common belief, this can have a very positive effect. At one client, a pending unannounced lay-off was going to remove nearly two-thirds of the team. All laid-off workers would receive a severance package. However, one individual refused to do his assigned work and behaved in an unprofessional and dishonest way that damaged teambuilding efforts. He was warned multiple times of his negativism and was finally recommended for termination—a week prior to the layoff. There was a lot of hesitation about taking this step since he was already on the list for the layoff, but proponents argued that letting him go would show the remaining team members that management was intolerant of this type of toxic behavior. Eventually management relented and terminated the person.

After the layoff, many of the remaining team members thanked me for behaving fairly and stopping the insanity. They saw the action as positive and as a sign of being able to trust management. Sensible action and control was being applied to the situation.

Actions on the Team

The team is by far the most visible part of the project. Its members are the interfaces and conduits into the project for the customer, management, and subcontractors. At the same time, people always play a significant part in project failure. It may be because management is levying unrealistic constraints, the skill sets are inadequate, there is poor team member performance, or the project manager is failing to do his or her job. Regardless of the cause, address it aggressively.

Bad habits and poor attitudes are repressive to the project; insubordination and obstructive behavior is even more detrimental. Allowing such problems to linger will negate positive actions on the project. Enumerate the personnel issues and rank them by severity. To this list, add the overall impact the resource will have on the project, including corrective action and eventual replacement. Use this to relay the effect of the team's liabilities to the steering committee.

The best choice for handling such a situation is to coach people to modify their behavior. This task belongs to the resource's functional manager and is surely outside the project's scope. Regardless of who does it, add time to the schedule and a risk element accounting for its possible failure.

In most cases, projects lack a budget for on-the-job training. For a troubled project, the burden of training someone to correct poor behavior is out of the question. It is best to replace the resource swiftly. Do it as quickly and decisively as possible. Having problematic resources stick around for any reason (i.e., they have history, might provide background, etc.) only prolongs the pain of leaving. People who are in leadership roles will have some of their past reports coming to them for direction and the chain of command may become blurred. People who are friends with the affected individual may feel remorse or anger over these events. The animosity, which will last as long as they are on the project, will decrease productivity. Therefore, plan the restructuring to happen over a very short period, preferably one day. The decision to replace staff over a short defined period removes the anxiety that additional layoffs are planned, is far less painful, and helps teams form more quickly.

CASE STUDY 8-2:
TEAM MEMBERS WHO DO NOT FOLLOW THROUGH

A client had severe deficiencies in its testing environment. The computers used to test the product were five years old, which meant they were significantly slower and had less memory than the minimum product requirements. For example, these computers took nearly two minutes to initiate the application. To run one test took in excess of 140 seconds—and, there were tens of thousands of tests. I assigned the quality assurance lead the task of generating and submitting a purchase requisition for new computers, while I secured financial approval. After a week, finances were approved, but the quality assurance manager had failed to start the task. She was given a three-day deadline to have the requisitions turned in (it should have taken one day). Again, she failed to complete the task. She said filling out the requisitions was a waste of time since they would ultimately be declined. I requested an immediate replacement for her and completed and submitted the requisitions.

Many felt the team would have difficulty functioning without their well-liked lead and would be angry that I had removed her. Two weeks later, with the deployment of the new computers, the application started in five seconds and a single test ran faster than the testers could record the results. The frustration waned. The team was happier, working faster, had significantly less stress, and knew that I was willing to take action.

After punitive actions are complete, the team needs to heal. This can be accomplished in many ways. One of the best is to address the deficiencies in the project that directly affect the team. During the audit, numerous conditions were found that could be corrected. Every project is different, but some examples are:

- Replace slow, outdated computers.
- Fix incomplete development and test environments.
- Provide direction.
- Improve the tools for doing the job.
- Provide training on tools required.
- Address slow response from management.
- Make decisions and take responsibility for them.
- Remove nonessential interruptions that take time away from more important project tasks.
- Resolve action items affecting work progress.

It is worth pointing out that pay rate is missing from the list. If people have stayed on a project that is as stressful as a red project, they must like the pay. Otherwise, they would have left a long time ago. What will appeal to them is to feed their careers and make them feel appreciated.

CASE STUDY 8-3: SUCCESSFULLY ADDING RESOURCES TO A RED PROJECT

Adding resources to solve problems on a project is usually frowned upon. This is especially true when they are being added to areas where their skills are weak. However, under the right circumstances, it can be very beneficial. For example, it worked very well on a project where a specialized tool was used to do a part of the integration and only a few people worldwide were trained in its use. Bringing in additional trained resources was impossible. The schedule had slid significantly, and management decided to mitigate the risk by having two senior programmers learn the tool. Both of these programmers were FORTRAN programmers and knew little of the tools, code base, or Java. It would be about three months before they would need to be competent with the tool, so the decision was made to invest the money to train them. They would do the simple integration tasks while the experienced resources would do the complex ones. There was a lot of skepticism about the plan, especially by the experienced staff. They relented and made a superior effort to train the two newcomers. It was a stellar success.

There were many reasons for choosing the specific individuals. Adaptability, technical competence, and attitude were critical. It must be said, playing to the technical person's desire to learn new tools and remain marketable was vital to success. They knew this was excellent education, it would look beautiful on their résumés, and it would get them out of their FORTRAN type cast.

Canceling Overtime

Many troubled projects have teams working overtime to compensate for missed milestones. Often this is futile, because the reason tasks are late has little to do with the team member's actions. The overtime is probably a result of changing requirements, slow decision-making, poor communication, and open action items. Prohibit overtime until these issues are resolved. This gives the team a break and cuts expenses. After resolving core issues, there may be a need to work some overtime, but this is rare for the following reasons:

1. People work more efficiently without overtime.
2. Resolving problems boosts morale.
3. There is less rework since people have a clear plan.

Although compensation is a lesser concern, cutting overtime for hourly staff, when overtime is the norm, is effectively a wage cut. Monitor the situation and see what happens. Experience shows that the increase in quality of life outweighs the pay reduction.

Handling Team Members Who Are Prima Donnas

On occasions, people think they are critical to the success of a project. This feeling of indispensability can manifest itself in an arrogant and divisive attitude. Seriously consider replacing these individuals. They hamper team building and damage the project by threatening to leave or by not performing to the same level as others. If this is indeed the case, look into replacing them as early as possible. People are rarely indispensable.

Dealing with Management Problems

Issues with management are difficult, and at times impossible, to resolve. The key is to be objective, lay out the facts, determine the corrective course, and find the appropriate person on the steering committee to assist in the implementation. Some corrective actions to consider are:

- Removing the project from the manager's responsibility.
- Have a steering committee member work with the troublesome manager.
- Develop process changes or workarounds to offset the manager's deficiencies—effectively micromanaging the manager.

Indecisive managers are a major problem, so address this as soon as possible. Remember the credo discussed earlier—it is not if the recovery manager assumes authority, but when. Unless this issue is resolved, the project will continue to founder. Create a way to circumvent ineffectual decision-making. The problem's source may be other than management. It may be other process two or three levels deep. The problem may be that the managers simply need to do better follow up on issues. Aside from the suggestion above, to remove the offending manager's influence, it may be as simple as managing his or her workflow. However, always keep in mind the options of making the decisions or doing the work for them. Just keep a good paper trail to defend the actions taken.

Many management problems result simply from a lack of participation in the project. Management is reacting to reports or spreadsheets instead of visiting the project to see and hear what is actually happening. Because of the attention given to a failing project, this should rarely affect the recovery; however, the attention should be constructive and beneficial. Highlighting the lack of attention will surely help other projects avoid the same situation. Therefore, include this issue in the findings report.

Developing Plans with Subcontractors

Identify subcontractors with substandard performance, and determine the root cause of their noncompliance. These causes need to be addressed, whether they are internal or with the subcontractors. Subcontractors need to be aware of the corrective action plan, so it is best to keep them apprised of the assessment. If they are hostile, carefully calm the situation. At times, there is no other option than to be forceful. In Case Study 3-6 (pg. 41), notifying the subcontractor of the concerns resulted in a hostile backlash. Communication was limited to contractual requirements as the client turned over negotiation to its legal team.

Sources of issues with a subcontractor fall into the following general categories:

- Internal project issue—the project team is not providing the deliverables required for the subcontractor to complete its job.
- Improper, ambiguous, or errant statement of work.
- Subcontractor incompetence.

Immediately start enforcing the contract and a change management process. This creates a fair and even playing field. Other than that, treat them as any other team members.

Boosting Morale with an Early Win for the Team

At this stage, a full recovery plan cannot be established. However, action is required to settle management's nerves. In addition, the team's morale and trust must be built. Many of the case studies in this chapter demonstrate methods of boosting morale, but to build the customer's trust takes action that will be visible outside the group. To do this, find an item on the project that the customer sees as a sign of the project floundering and work with the team to determine how to turn one or more of these into a sign of progress. This can have a strongly positive effect on the project team, the customer, and upcoming negotiations. A success, even small, can change attitudes quickly about proposed changes or new processes.

CASE STUDY 8-4:
BOOSTING MORALE WITH AN EARLY WIN

When selecting an item to demonstrate an early win, it is beneficial if it has significantly high value for the customer. It reinforces the win from both the customer's and team's standpoints.

One client had numerous bugs in its sales product, and the product group had no process to correct them. Bugs sat in the product for months waiting for a project to deploy. The end user, the company's sales staff, continuously complained. The project team defined a process to prioritize bugs and release monthly fixes. The first release was about three months after I started. The customer was very doubtful the team could do the task.

The development team created single sheet specifications for the bug fixes and end users sat with the developers to ensure they understood the bug's extent. The bug fixes were deployed according to schedule. The process worked just as planned, and the customer was ecstatic. This successfully improved the customer's perception of the team.

Improving Communication with All Stakeholders

Communication problems plague every project. In red projects, it is worse because of people's uncertainty, denial, and concern for being held at fault. Recovery managers must act as facilitators to assure good communications. In this respect, they are responsible for:

- Updating the stakeholders through regularly scheduled status meetings.
- Facilitating communication within the project team, as well as with management and the customer.
- Setting guidelines for proper communication with the customer in each of the project's groups.
- Providing fighter cover to give individual team members relief from outside disturbances, namely requests directly from management or the customer.

The recovery manager must communicate with both executive management and the project sponsor on the one hand and the project team on the other. In short, between the project's management and the people actually doing the work who report directly or indirectly to the recovery manager. Quality, as opposed quantity, of communication is important.

Fighter cover, a military term for the support fighter planes provide troops, is very important. Chapter 7 offered the bold suggestion to funnel all communication through the recovery manager. This is one of the strongest forms of fighter cover. It surprises many people to see how willing, actually pleased, the team is to have this restriction. It stops the constant interruptions, changes in direction, and the need for the team to tell the customer or management "no." It is very difficult for individual contributors to contradict a superior, especially their boss. By requiring that communication go through the recovery manager, the recovery manager takes on this task and removes the frustration from the team members. It also gives the recovery manager visibility into the project, and the opportunity to manage the plan better.

Preparing to Negotiate with Management

Besides taking care of the project team and trying to determine what needs fixing, a recovery manager must understand stakeholder expectations and determine how to get the customer and supplier to agree on an acceptable recovery plan. The recovery manager needs to understand how each stakeholder will react to proposed plans, who needs the most explanation, and who are the skeptics—the friend and the foe. The recovery manager must accurately anticipate the type and amount of effort required to gain acceptance of the plan.

The recovery process's early stages have little progress to report, although a significant amount of discovery may be happening. Management, however, wants to hear that burn rates are decreasing and delivery dates improving. Initial meetings will consist of reporting on newly implemented procedures and processes to remedy the situation. Customers, maybe even management, may not understand, or want, the added control. Control constrains their ability to meddle with the project.

CASE STUDY 8-5: NAME THE ONE THING THE CUSTOMER WOULD LOVE

A project to develop a new electronic device had completely stalled. I called a team meeting and asked one question: "What is the one thing the customer would look at and say 'Wow, I wish I had that today'?" After numerous meetings, the team came up with the answer—the ability to print a customer record. As a result, the print feature became the highest priority item to develop. It was unimportant if it met all the customer's requirements; a prototype was all that was necessary.

The prototype was shown to a select set of customers with the explanation that it needed significantly more work. The result was as anticipated. Word spread like wildfire that the team had made tangible progress. At this point, the customer was unaware that the project, a big-bang deployment, was going to be phased. This demonstration helped in the negotiations, as it would be difficult for the customer to deny the value of releasing the feature early.

In actuality, a project may continue to decline. For instance, burn rates may initially increase in the rush to find and solve problems, but schedules, which were unrealistic to start with, may appear to degrade. Uncovering the project's true status may shock some stakeholders. They may require significant education to understand the issues and the effort required to fix them.

The basic processes put into place in the early stages of fixing a red project will significantly affect management—the steering committee, project sponsor, and executive management. The new processes hold them accountable, something different from the past. Chapter 7 discusses these remedial actions. For example, a change management process will highlight the number and frequency of changes, while meeting minutes will assign action items, and thorough estimation processes will draw attention to a change's real cost and schedule impact. This is bound to make stakeholders anxious. Therefore, as part of the recovery manager's education on how to work with the stakeholders, he or she must meet with each one and understand the politics of the project in order to appreciate each stakeholder's position.

Since recovery managers lack a hierarchical advantage over stakeholders, they must learn how to persuade each stakeholder to be an advocate for the recovery manager's cause. Therefore, when implementing or negotiating new processes or fixes, the recovery manager needs to start lobbying the stakeholders and use the information gleaned in the initial interviews to help tailor the presentation to accommodate each member.

Recovery managers must make two types of changes to the project. The first is to bring the project back into its contractual bounds. This will affect both the customer and the supplier, but it will affect them unequally. On rare occasion, it may affect solely one party. Regardless, remove out-of-scope items from the work. If, in the process of building a recovery plan, out-of-scope items are considered more valuable than the original items, then they can be added, but only with a commensurate combination of more funding, increasing the timeline, or removing contractual scope. Add items back into scope that the supplier has failed to address without affecting the project cost.

The second change is an adjustment in the project to accommodate lost time and additional expense. It is insufficient to return the project to its original baseline. Since time was lost, the only option is trimming the baseline scope to bring the project back to a new and acceptable financial or schedule baseline. This change starts with an understanding of where the value for each stakeholder lay in the project. For the customer, this will include various product features, the delivery date, and other incidental deliverables. For the delivering organization, it will include the funds for completing the project or business references. Since the project is in trouble, a reduction in some of these benefits for both parties is likely. Therefore, the recovery manager must know:

1. The relative importance of the product's components.
2. The significance of removing a component—the consequence of failure.
3. Each component's ranking of features—the wish list.

From these lists, the recovery manager can develop a set of the components and features that may be removed with minimal impact. To decrease the project's cost and timeline, first remove the components having the least consequence of failure.

Then, remove items on the bottom of each component's wish list. Continue to do this until achieving a reasonable scope, timeline, and budget to meet recovery guidelines. Validate the results with the stakeholders, and tune the solution to meet their needs as closely as possible.

There will be conflicts between groups on the importance of items, so these changes will inevitably require compromise. Once the best blend is determined, start building alternatives for later in the process. Three plans are optimal—one to meet the recovery guidelines, one with fewer features, and one with more. In step three, the negotiation step, where these will be packaged with all the other plan documents and corrective actions for presentation, the stakeholders may modify the recovery guidelines and ask for the addition or removal of features. If you have known alternatives, adjustments will be easier to make. The remaining wish list items can fine tune the agreement.

Before the negotiation meetings, the recovery manager should meet privately with each stakeholder to discuss the upcoming changes. The goal is to explain the anticipated effect, obtain support, and understand any objections. In summary, the task is to size up the stakeholders and determine how to get their support. Although it may be obvious which individuals are critical in achieving a successful implementation, meet with as many stakeholders as possible. Lobbying key stakeholders prior to meetings improves the chances for a quick resolution. Chapter 14 will cover this in more detail.

Although one-on-one meetings take a significant amount of time, the value is immeasurable. A group meeting can become a feeding frenzy; private meetings rarely have this atmosphere. It may take a couple of meetings to understand their positions and interests. As time goes on, these meetings may be replaced by phone calls. Email is the wrong tool for communicating with stakeholders. The most critical aspect of these meetings is to understand key stakeholder's reactions and prevent them from forming an incorrect interpretation of the options. Emails allow readers to form their own impressions without the sender's moderation.

Steering Committee and Status Meetings

Regularly scheduled status meetings can be a burden, but they are essential to success. If they are already part of the project structure, review their effectiveness. Reevaluate and change standing meetings regularly to keep them pertinent; if they are ineffective, cancel them. A few common failures of status meetings are:

- Absence of key decision makers.
- Failure to review, distribute, or follow agendas—a static agenda is too generic and irrelevant.

- Failing to remove agenda items no longer relevant, minimizing time for reporting on new problems.
- Not capturing, assigning, and tracking action items.

To successfully correct an errant project, the recovery manager must coordinate and drive these meetings. Management will want to know everything being done to make things right. Work with the meeting chairperson to set the agenda. By driving the status meetings, the recovery manager will be able to provide management with the data it requires in a manner advantageous to the recovery manager and the project. This has many benefits since it:

- Exhibits a proactive stance on the project.
- Sets the agenda, presenting topics in a comfortable order.
- Conveys the recovery manager's sense of urgency.
- Reduces the number of surprises.
- Sets the meeting tone, removing the aggressive stance of individuals.

CASE STUDY 8-6:
DRIVING THE STEERING COMMITTEE

A project's steering committee met every other week. There were supposed to be five representatives from the business unit and six representing the Information Technology (IT) group. Only three people from the business unit attended, representing only two of the three user groups, and four IT members. The business' General Manager and the CIO were both absent. I met privately with the end user representative who missed the meeting. He avoided the meetings since they were "a total waste of time." I promised changes.

Three days prior to the next meeting, I called the chairperson and proposed an agenda. He made a couple of adjustments. More importantly, we agreed to continue to follow this plan.

The IT director who occasionally attended complained that the meeting agenda should be prepared by the chairperson, but it was obvious that I was preparing and running the meeting. I asked if the meetings were effective and less contentious. The affirmative answer was evidence that what really mattered was the efficacy of the meeting.

The recovery manager and the chairperson should work together to create a meaningful meeting that encourages attendance. Inform attendees that decisions will be made in their absence and their lack of objection will be considered approval. If a key decision maker's absence impedes progress, escalate the situation.

Review meeting agendas with the chairperson face to face. Capture the chairperson's comments and change the presentation in an agreeable fashion. This will minimize surprises and help build trust. The chairperson should be able to supply insight on how to approach sensitive issues with other meeting attendees. He or she may even have a conversation with other members prior to the meeting to get everyone into the right mindset.

Properly preparing for status meetings turns them into a review of known status. It creates an environment with few surprises, fewer disagreements, and a higher likelihood of achieving the desired results. It also shows the recovery manager's competence and supports him or her in taking control. This is the first step in reducing the frequency of the meetings. This extra work early in the recovery process will have a quick payback.

CASE STUDY 8-7: HANDLING OPEN ITEMS RAPIDLY

Steering committee meetings are usually infrequent—often not even biweekly. Thus, waiting for a steering committee meeting on severely troubled projects is ineffective. To bring the project under control and ensure the steering committee is informed, meet more frequently with a key steering committee member. This should start early in the analysis phase as the solutions start forming and the recovery manager begins imposing his or her management style.

On an overseas project implementing a manufacturing execution system, this entailed a daily review of an open-item list with the customer's key steering committee member. If I was onsite, this meeting would happen in person; if I was remote, over the phone. New items were added and old items closed when both parties agreed. After this 15-minute morning meeting, the open items lists would be shared with the rest of the steering committee via email.

Debunking Myths and Promoting the Project

If a project is in trouble, the assumption is often that the project is bad or jinxed or that the project team is unqualified to do the job. The recovery manager is responsible for correcting these perceptions.

Projects are not jinxed; some simply have a set of conditions that make them difficult to manage. This perception is usually a result of management's lack of experience with the given set of circumstances and a lack of awareness about how to handle them. A common situation occurs when a company decides to enter a new line of business and fails to hire domain experts. The recovery manager needs to identify these items and propose methods to get around them. Implement processes; log, track, and report on risks; and quietly replace underperforming team members. The recovery manager needs to replace myths and superstitions with facts.

Promote the project and the team. Although reporting the actual project status is critical, status meetings often report only problems. When creating reports, include what is going on right along with what is wrong. Make sure all problems listed include a description of the actions required to fix them. This is very important and too often overlooked. Review the team's hard work and accomplishments with management. Have management acknowledge this even though a solution may be only a temporary fix.

An example might better illustrate this. Assume a project team has been having significant difficulty deploying its product, and there is insufficient time to develop the fix for the upcoming release. However, as a stopgap, the team has implemented improvements to respond better to a deployment failure. Explaining to management and the customer that this is a temporary solution will reduce confusion as to its purpose, and it will be perceived as progress.

Communicating with the Project Team

The aforementioned steps are primarily outward facing. It is also important to work with the team in the same manner.

At least once a week, the recovery manager should be available to team members in an unstructured environment. Walk around to the team's work area or, for dispersed teams, telephone members at a convenient time for them. These discussions should be impromptu, so people are unconstrained by an agenda or the need to prepare.

The recovery manager's role is to listen, prompt for questions, ask for clarification, and mention team accomplishments. Otherwise, he or she should only talk when answering a question. The recovery manager should take notes; few things make people feel better than knowing their ideas are worth writing down. Follow-up is required for any subject left open. All team members must understand they are valuable to the project. Often startling facts can be uncovered in this process. As comfort builds, people will mention subjects they think are immaterial but turn out to be important. Listening is the key.

Just as with management, the recovery manager needs to prepare the team for changes. Implementation of a meeting minutes process often meets with significant resistance because it entails more work and the benefits are deferred. Explaining the reasons, benefits, and examples of where it could have helped in the past will decrease the resistance and improve reception of the idea. Discussing this individually, and as a group, will allow the team members to express their concerns and will provide useful information about the individuals.

Good news is important. The team must hear the successes. The recovery manager cannot assume all members know the team's successes. Distribute management's compliments to all team members. Morale is important; good news and compliments are critical in building it.

Communication Guidelines

Channels of communication, and the information going through them, are very important. Information is power, but misuse of this power (i.e., hoarding information) is destructive. The recovery manager must control the information flow without obstructing it. Take the opportunity to educate each team member on what is important for the recovery manager to communicate. Meeting minutes will help this process because it allows the recovery manager to see occasions where team members make inappropriate commitments. The recovery manager can then correct the situation.

Minimize the possibility of blindsiding anyone by establishing team communication guidelines. This may include restricting all communications or identifying specific subjects the team can and cannot discuss with the customer.

The team must understand the power of information and how properly channeling information can be beneficial. The most innocent of comments can have serious repercussions. The team needs to be educated on scope and critical issues so its members know how to avoid committing to additional scope. By doing this, the recovery manager will find other issues needing to be addressed. As already mentioned, information is power and some team members may want to hold on to that power.

Chapter Takeaway

- Assess the project team members and ensure their skill sets match the requirements.
- Create a skill set matrix, and make sure all skill requirements are covered; remove excess personnel from the project.
- Reorganize and remove team members in a single, concise move. Prolonged reorganizations increase anxiety.
- Successful projects have no room for prima donnas.
- Determine what is needed to return the project to its baseline scope.
- To negotiate a solution:
  - Understand the stakeholders and their concerns.
  - Prepare the extended team (steering committee, project sponsor, executive management, customer project team, project team, subcontractors, and suppliers) for change by prenegotiating with them.
  - Determine which stakeholders are most critical to the success of each proposed change and focus lobbying efforts on them.
  - Understand each stakeholder's consequence of failure and wish list.

- For all steering committee and status meetings:
  - The recovery manager should drive the agenda.
  - Decision makers, or their authorized delegates, should attend.
  - Attendees should be prepared in advance for all items requiring a decision.
  - The meeting agenda items must be relevant and current.
- Communication best practices are:
  - Communicate directly with individuals; group meetings can inhibit open communication.
  - Listen and take notes.
  - Close all open issues.
  - Ensure everyone knows scope and urgent issues.
  - Manage, do not inhibit, communication.
  - Communicate weekly with each team member.
- Lobby the extended project team to:
  - Break the myths surrounding the project and replace them with fact.
  - Create an early win for the team.
  - Establish support for the change.
  - Enumerate and announce successes to the teams and superiors.
  - Promote the project and the team.

9

Considering Options for Realigning Technology

"Technology is so much fun but we can drown in our technology. The fog of information can drive out knowledge."

—Daniel J. Boorstin, American Historian, *The Image*

Technology's contribution to a project's failure is difficult to assess. Most people look to technology to solve problems, not to create them. Further, most project managers and executives do not have the skill to assess current technologies. This limits the ability of the manager to discuss technology issues based on their attributes. It is crucial to have objective data and a thorough analysis. Therefore, a technical background is helpful in seeking out unbiased sources.

Determining whether technology is contributing to the problems on a project and, if so, evaluating the options to solve them is a major task. Nearly religious beliefs in the benefits of one technology over another hamper the recovery manager's goal of objectivity. To select the correct option requires a blend of business and technical knowledge. Garnering the cooperation of an unbiased architect (on or off the project) to review the options and assess impact is time well spent.

The options for solving technology problems are specific to the situation, but there are some common issues and resolutions. The following sections provide direction on general issues for custom development and product implementations.

First, determine if the technology is actually needed. If the project is trying to accomplish something too advanced for the team's skill set, maybe it is better to do nothing. If no reasonable alternatives to the technology exist, ask whether the technology is needed at all. For example, suppose the project is implementing a customer enrollment process, but the team developing the middleware piece is struggling. Maybe it is possible for the customer enrollment forms to be printed and manually entered. Although this may seem archaic, the completed forms may be error free, thereby creating enough value. Manual entry is always a possible stopgap measure that provides time to assemble a team that can complete the integration while providing the customer with the experience of an integrated system (assuming this is the primary goal).

When addressing technology issues, tradeoffs must be made. Is the proposed tool meeting long-term needs instead of the project's needs? Are there more features in the product than are really needed now or in the future? Are there nonessential requirements that, when removed, will allow selection of a less complex technology? If a tool's functionality appears too advanced for the intended use, determine if another tool would be a better fit. Make sure the implementation is the best fit for the project as opposed to someone's favorite toy. A motor home has many neat features, but it is an inappropriate vehicle for daily grocery shopping in downtown Tokyo.

In the end, many technology decisions are business decisions. To develop a complete list of recovery options, the business goals must be understood and may trump any technical analysis.

General Issues to Consider When Assessing Technology

Whether the project is doing custom development, using common-off-the-shelf products, or both, some common questions need to be answered. Start by determining the impact of technology issues on the project by comparing the original proposal's cost, schedule, and scope of the technology component to the current commitment. This will indicate if technology is inappropriately influencing the project. If management is pointing fingers at technology as the source of the project's problems, check the reasoning. When difficulties arise, people forget their commitments. For a complex implementation, the project may be on track. Were the technology problems predicted? Review the risk register, and determine if there is anticipated risk firing. If there is, then management's concerns may result from a failure to understand risk. Remember, failure is deviation from the plan; executing predicted risk is part of the plan. People may misunderstand that. If business conditions have changed, making the risk intolerable, complete a risk reassessment and reevaluate the technology needs.

Ensure that the technology's scope is within the recovery guidelines. If not, determine which is the issue—the guidelines or the technology. The project charter or contract may be missing verbiage about the technology's relative importance in the project. As mentioned in Chapter 6, scope and the triple constraints often omit the influence of technology; it is hidden in implementation details. Implementing technology for a greater good can negatively affect the project. When the scope does not reference technology, the recovery process needs to bring it to light.

The opposite can also be true—the technology can be the project's goal. Whichever is the case, understand the actual business objective and bring the project back to that baseline. Analyze the current scope (the scope people are actually working on, rather than the original scope plus change orders) and determine whether the technology was chosen because of new scope or if scope has increased to meet the technology's features. Capture any issues with the technology that are a result of a change in scope.

At times, the only reason behind technological choices is the existence of new technology. People pick a direction because it sounds good or because they want to use something new. Alternatively, people may choose an implementation because it has neat features or is readily available and covers the requirements. Sometimes these choices meet some perceived future needs. In such cases, the work entailed to implement the technology may be inappropriate. Do not use a sledgehammer to kill a fly. If you suspect this may be the problem, reevaluate the technology and potentially replace it.

Dealing with Technology Induced Scope Creep

Just as the amount of junk in a garage will swell to fill the space, scope can increase to match the features of the technology used. This is called the Garage Syndrome. Two examples may help explain this.

1. A project team provides schedule estimates to create documentation manually, but the programming tool selected has a feature to generate documentation automatically. Unfortunately, a bug in the tool prevents the use of this feature. The developers should not work on solving the issue. Even though it would save time if it were working, it is outside the project's scope and only distracts developers.

2. A processor that has limited internal memory also has a feature to use secondary storage. If the greatest amount of data to be stored is within the internal memory's limits, there is no reason to accommodate external storage. In fact, incoming inspection should not test this function, since, if the feature fails, there would be no affect on the product.

Establish a minimal implementation. Understand the reasons for choosing a technology and compare those to the project's requirements to determine if there are ulterior motives for the selection of a particular technology. In the second example above, designers should exclude any design around the external memory's eventual use unless the statement of work expressly asks for the design. Building an extensible solution to accommodate the feature when it is missing from the roadmap is wasteful. Too many details are unknown.

Agile directly addresses extensibility, as will be seen in Chapter 11. It is mentioned here because it is a good argument to use with most engineers and architects, who have significant respect for the agile methodology. Create a clean simple design, uncluttered with things that might happen. Add future needs when they are defined.

Determine if the technology is a fit with respect to the maturity of the organization installing or using it. The team's experience with the technology is critical if deadlines are to be met and risk minimized. If the architectural goals are outside the team's comfort zone, three options should be reviewed:

1. Switch to a different, preferably known, technology.
2. Use another in-house option with which the team is familiar.
3. Acquire knowledgeable resources (see Chapter 8).

If switching technology is worth investigating, understand the level of rework and the effect of unknowns in the new technology. In general, switching to another new technology is a mistake. New products always sound good in the sales brochures, but, in reality, they will present just as many challenges as the one under suspicion. This is often referred to as the devil known versus the devil to be met. Switching to a silver bullet technology, one perceived to fix all the problems, is always wrong.

Identify any political issues and determine the methods to circumvent them. This is an issue with both internal development and common-off-the-shelf (COTS) solutions. For COTS implementations, a relationship between the customer or supplier and the COTS vendor may restrict moving to a different tool. This relationship may be a large part of the decision to use the product. These relationships could range from strategic alliances to design agreements. For internal development, it is likely the technology is tied to a manager's decision, and someone is going to lose face if the project or custom development fails. This can make some options political and emotional.

Developing Custom Technology Components

Custom development always sounds good since, in theory, it meets all of the customer's requirements, but these projects are never as simple as they appear. The first question should be whether the project team made the correct make-buy decision. This is an emotional question because one or more manager's careers are most likely at stake, and the technical team can be very excited about the opportunity to do the custom work. Nevertheless, broach the subject and evaluate the options.

Assess the team's experience with custom development. Use this to rate the team's probability of success. Unfortunately, custom product development is usually missing from an internal team's portfolio. The company's real focus is manufacturing, health care, aerospace, insurance, or something else, and the product is being developed to help the core business. The same questions apply to subcontract development, where you need to be sure that the subcontractor has domain knowledge in the customer's line of business.

The impact of maintenance on a custom product is significant, as there is no vendor to provide free upgrades. Every upgrade is a development project. Even the common features that come with COTS packages (i.e., printer drivers, tax forms, postal regulations, and the like) need to be created from scratch for a custom product. The organization has to completely understand, specify, and build the change. Stakeholders get very tired of the continual expense for features that competitors get free.

Enumerate the COTS packages available and how they align with the project's requirements. Estimates for custom development are often favorably biased. When faced with the opportunity to build a product from scratch, an evaluation team will underestimate the work required to do the development and subconsciously understate the positive and overstate the negative features in the COTS product.

Determine the impact of moving to a COTS product. It is unlikely to cover the project's original scope. Enumerate the compromises in the list of required features. Estimate the effect if these features are unfulfilled. List potential workarounds for the missing features. As with anything, be skeptical and assume the initial impression of the product's functionality is more than what it can actually do. There will always be issues arising in the installation.

Handling Issues with Common-Off-the-Shelf Products

Implementing a COTS product is usually the lowest cost and lowest risk option. However, problems can still arise, and the recovery manager needs to determine how many, if any, of the problems are due to the product selected. Hidden costs and overstated functionality are the most common reasons for failure. Validate that a solid due diligence was performed on the vendor and the product prior to its purchase.

Determine if the training was adequate for both the internal and vendor resources and whether the vendor has used the product in the same manner required by the project. Make sure at least some of the staff has several years of experience with the product.

Look at other COTS packages that might be a better fit. Maybe simply switching to another version of the same product (older and more stable) will solve the problems. Older versions have a longer track record and may reduce the project's issues. Investigate what the organization's competitors are using, as well as products used by the team in the past.

If the product is new, or at a new major version level (X.0), then get lists of others using the same product version. Major revisions levels have significant changes. In many cases, these versions are bug laden, and the vendor has limited experience with them. Determine the installed base and identify the technicians who helped other clients with installation, implementation, and training. Try to get these resources on the project, even if only on an on-call basis.

Assess the vendor's knowledge in the business domain (i.e., manufacturing, aerospace, finance, insurance, healthcare, etc.) and environment (i.e., weather, indoors or outdoors, computing platform, etc.). Establish if the product has been used in the business' domain. If it has not, the vendor may have difficulty assisting in the product's implementation and solving issues.

Determine if implementing the product requires installing and using all of its components. Many products have a variety of functions inapplicable to the project at hand. Scrutinize the features to ensure that only those needed are being installed and used. Installing features outside those required opens the door to scope creep.

Investigate the product's stability and longevity. Ensure the product is far from its end of life (EOL). A common fact in the world of mergers, acquisitions, and downsizing is that some products are no longer part of the vendor's core business. In this situation, the deployment group may be reassigned to the core business, leaving the project with few resources.

CASE STUDY 9-1: MODIFYING THE PROJECT
TO COMPENSATE FOR A PROBLEM TECHNOLOGY

A message bus was the chosen architecture for integrating multiple computer systems. The tool had the ability to route and transform messages based on the destination system. The project's delivery date was a hard constraint since the software had to be in place to accommodate new governmental regulations on the first of the year. The decision was made to use two other tools to do the transformation functions. Legacy systems would use an existing older technology with which the development team was already familiar. For the other portions of the project interfacing with new systems, another product, also being installed as part of the project, could do the transformation. This was a good solution since it removed the reliance on the lesser known newer technology. Although a new product was used, there were existing resources with experience using similar tools. By removing scope from the riskier technology's implementation, no team was overloaded.

As it turned out, eight months later, when the transformation functions were migrated to the message bus transformation feature, it required the purchase of another product. The original decision was better than anticipated.

Resolving Conflicts Between Business Goals and Technology Implementation

At times, technology is part of a new strategic direction. Regardless of the challenges encountered, it must also be part of the solution. This often results in a conflict over the importance of two or more aspects of the project. If the project's goal is to deploy more than the technology, the recovery manager must determine technology's relative priority in the implementation.

For instance, if one group feels technology is of prime importance and another focuses on the delivery date for the overall product, then there is a conflict. If one of these two is the project sponsor and the other the project team, the solution is easy. If, on the other hand, they are two groups inside the customer organization or one is the project sponsor and the other is the executive management, the conflict needs to be negotiated and clear direction given. This can be determined by querying the project sponsor on the triple constraints. If the customer needs the project completed by a certain date, then the most important constraint is schedule. However, if the project is treating the technology as most important, then scope is the primary triple constraint. This points out where the real conflict lies in the project, as the two requirements are contradictory. Essentially, there are two projects in the same project. This issue needs to be resolved prior to making recommendations on the technology's use.

When this happens, one option is to decouple the two deployments and run them as independently from one another as possible. Another option is to compromise one of the two projects so the triple constraints match. Solving the deficiencies in the compromised area will require a full explanation of the impact and definition of the follow-up actions. For example, assume date is the most important for business (it usually is over technology), requiring a compromise in the technology installation. In this situation, it needs to be clear that the deployment will be incomplete when compared to the original promise. Something will need to be reworked later. Maybe a functional component will be disabled, a database will be unnormalized, or data is incompletely defined. To correct any of these items will require follow-on work.

CASE STUDY 9-2:
COMPANY POLICIES THAT HAMPER THE PROJECT

Conflicting goals do not need to be within the project, they can be between a project objective and an organization's policy. For instance, a client deploying software to its sales force over the Internet failed to test the deployment using computers outside the company's firewall. This was the result of a policy that required all computers in the facility to be protected by a firewall. Numerous bugs were missed, and the deployment was a disaster. The customers were very upset.

While attempting to fix the situation, I failed to persuade the company to relax the firewall policy. Instead, I sent testers home to test the software against the firewall. This violated two other company policies: (1) contractors had to work on site, and (2) the company's own software was unlicensed on the home machines. However, I made the point and the company relaxed the policy allowing computers to be connected directly to the Internet (around the firewall) as long as they were disconnected from the internal network, a solution that should have been accepted in the first place.

Environments for Building and Testing the Project's Product

Technology issues include the tools and the environments employed in building, testing, and using the product. All too often, a project is missing the correct environments in which to develop and test the project's product. It may be that the environments are deficient, totally missing, or inadequately represent the end user's conditions.

CASE STUDY 9-3: DEVELOPMENT ENVIRONMENTS

Developers need to be able test code in a repetitive and predictable fashion. This may require dozens of tests in a day. They need to quickly reset their environment to a baseline. This is commonly done by creating virtual machines on one workstation. The project manager needs to ensure the developers have the required tools.

One client refused to purchase this $300 piece of software that would easily replicate environments. As a result, developers wasted days restoring their workstations to rerun tests. The company's policy to not purchase developmental tools outside the basic suite they already used was so engrained in the group that I had to first convince the developers of the need for the software by purchasing it on my own and encouraging the developers to test it. Once the developers saw the value, I had to convince executive management to buy it. The resulting increase in efficiency reduced development time by approximately 20 percent and the end users noticed the improvement in product quality.

This can cause numerous problems by wasting time trying to set up these environments or reconfiguring equipment to function as the missing environment. The recovery manager should properly define the environments in the quality plan.

The key elements for each project are to have environments that:

- Are distinct for development, integration test, system test, acceptance test, and production. The last two environments need to be nearly identical, including resident data.
- Have an independent software stack; the hardware can be virtualized.
- Have procedures to refresh the data in the lower environments—development, integration, and system test—to properly represent production conditions.
- Have procedures to replicate external influences.
- Are clean for each deployment to properly test the actual production release.

If the company is running multiple projects, each requires an isolated environment for testing. Without this, individual projects will start conflicting with one another, and the test results will be inaccurate.

Ensure the recovery plan includes:

- The effort and budget to create the proper environments for the product.
- A scheduling process for the final three environments' use across all projects.
- Headcount to manage and schedule the environments' usage.

Chapter Takeaway

- When defining the triple constraints on a project, technology is part of the scope.
- It is best to have an unbiased architect help in analyzing the options.
- When problems arise, options for reducing technology's impact include:
  - Reducing the implementation.
  - Replacing with known technology.
  - Replacing custom development with a COTS product.
  - Ensuring products are stable and meet the project's needs.
- Make sure vendors and subcontractors have domain experience and that the technology has been used in that domain.
- Determine what political ties exist between the technology and the organization.
- Refrain from designing for the future unless specifically in the statement of work. If it is required, insist on a test plan.
- Ensure a complete set of environments exist for testing.

10

Assessing How Methodology Affects the Project

"It is common sense to take a method and try it.
If it fails, admit it frankly and try another.
But above all, try something."

—Franklin Delano Roosevelt, 32nd President of the United States,
Address at Oglethorpe University

As technology is the architects' and engineers' religion, methodology is the religion of a pedantic PMO and executive management. They believe that the organization's methodology, whether chosen by formal or informal means, *must* be used by all projects. According to them, a failing project is simply not following the defined methodology, and the solution is to replace the current project manager with one who will enforce it. This philosophy—one size fits all—really fits no project. The single methodology will fit some projects just fine and others not at all, while some will be operating fully exposed. Yet deep down the PMO and management know that this answer is incorrect; they need help from someone with the art, magic, or special potion.

First, some myths need debunking. One is that methodology brings standardization and commonality to projects so that senior management knows what to expect. Members of senior management achieved their positions because of their ability to handle variations in business conditions; in fact, they capitalize on this ability. What frustrates them is someone who is unable to concisely justify and summarize variations in the project's expected progress, and then provide updates on its status.

No one likes surprises. The problem is middle management—the layer between the project and the executives—which has been telling the executives that they are doing their jobs and that all projects are fine. Then, one day, a project derails, and there is a train wreck to fix. Now, it is time to blame the innocent and reward the guilty, which does nothing to move the project forward.

Why the soapbox? To bring attention to the fact that in many cases the methodology is the problem. The organization's project management philosophy may be a poor fit for the project. Because of this possibility, the recovery manager needs to have a portfolio of process tricks ready to implement based on the problems he or she uncovers. In more general terms, since an organization has a portfolio of projects, it needs a portfolio of processes.

The three most useful tools for helping when methodology issues are uncovered are phasing the project, implementing an agile approach (short, time-boxed phasing), and using the rigor of critical chain methodology. The key is knowing what portions of each methodology are applicable, when to use them, and how to convince management they are required.

Methods of Developing Schedules and Estimates

An actual project schedule is built after a recovery plan is accepted. Until then, a tentative schedule is required; having one is critical when negotiating a final plan. Using a tentative schedule will start to point to the problems in the project and allow testing of theories for fixing the project.

Schedules are unique to each project. Beyond the imperatives of design, build, test, and deploy, projects tend to have few things in common. Before starting to build a schedule, it is important to review the audit findings and determine if the project team is using a reliable estimation process. If necessary, the recovery manager should take the time to educate the core team on an estimation process. Both agile and critical chain methodologies (Chapter 11 and Chapter 12) approach estimation with rigor. For now, suffice it to say that you should implement a reliable process. Doing so will provide a modicum of consistency and will allow you to better understand the repercussions when the task's parameters change.

The level of the accuracy for estimates of a project's constituent tasks depends on the project's clarity. As with time estimates, domain experience is critical. It is common to miss tasks as a result of both optimism for the upcoming project and ignorance of the work required. The more innovative the projected product, the larger will be the variance in the estimates. This is an area where iterative methodologies, such as agile, benefit the project the most.

The task's clarity will, in turn, affect the time estimates. The poorer the understanding of the task, the more likely it is that time estimates will only be guesses.

Dependencies for known tasks are usually easier to determine. Obviously, if the team is unaware of a prerequisite task, the dependencies will be incorrect.

Estimates are associated with a number of assumptions. The parameters used in various estimation algorithms—the number of work hours per week, resource dedication, allowances for nonproject related training, overtime, and meetings—indicate but a few of these assumptions. Document the parameters for the project and review them with the team for their validity. Determine ways to minimize their effects when variations occur.

People dislike giving estimates for good reason—estimates are always wrong, simply because they are just estimates. In most cases, managers treat estimates as quotes and reprimand people for deviations. If a task completes early, the person is reprimanded for padding the estimate; if late, the reprimand is for missing the deadline. Thus, team members are motivated to pad heavily and never complete a task early. Start by educating the team on providing unbiased estimates.

Educate stakeholders and management to understand that estimates are not quotes and that it is okay for people to miss their estimates. Everyone being late is a problem. Padding estimates is a problem. Missing one deadline, however, is acceptable. For this reason, understanding the schedule's derivation is critical to a manager's perception of it. If the estimates for the schedule were given to guarantee making the date, the schedule would contain significant pad. In this case, most people would complete their assignments on or ahead of time, but this is rarely the case.

Management's reaction to people missing an estimate (going either over or under) conditions the team members' style of generating estimates. The stricter management is about treating estimates as quotes, the more padding the estimates will contain and the more unrealistic schedules will be. Padding schedules creates a justifiable feeling that there is plenty of time to complete the task. If the time line is excessively padded, there will be a lackadaisical approach to completing tasks. Functional managers (managers of the project resources) know the tasks have padding and slip in extra, nonproject work. The project team members, knowing this will happen, add more pad.

Because of the padding, tasks should be completed on or before the estimated completion date. However, since functional managers know they have extra time, they assign nonproject tasks to the project resources. These extra tasks chew up the allotted time, including the risk allowance, for the original task. When the resources finally get to work on the original task, they run into unexpected issues, and the task becomes late. Even if the task could finish early, people use the additional time striving for perfection. They are unwilling to admit a task has completed early, as management will then unleash its wrath by accusing people of padding their estimates, the same padding management used to slip in other assignments. This vicious cycle must be broken to get estimates that are uniform and realistic.

There are as many ways to build a schedule as there are project managers, but there are only a few proper ways. Chapter 5, "Validating the Schedule's Derivation" discussed the two best methods of scheduling: forward pass and backward pass. Of these, the best planning is forward pass scheduling; use the original start date, add tasks, and then plug in their dependencies. Never use milestones to constrain the schedule; let the dates float. This will do a reality test on the milestones. Schedule the resources to work no more than 35 hours a week. Ensure all nonhuman resources (tools, environments, test facilities, etc.) are not overbooked. Make sure to exclude holidays from the work days for the region the project team is working in and for the resource's own culture. A team of U.S. citizens working in Israel is restricted from working on Yom Kippur, but is also going to have time off at Thanksgiving and Christmas, as well as travel and shopping time. Christmas/New Years, Passover, Yom Kippur, Chinese New Year, Diwali, Ramadan, and other major holidays all take more than the actual holiday's calendar time. Christmas, for instance, wipes out nearly two weeks at the end of December, and in the United States productivity drops from Thanksgiving (the fourth Thursday in November) until New Years. Be aware of an organization's blackout days—times when project deployments are prohibited. Determine these rules and incorporate them into the schedule (even if only noting that they will need to be broken).

After determining a realistic end date, adjust resources and double check dependencies to pull in the delivery date. When the primary triple constraint is the delivery date, some schedules are impossible. Regardless of the money and people thrown at them, the milestones will be unachievable. To reshape the project so that it can come in on time, rank its components from the greatest to the least consequence of failure if they were to be removed. Remove items from the bottom of the list until the schedule fits. Then add smaller features from the wish list to achieve an acceptable value. Either present a schedule that fits (removing scope and adding resources to make the delivery milestone) or present the forward-built schedule with realistic resources and an achievable delivery date. The latter underscores the need to remove scope, change requirements, add resources, or move the end date. These are contentious issues, and it will take significant skill to negotiate the changes, but presenting a nonrealistic schedule is unethical (refer to Chapter 14 for more about negotiating the schedule).

Make sure to record all the assumptions in building the schedule. The two most often missed assumptions are skill level requirements and dedication of resources to the project. Build the schedule assuming that the identified resources are available for the task assignments. Log the assumptions. If, at the time of assembling the team, the assumed resources are unavailable, then recalculate the schedule and report the new delivery date. When presenting the schedule, make sure that people understand that changing resources will affect the project.

The team and all dependant parties (vendors, other teams, and the customer) must agree to the schedule. The extended project team must trust and believe in the schedule. Too often, the team will leave schedule creation to the project manager, who prepares a schedule without taking into account the underlying project realities. Only the team members know the details of building the product. The recovery manager can keep them in check but cannot develop the schedule in a vacuum.

Gathering Project Progress Estimates

The schedule has a greater purpose, one that goes beyond coordinating the recovery manager and the team. It is a tool to report status to management and the customer—it must cover the good, the bad, and the recovery plans for consistently missed deadlines. The estimation process must include gauging project progress, since team members must estimate their progress on each task. Team members need to report their status on a regular basis and this information must be incorporated into the schedule.

As discussed in Chapter 5, "Understanding How Team Progress Is Reported," asking resources to estimate the percentage completion for a task will yield inaccurate information. The question should focus on how much time is required to complete the remaining work.

A Hypothetical Example for Comparing Methodologies

For this discussion on phasing, agile, and critical chain methodologies, a hypothetical example will be useful. Assume a project is behind schedule and over budget. The customer's management has complained that the development effort is missing critical deadlines and the project must be brought back on schedule. Frustration is increasing because of inefficiencies, which result in high labor costs, eroding market share. The costs arise from rework, low quality, and an inability to determine the location of the work in progress (WIP). As the delivery date of the system extends further, the customer becomes more intolerant.

The proposed system automates the workflow process by routing and tracking work items through the fabrication facility. In addition, it provides online, customer-generated specifications to the workers based on each item's location, as indicated by the workflow system. As end users start to work on their assigned item, the system will automatically download the processing instructions to the equipment. The system provides functionality to solve the issues of tracking product and minimizes the need for rework by eliminating operators' errors in choosing the incorrect processing instructions for the equipment.

As specified in the customer requirements, the system will be installed and the data converted over a three-day weekend. Workers returning after the long weekend will start using the new system they had been trained on during the previous weeks.

Phasing the Hypothetical Project's Deliverables

Phased project deployment has been around for years. Unlike the other methodologies, there are no books devoted to the subject, so common sense must prevail. The steps to phasing a project are:

- Rank the project requirements' importance.
- Set the features' dependencies.
- Determine logical release units for sets of features.
- Create multiple overlapping schedules for deploying the feature sets.

CASE STUDY 10-1:
PHASING TO PROVIDE MORE ENTERPRISE OPTIONS

Phasing brings advantages beyond those discussed in Case Study 5-1 (pg. 65) by providing additional options for the enterprise. One project, to supply a new customer information maintenance system, was floundering because of an ever-increasing set of requirements and a monolithic deployment. The recovery recommendation was to phase the project providing three sets of deliverables: (1) a view and download of the legacy system data; (2) report printing and history, and (3) a new user interface for updating customer details. Senior management and the stakeholders accepted the project plan.

Shortly after phase two began, the organization launched a much larger and higher priority project that had significant revenue impact and many challenges. Because this new project was short on resources, executive management decided to cancel the third phase of the project, making those project resources available to the new project. The impact on replanning was minimal since the phases were independent.

The actual methodology used in each phase is based on the type of work being done. The customer assigns priorities based on the business value of each feature. This information was already gathered in the customer interviews. As a refresher, this included:

- The relative importance of each component.
- The significance of removing a component—the consequence of failure.
- The component feature ranking—the wish list.

Proceed cautiously. What is important for some is unimportant for others. In the hypothetical example, the quality manager may have little interest in the WIP's location but surely wants to see improved rework trends and adherence to procedure. Customer service wants to know the product's location and its estimated delivery date. For this reason, the project sponsor will need to negotiate with each group to determine the correct priority.

Assume WIP tracking is the most important. This will give the business the ability to estimate completion dates and expedite given units. The specification and process instruction download already have manual processes that will suffice for a couple of months, so the preference is to deploy the WIP module, then instruction download, followed by the online specifications.

Analyze this for dependencies. In this simple example, it should be apparent this sequence would work. By knowing where the WIP is, it is feasible to provide the recipes or the specifications for performing the work.

In a different situation, the most important issue may be reducing operator errors caused by manual selection of the process instructions. In this situation, there are three options:

- Determine what parts of the WIP system are needed to identify where the material is located to download the required instructions.
- Provide a manual run card with the equipment recipe in a scannable format.
- Show the required dependency and persuade the customer to change the deliverables' order.

The resolution of this is based on project details, which are beyond the scope of this discussion. The salient point is the decisions on priority may be obscure and may take significant effort to establish.

After laying out the dependencies, examine the work to determine the logical release units. This action groups the work together to meet the priority placed on the requirements while minimizing cost and risk. Further work decomposition may be required to minimize risk and maximize the chances for a successful deployment. In the example, the download of equipment instructions and specification viewing may be sufficiently isolated so that they can be deployed concomitantly without encountering any conflict in resources or other factors that might complicate the deployment. This will result in a two-phased approach—deploy the workflow module followed by a simultaneous deployment of the online specifications and the process instruction download. If, due to complexity, instruction download needs to be broken down further, separate it into two or more releases.

After determining the options, the customer and the project executives must approve the solution. After approval, realign the teams and focus them on their work. Of course, this is only part of a complete recovery plan. Address all problems uncovered in the audit in one recovery plan—doing bad things fast and efficiently just gets the project back into trouble, albeit more efficiently.

CASE STUDY 10-2:
PHASING A PROJECT TO REDUCE RISK

As mentioned in Case Study 5-1 (pg. 65), many customers are enamored with the big-bang deployment. On a large manufacturing execution system (MES) deployment and equipment integration project, the client wanted to release all the features in one three-day deployment, but the audit showed that some components needed to be redesigned. The original deployment date was in June. A realistic look at resource capability and dependencies showed the MES would not be ready until November; the new graphical user interfaces (GUI) and underlying custom services would not be ready until the following August (16 months away); and the equipment interfaces needed approximately another two years to complete. After significant debate, the customer accepted the recommendation to deliver the project in three phases. The first phase would allow the customer to take advantage of the MES' additional features, and the second phase would deliver the GUI with other custom modules. Equipment interface delivery would happen after completion of the first two phases. This provided functionality at the earliest possible date and gave time to redesign and code the poorly designed pieces. Although neither the customer nor supplier was happy, it was the only option considering the current investment in the project.

Using Agile in the Hypothetical Project

The areas where agile shows its greatest advantage is when the customer is having trouble visualizing how its requirements translate into the product or the supplier is struggling with the technology's implementation. It is difficult to use agile for large projects when there is a need to share resources across multiple projects.

Agile addresses resource constraints by dedicating resources to a task. The proponents of both agile and critical chain are adamant that multitasking is inefficient. To accommodate this, agile methodology brings the developers, engineers, and customers together to work in a series of iterations. Limiting the time allotted to perform each iteration (time boxing), the developer and the customer must make sacrifices in scope and thoroughness to achieve the anticipated functionality. The number of iterations allowed is limited. If anyone tries to include any frills into an iteration, there will not be enough time to complete the required scope of the project. This methodology is excellent at getting the customer to prioritize requirements and sacrifice the least important features.

CASE STUDY 10-3: USING AGILE FOR MAINTENANCE

One IT organization treated all work as a project. It would bundle maintenance, bug fixes, and enhancements into one set of requirements and deliver all in a project. Since the projects had nine- to twelve-month delivery cycles, the customer had an inordinately long wait for bug fixes.

The organization had a project underway to enhance a sales tool, but the project had experienced numerous failures. I determined that trying to do all the work required for the project release was too challenging. The project would be late because of the amount of work. Therefore, I decided to run the bug fixes as a subproject. Working together on a plan with the development and quality assurance teams, two resources from each group were dedicated to fix bugs and test functionality. All the known bugs were compiled in a spreadsheet with formulas to accumulate the estimated time for building and validating the bug fixes. In two meetings with the customer, the bug fixes were prioritized for the first release due in five weeks. I promised the customer there would be another planning session in four weeks to determine the second release's scope, but the customer was skeptical. The architect developed single-page specifications to define the bug fixes and the test procedures. We assigned end users to work with the developers to ensure the fix was correctly implemented. The bugs were fixed and deployed according to schedule. Second, third, and fourth scheduling meetings were held, fixes deployed, and the scope of the project's final delivery was greatly reduced. The word agile was not used to describe the process; the executive management would have never allowed an agile process.

The process worked so well, it was eventually removed from the project and used as the basis of a maintenance group. As will be discussed in Chapter 15, maintenance is an example of work that fails to meet the definition of a project.

Using agile to implement new technology has two advantages. First, since the long design phase is removed, the developers start working with the technology much sooner. This uncovers deficiencies earlier, leaving more time to solve the issues or develop workarounds. The second advantage is the customer is aware of the issues firsthand and can apply its knowledge of the feature to suggest alternate methods to remove the problem.

Agile resembles a phased approach with much shorter cycles and less overhead. The products of these cycles, however, must show value to the customer rather than be production quality. Because of the relatively short iterations, the stakeholders and executives get consensus from both the customers and the developers on the progress, challenges faced, and comprises required. Stakeholders can see the progress and direction more clearly.

In the hypothetical project defined at the beginning of this chapter, there are many ways to implement agile. For the sake of discussion, assume the project is phased as defined in the prior section—MES, specification system, and equipment integration. Phasing is common since agile projects arrive at usable product sooner and logical chunks may be deployed earlier, resulting in a quicker return on investment (ROI).

After developing the infrastructure for the first phase's workflow module, the customer would be an integral part of the user interface design, implementing screen components to best accommodate the operator. End users would test the screen usability. The combination of time boxing and the focus on customer needs stops the developer and customer from adding bells and whistles.

The same design process would work for the specification display. With the specification system, further benefits would be gleaned by determining the best specification format and feeding data back to the customer's engineering department for format changes. Without the customer's and developer's tight coupling, this would have required development work or the overhead of change orders.

The cooperation, short development cycles, and flexibility in the process removes issues with poorly defined requirements, inadequate understanding of a tool's use (by the implementation team and the customer), scope creep from adding unimportant features, and lack of status visibility—all valuable qualities in recovering a project.

Chapter 11 is a primer that provides enough information for a rudimentary discussion of the subject. For more information on agile, please refer to Recommended Reading.

Using Critical Chain in the Hypothetical Project

Critical chain is another methodology that works well when reining in the terror of large complex projects, especially if there are significant external dependencies. Critical chain, based on the theory of constraints for manufacturing, focuses on defining and mitigating the bottlenecks, as well as properly defining tasks in order to reduce the chances of wasting time.

Resource utilization is crucial. It supports this by doing the following:

- Implementing a strict estimation process for all resources.
- Analyzing resource requirements across all projects.
- Resource leveling schedules.
- Placing buffers prior to resource leveled critical path tasks to ensure efficient use of resources' time.

The key element in implementing critical chain is time management. The estimation process, building time buffers into the schedule, and staggering the launch time of projects significantly reduce projects' duration. As a philosophy for the organization, it is very thorough and easy to understand. However, a project recovery only uses a subset of the methodology. Critical chain provides the most benefit for projects with resource constraint issues or the need for schedule compression, but it fails to provide agile's benefit for poorly defined projects.

Critical chain starts by implementing a process to develop task estimates. It contends that individuals are habituated to pad estimates for the worst-case scenario. People providing time estimates include time for interruptions, meetings, working on other projects, and other tasks. This overstates the time to such a degree that the person takes a lackadaisical approach to working on the task and actually starts it late knowing there is plenty of time. There is no desire to start the task on time or finish early since management rewards neither. Usually people completing tasks early are met with a reprimand for padding estimates, creating more disincentives.

Starting tasks late because there is plenty of time to finish them, is called the student syndrome.[4] It is easy to comprehend when thinking about students who have a term paper assignment they can start any time in the term, but instead start it so late they have trouble finishing on time.

To correct this requires retraining everyone on the project to supply task estimates that have a 50:50 chance of being achieved. In other words, estimates where they believe they will be able to finish the task, uninterrupted, on time or ahead of schedule 50 percent of the time; the rest of the time they will be over the due date. As a result, people are rewarded for finishing early, and they are not reprimanded for being over their estimate. Those who maintain other than a 50:50 average are coached, never reprimanded. This schedule, in theory, is devoid of float. Statistically, the early delivery on one task negates late delivery on another task. Realistically, however, risk will make more tasks late than early, so a buffer is added to the end of the schedule to ensure there is room for cumulative risk.

Retrain managers, along with team members, on estimation processes. They must follow the rules of prioritizing work, utilizing resources, and eliminating multitasking. Managers' reactions to late completion of tasks is critical in deprogramming negative behavior. Teach them to look at the overall project and the use of the project buffers to determine if a project is in trouble.

Consistent estimates based on a standardized technique with understood limitations and attention to resource loading will minimize the schedule's duration. This, coupled with phasing the project to reduce scope-induced risk, will provide the earliest delivery at minimal risk. An additional benefit is the schedule's transparency provided by the clear identification of buffers. See Chapter 12 for a primer on critical chain methodology.

Chapter Takeaway

- Methodology is critical to the smooth running of a project, but no methodology is a solution in and of itself.
- Schedules are often unrealistic because of a number of issues, including:
  - Squeezing a project into too short a timeframe to meet a fixed project end date.
  - Estimates lacking standardization or realism.
  - The delivery attempting too much.
  - Too many scheduling assumptions ending up being false.
- Phasing a project can help by:
  - Effectively reducing each phase's scope.
  - Decreasing the overall complexity for each delivery.
  - Releasing the product earlier.
- Agile methodology can help projects where:
  - The customer has an incomplete understanding of the product.
  - The supplier has an incomplete understanding of the technology.
  - Early release of partial functionality is beneficial.
- Critical chain methodology helps on projects:
  - Where resources are constrained and need better management.
  - That need to pull in the delivery date.

11

How Agile Methodology Can Assist in a Recovery

"Small deeds done are better than great deeds planned."

—Peter Marshall, Chaplain of the U.S. Senate

This chapter provides a primer on agile project management (APM). In particular, Case Study 11-2 examines an implementation process at a company that was skeptical of change. It then discusses the technique of applying agile methodology as a recovery tool and the logic of the compromises in the methodology's implementation that make it beneficial.

Agile Methodology's Basics

The genesis of agile as a defined methodology came from a need for continuous innovation, product adaptability, reduced delivery schedules, and reliable results. Its premise is that conventional project management practices—generating and rigidly following detailed plans and designs and adhering to these documents for the project's life—build in failure. Even with the most flexible change management system, most products need quicker response. Agile is not a new methodology. In a less formal process, it has been around for decades (see Case Study 11-1).

The primary goal of an agile project is to respond to change in order to deliver value to the customer. Compared to conventional project management, agile's iterative process with its ever-changing requirements appears chaotic and nontraceable. However, the minimal documentation required maintains traceability.

Classically managed projects often appear to practice administrative perfection, thereby losing focus on the product and the deliverables. Instead, people focus on building risk registers, change management processes, detailed design documents, meeting minutes, and a plethora of other documentation that bring projects back from red. However, no one methodology fits every project. The need for these processes is greatly reduced when people work responsibly and complete their assignments, stay focused on goals, hold to commitments, and work ethically. Given a hard working, ethical team driving toward a common goal, much of the administrative bureaucracy can be removed. To do this, there must be tolerance for people's mistakes; management must resist the practice of creating new processes to prevent reoccurrence of these issues. The key is people. Agile teams consist of success-driven, above-average people. People in agile projects are not resources thrown at a project to fill the open slots. They are individuals handpicked to achieve success in building the desired product.

Since most classical project management processes fail to add value to the product, they violate the lean principle of reducing waste. Although some administrative functions are required for compliance to customer requirements, the level attained in today's projects stifle adaptability in product design and development and consume inordinate amounts of the team's time.

The concept behind an agile project is to deliver products that provide value to the customer. Classically managed projects lose sight of this goal by focusing on process, cost, and control. To implement the lean concept, a number of project management philosophies must change. Project methodology must become more adaptable as business needs change customer requirements. Processes should focus on delivery rather than on compliance with procedures. One must look at the value of each action on the product and eliminate nonvalue-added tasks to minimize waste. The project team continually needs to strive to meet the four tenets of lean thinking:

1. Specify value.
2. Identify the value stream.
3. Enable continuous flow.
4. Instill a pull mentality.

Agile's iterative, feature-based delivery has an advantage over classical project management techniques in achieving these goals. Getting somewhat functional products to the customer for review, comment, and change will provide a faster delivery, happier customer, and lower risk. In short, instead of focusing on procedural excellence, agile projects focus on technical excellence.

The agile methodology includes the maxim that projects for new products are not repeatable. By being unique, they encounter new and unforeseen issues that require unanticipated change. Therefore, managing projects that develop new products need a different methodology from those defined by conventional project management philosophy. Interactions with customers must be adaptable, people must be receptive to change, and the processes must be lean.

In this environment, the project manager moves away from being a paperwork administrator to someone who focuses on articulating the product vision, encouraging interaction, facilitating a distributed decision making process, insisting on individual accountability, and steering the project. In other words, the project manager is a leader.

To create a lean project, processes must be simple and minimally adequate; this requires eliminating wasteful processes. It is the project manager's responsibility to facilitate this. Many elaborate processes are implemented to eliminate mistakes or accommodate deficiencies in the team. Project managers need to avoid this practice. Instead, they must:

- Educate the team and be tolerant of mistakes.
- Educate the executive management on tolerance.
- Concentrate on what is minimally sufficient for compliance and control.

To achieve this, they must be highly critical when selecting team members. One of the many problems with current management practices is the process for building a project team. Project resourcing goals fail to get the best people for the project; they are geared toward using the people in a resource pool. To produce robust products in a timely manner, better than average people are required. Rather than getting resources with technical skills, they must have the qualities for this style project. The project manager and project team need complete authority over the selection and retention of people on the project. They must have the authority to build teams with the following qualities:

- Above the average in skill set.
- Adaptive to changes in requirements.
- Self-organizing.
- Self-disciplined.

An Agile Project's Lifecycle

The agile project management model has five phases—envision, speculate, explore, adapt, and close (see Figure 11-1).

Figure 11-1: Agile Flow

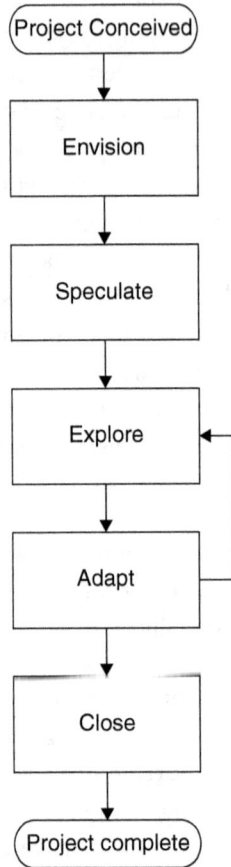

The Envision Phase

Envisioning, rather than detailed requirements, paints the deliverable's high-level definition. The envision phase generates a number of concise project documents. A standard set of documents are a vision box, an elevator statement, a vision document, a feature breakdown structure, and a project data sheet.

Envisioning includes team selection, formation, and grounding in the precise methodology to be used. Since an agile project's structure is flexible by definition, even experienced teams must review the methodology to understand the practices used in each application of agile. Table 11-1 concisely presents the work performed during this phase.

One key aspect often overlooked is agile's use of quadruple constraints (scope, schedule, stability, and budget) versus the more familiar triple constraints. The addition of stability to the normal triple constraints introduces the notion that quality (whether the product covers all the requirements) is sometimes a secondary goal. In classically managed projects, the assumption is quality cannot waiver. Adding stability to the list of project variables resets the team's thinking so it focuses on showing the customer value rather than wasting time adding features and functions that will be rarely, if ever, used. The system can be developed to handle a majority of situations, instead of every situation.

Table 11-1: Agile's Envision Phase

Step	Actions and Deliverables
Define the three key guidelines for the project in a one- to three-day process of working with the customer, project sponsor, or both. This is roughly equivalent to a project charter.	Generate a two- to five-page document including: • A vision box that conceptually holds the product. Its design shows the primary functions and features of the project's product. It forces the team to think of concise selling points and helps define the value. • An elevator statement, a one- or two-paragraph product description. • Customer satisfaction measures, key technologies, operational constraints, competitive analysis, and financial indicators.
Create a feature breakdown structure to define the product architecture and features. This is analogous to a work breakdown structure but it identifies features rather than tasks.	Generate the development team's initial list of guiding principles. As opposed to classically managed projects, agile projects differ drastically between projects, even if they have similar products. Add or remove project deliverables, such as compliance materials, communication tools, or practices, to satisfy specific customer or product requirements. Develop a project data sheet to identify a variety of project level parameters—customer, project manager, project objective, trade-off matrix, exploration factor, delay cost, features, customer benefits, performance and quality attributes, architecture, and risk. All projects have four primary variables—scope, schedule, stability, and budget. A trade-off matrix reduces the variables by making one fixed (i.e., must deliver by a certain date), a second flexible (i.e., should be approximately X dollars), and leaving the other two as variables. This establishes a foundation for limiting the types of change. This is very similar to traditional triple constraint models in classical project management, with the addition of stability.

(continues)

Step	Actions and Deliverables
	Determine the risk and uncertainty in the project. Looking at the technology's maturity (leading edge to well understood) and the requirement's stability (erratically fluctuating to stable and unchanging), and assign a numeric value to the amount of exploration required.
Participant identification	This practice defines the individuals involved in the project and their contribution. Broadly categorized, customers define features, project team members build the product, and stakeholders apply constraints. Define these roles with enough detail to clarify their interaction with the team and each other. Outline the project manager's responsibility to the customer, the team, and the stakeholders.
	The goal of an agile project is to be adaptive. The key to this is having self-disciplined team members. The project manager must have complete control over team member selection to ensure the team has an above-average skill set. Without this, the chances of success are greatly diminished. Acquire qualified, self-disciplined team members with a customer-first attitude.
Customer/developer team interface	The project must have a product manager. Project sponsors can fulfill this role as long as they understand the end users' needs. Product managers manage the customer, while project managers manage the team. Product managers are responsible for ensuring information flows to and from the development team completely and without losing the product vision.
Process and practice tailoring. Agile projects need to be tuned to the situation to which they are applied.	Establish collaboration and communication guidelines for the organization. To minimize the command and control aspects of a project and promote self-organization principles, the project manager must guide the team in understanding what communication is required.
	Define the milestones, gates, and project artifacts. This must be a minimal framework to provide the customers and stakeholders with a gauge of project progress and add product value.
	Some projects need more, others need fewer processes, so define the minimal number of processes in the project.
	Planning for items with long lead times (customer focus groups, acquisition cycles for capital items, etc.) needs to start early to guarantee acceptable results.

The Speculate Phase

Speculation, rather than detailed planning, follows envisioning. Since agile projects focus on features rather than tasks, this phase defines what features to build and the order of development and release. This phase will assist the project team by:

- Determining how the product and feature sets evolve.
- Balancing customer anticipation with product adaptation.
- Identifying high value and high risk features to build early.
- Helping understand business goals and customer expectations.
- Framing the budget and schedule requirements.
- Providing tradeoff data to evaluate changes.
- Coordinating feature and activity dependencies.
- Defining the adaptive process in the context of this project.
- Explaining how to analyze events occurring during the project.

At the end of this phase, the project has a tentative schedule, with a concept of the number and order of iterations; the features are assigned to the iterations. The iteration plan mitigates project risk by pulling riskier features into early iterations. This phase generates the equivalent of a classical project's schedule. Table 11-2 outlines the recommended steps in the speculate phase.

Table 11-2: Agile's Speculate Phase

Step	Actions and Deliverables
Product feature list	This step expands the list of features formulated in the envisioning phase by adding the detail required for the development team to complete the feature.
Feature cards	Develop feature cards for each item listed in the product feature list. Feature cards are 4" × 6" cards containing the feature ID, name, description, planned iteration, feature type (customer or technology), estimated work effort, uncertainty of requirements, dependencies, and acceptance tests. These are inputs to the release, milestone, and iteration planning steps.
Performance requirements cards	Performance requirements cards define the performance characteristics of a set of features. They identify the acceptance tests and are assigned to given or multiple iterations. They contain the performance ID, name, description, anticipated difficulty to achieve, and acceptance tests.

(continues)

Table 11-2: *(continued)*

Step	Actions and Deliverables
Release, milestone, and iteration plan	This step is the equivalent of developing a high-level schedule. Assign features cards to iterations based on the level of risk (the higher, the earlier), the feature's value to the customer (the greater, the earlier), and interfeature dependency. Planning iterations may take various forms. In some cases, develop a complete plan to enumerate each iteration. Identify risks that affect planning. Identify any unmitigated risks as early as possible to avert additional costs and minimize project cancellation cost. The primary functions are to identify schedule target and establish project milestones and iteration periods.
Iteration 0	Iteration 0 is the iteration where the team works on noncustomer features. Since many products need new technology, this is the step to do the proof of technology.
Iterations 1 through N	All iterations should focus on delivering value to the customer and minimizing risk. To help restrict changes, each iteration is a fixed length of time (time boxed). Make tradeoffs to complete an iteration on time. All iterations should have a defined theme identifying the type of features delivered in the iteration. Rework and contingency should be factored into the iterations to account for issues remaining from or uncovered in previous iterations.
Next iteration plan	Prior to starting each iteration, team members sign up for work they will do in that iteration. Two critical points should be kept in mind: • Team members choosing what they work on is essential to accountability. • Making task assignments immediately prior to building the feature provides for maximum flexibility.
First feasible deployment	Throughout the planning process, the team should be looking for the first opportunity to deploy the product. This increases the return on investment (ROI) and customer feedback. It increases value and lowers the cost.
Estimating	Estimates are feature based in agile projects, instead of task based. They need to account for all work to make the feature deployable.

(continues)

Step	Actions and Deliverables
Scope evolution	As opposed to myth, scope cannot change indiscriminately. Scope can change within the bounds of the iteration's vision and theme. Allowing the customer to change their minds for each iteration provides power to agile projects.
Risk analysis and mitigation	Agile projects handle certain types of risk better than classically managed projects. This is accomplished by: • Heavy team involvement in planning and estimating. • Early feedback based on delivery velocity. • Constant pressure to balance the number and depth of features within the schedule constraints • Close interactions between technical and customer teams. • Early error detection and correction.

The Explore Phase

The explore phase's goal is to develop and deliver tested features in a short timeframe. Repeating explore and adapt processes (see Figure 11-1) allows for continual addition and alteration of features and functions, evaluation of progress, and adjustment of subsequent iterations to attain better results. The project manager's role is to facilitate the creation of a self-organized and self-disciplined team. To do this the project manager must transform the individuals into a team by:

- Focusing the team on delivering results.
- Developing each individual's capabilities.
- Removing roadblocks from the project.
- Acquiring the required resources.
- Coaching the customer.
- Creating and orchestrating the team's workflow and interactions.

By definition, each iteration, save Iteration 0, must produce value to the customer. The output can be evaluated and adjustments made to future iterations to achieve the value needed in the product at the earliest possible time. Iterations are complete to an acceptable quality for deployment. This is a key concept to getting the quickest return on investment.

Table 11-3 shows the steps in the explore phase.

Table 11-3: Agile's Explore Phase

Step	Actions and Deliverables
Workload management	The team maintains and the project manager enables workload management. To maintain accountability, self-organizing and self-disciplined teams manage their own workloads. The project manager monitors their effectiveness and provides assistance in maintaining the validity of the planning assumptions.
Low-cost change	Keep two points in mind: (1) the iterative development cycle enables change; and (2) the goal is to deliver future value in the product by making it easy to adapt to new situations. To do this, five factors should be watched:

• Minimizing technical debt (the difference between doing something the right way versus getting it released quickly) is the single most important philosophy in delivering a maintainable system. Keeping technical debt to a minimum and refactoring creates a product that is easier to change and is responsive to customer needs.

• Keeping the design simple is a key concept enabled by the iterative style of agile projects. Since the design will evolve during the development process, there is no need to include complex solutions for anticipated problems. If a problem is not immediate or fully defined, there is no need to implement a solution. Address actual problems more completely.

• Integrating frequently within an iteration for testing builds in quality and highlights potential design issues.

• Testing ruthlessly must be a continuing objective of each developer.

• Practicing opportunistic refactoring keeps the design clean and up to date. This must be the management team's and developers' guiding philosophy. Developers take inadvertent shortcuts when modifying any product. In addition, new technologies may be developed rendering parts of the product more difficult to maintain than need be. Refactoring the product will address both of these issues, improve the responsiveness to the customer, increase the design's longevity, and boost profit.

(continues)

Step	Actions and Deliverables
Coaching and team development	Second to getting the right people, improving team member's qualifications is critical in having a high-performance team. Customer and stakeholders, in addition to the team, receive coaching. The project manager's responsibilities are:

- Focus the team on delivering results. Because of the nature of agile projects, maintaining focus in each iteration and its relation to the final project is a difficult task. The project manager coaches individuals on maintaining focus and adding only essential functionality. Since there is a fine line between what is essential and what is nice to have, the team needs assistance in making these decisions.

- Develop each individual's capabilities—both technically and interpersonally. Everyone has room for improvement. Individuals should be fostered in adopting behaviors including:

  — Accepting accountability for results.

  — Willingness to work in a self-organized environment.

  — Analyzing situations to determine root causes.

  — Respecting one's colleagues.

  — Engaging in intense debate and interaction.

- Mold the group of individuals into a team. Developing each individual's capabilities goes a long way toward building a team. The project manager must further this by exhibiting trust in the group and facilitating interaction and debate to achieve technical excellence. Teams will form without a manager's influence; they will form much faster with proper leadership. Teams must be able to aggressively debate issues and solutions and come to an agreement, rather than consensus, on a decision. To help, formulate a set of guidelines. These should include:

  — Everyone has an equal voice.

  — Everyone's contribution is valuable.

  — Attacks must focus on issues rather than other people.

  — People must respect each other's differences.

  — All members must participate.

(continues)

Table 11-3: *(continued)*

Step	Actions and Deliverables
	• The project manager must supply quality resources, eliminating roadblocks to keep the team focused on its tasks, reducing distractions resulting in enhanced velocity.
	• Orchestrate team rhythm. The project manager needs to assist the team in finding a rhythm, a smooth interaction process, to keep members coordinated. Similarly, this is found in critical chain.
	Coach the customers. Agile project changes affect more than the method by which team members interact among themselves, it also changes how they interact with the customer. In agile projects, customers are much closer to the project team and need coaching. This is vital to adding value. Just as the project manager must educate the team, the product manager (project sponsor) must educate the customer.
Daily team integration meetings	As a result of the speed of development, daily meetings, often referred to as scrum, are required. Short cycle times make problems surface quickly, and resolution is critical. These meetings should inform on (rather than discuss) progress and impediments. The goal of these short, efficient daily meetings is to:
	• Review the prior day's accomplishments.
	• Enumerate plans for the day.
	• Highlight issues, obstacles, and needs.
Participatory decision making	Including the team members in the decision-making process is one of the most effective ways to make individuals and teams more accountable. Participatory decision making involves the team, stakeholders, and customers. It ensures that all participants in the project are informed and their concerns have been heard and addressed. Participatory decision making is not consensus; it is a process to ensure all agree to support the decision.
	Involve the correct people in decision framing. The decision group is selected by a predetermined set of criteria, typically:
	• People impacted.

(continues)

Step	Actions and Deliverables
	• People providing input.
	• People required for discussion (i.e. subject matter experts, etc.).
	• Decision makers.
	• Reviewers and approvers.
	• People needing to know the decision's results.
	• Decision making is arriving at a common understanding.
	Evaluate all decisions for their effectiveness to achieve continuous improvement. Retrospectively look at each decision and note what could have improved the decision.
	Design and decision sets, as used at Toyota,[5] are critical to responsiveness. This technique entails looking at a set of solutions for a problem and delaying the decision as long as possible until a well-informed decision can be made. This accomplishes coming to a best answer as late as possible, allowing the maximum amount of data to be involved in the decision, hence reducing the risk.
Daily interaction with the customer team	As with team meetings, apprise the customers and stakeholders on a daily basis. This requirement is more important in agile projects because of the rapid development process and the need for trade-off decisions to meet the iteration milestones. The project manager has the responsibility for the communication to keep them supportive of the project.

The Adapt Phase

After each explore phase, the team needs to review the previous iteration's results and adjust the plans to achieve the best results. This is aptly called the adapt phase. This step is a feedback process that ensures the project achieves the correct results. The adapt phase makes changes to the project to ensure:

- The customer receives value.
- The project team is satisfactorily meeting its milestone, cost, feature, and quality objectives.
- The project team is adapting effectively to changes imposed by management, customers, and technology.

Evaluate the project to determine what adaptations are required. This includes:

- Product functionality.
- Product quality.
- Team performance.
- Project status.

Reflecting on these items and feeding the information back into the methodology will determine the next iteration's course. Table 11-4 outlines the steps in the adapt phase.

Table 11-4: Agile's Adapt Phase

Step	*Actions and Deliverables*
Customer focus groups	A set of customer representatives, different from the set working with the team, provides input on the product. This should be a larger group of customers with a wide range of duties. The technical team may be present, but it is there to listen and should avoid doing anything to stifle customer input. The facilitator should capture suggestions and provide them to the project team.
Technical reviews	Perform internal, facilitated meetings to review the project's technical aspects. Technically competent individuals assess the product, compliance material (documentation), defect levels, and other project statistics to determine the product's state.
Team performance evaluations	Review the team, ensuring that the right people with the proper capabilities are on the project. Team and individual performance needs to be evaluated and corrective actions developed for improving the team. Do this regardless of the iteration's level of success. Success can be for many reasons including low goals, hence demanding improvement.
Project status reports	A variety of reports indicate an agile project's progress. These include the percentage of features delivered to a customer, plan-to-actual features by iteration, and cumulative value of features delivered by iteration. Reporting depends strongly on the project's and stakeholders' needs.
Adaptive action	As the name implies, the result of this phase is process adaptation to ensure proper progress in delivering product value.

The Close Phase

Conduct the closing phase at the project's completion. In this phase, the team focuses on tying up loose ends, completing any documentation, and fixing the last few open items. In addition, it provides input to future project teams through retrospection (capturing lessons learned), looking at what went right and wrong, and determining what behaviors need changing and what processes require improving (minimizing waste while providing sufficient process and documentation). Last and very important to maintaining individuals' spirits and morale, there should be a celebration of the successful completion.

CASE STUDY 11-1: QUARTERLY RELEASE CYCLES THAT LOOKED LIKE AGILE

Long ago, when agile was only an adjective, the current agile concept was used without the process' rigor. New rapid development tools called fourth generation languages (4GLs) were available for simplifying the development of end-user systems. For classical COBOL/CICS developers, these tools were anathemas. Code could be developed and deployed without the need for many of the design specifications simply because the tool did so much for the developers.

In the 1980s, a large upscale retailer used such a tool primarily for reporting. The business unit needed a highly adaptable sales commission system for its sales staff. Attempts to build the system in CICS failed, so I recommended developing the system using the 4GL. In addition, I recommended segmenting the deployment based on region, since each region had separate business rules. The regions would be released quarterly. To appease the customer, the management information systems (MIS) group allowed the project to follow the proposed plan, but the MIS group was vocal about its skepticism.

Because I had an office with the commission group, I was able to develop the system while watching how employees performed their jobs. The system design and the end users' business process changed to overcome limitations in the tool. Quarterly, new pieces of the system were deployed, each region getting more functionality. That additional functionality was also deployed to the previously installed regions. The commission department's cost savings was huge and recuperated my fees every quarter. After three years, the MIS group finally relented and took over the system (leaving it in the 4GL) and kept the quarterly release process.

The Effect of Project Size on Agile Projects

As projects get bigger, there are many challenges. The biggest is the overhead required to maintain communication among the teams. Large projects need a hub organizational structure (as opposed to the standard hierarchical structure). This structure creates teams by functional area, whose members interact as peers, with each team employing the practices as if they were separate projects. This requires:

- Getting the right leaders.
- Articulating the work breakdown and integration strategies.
- Facilitating interaction among teams.
- Framing project-wide decision making.

To do this, the project manager must focus on interactions rather than activities.

A Critic's View of Agile

Agile has many opponents, whose major criticism is unbounded scope. At first glance, this may seem a legitimate concern. In actuality, however, time boxing tightly controls scope. Scope may change, but it is primarily trading one item for another to maintain the time box's restrictions. Customer-driven prioritization maintains the target on a value-rich product.

The second major criticism is the lack of traceability, but this can be achieved by maintaining simple document control on the feature list. The outcome of each iteration provides traceability and shows the product's evolution. It is the project sponsor's responsibility to control this issue.

CASE STUDY 11-2:
ANALYZING AGILE'S USE IN A RECOVERY

Full implementation of agile project management requires a top-down approach. Its reporting, resource dedication, team structure, and customer relationship need buy-in at the company's upper echelons. Educating superiors and customers on the benefits of agile project management may be difficult, especially if they are unfamiliar with project management principles or have an inflexible belief in classical project management. Implementing a pilot project is the best way to quell these fears. Unfortunately, this luxury is unavailable in project recovery scenarios, and the recovery becomes their pilot.

Getting people to change to an alternate method with which they are familiar is difficult. Getting people to change to something with which they are unfamiliar is even harder. Therefore, changing to an agile methodology can be very challenging. There needs to be a way to demonstrate its power without making executives commit to something perceived as too risky. Agile's methodology helps since the last phase, adapt, allows for slow adoption. Proposing and executing an iterative approach to the implementation shows its benefits more quickly than one might expect.

An actual example will illustrate this. A company had developed an application deployed at numerous franchised and internal locations throughout North America. The product had feature upgrades developed and deployed on a nine- to twelve-month cycle using the plan, define, implement, and manage (PDIM) waterfall methodology. For maintenance, though, the company used follow-up projects rather than a maintenance group. There were no technical constraints inhibiting distribution of releases on a much more frequent schedule—the Internet-based distribution infrastructure was already used for project and data releases.

The customers (franchised dealers, sales, and order processing) were displeased with the turnaround time for minor enhancements and bug fixes, but executive management was unwilling to try new methodologies because the product had been plagued with many main-tenance and management problems (mostly from long lead-time monolithic releases).

After the audit, I determined agile was feasible for the bug fixes and implementing minor feature changes on a much shorter cycle. To do this would require overcoming significant political pressure. The proposal involved implementing agile methodology in steps to show it could be beneficial. The approach proposed was:

- Demonstrate the ability to release bug fixes separately from the project cycle.
- Work with the customers to prioritize the feature list, initially restricting the changes to the simplest of enhancements and critical bug fixes.
- Segment the project (which was on a nine-month cycle) to create a small team to build and test the features in short iterative cycles.
- Show success in deploying minor feature enhancements.
- Improve the process to include more significant enhancements.

Although a number of factors had to be considered, the biggest was overcoming the team's and customer's negative attitudes and limiting the number of items to be fixed in each cycle.

Because of previous issues, the team was highly demoralized. Management had denied training on tools, and many members felt incapable of meeting the request. Most were skeptical of my radical ideas, and a few members' actions bordered on insubordination. The first task was finding allies. Developers and the product manager were quick to step into that role.

I wanted a release every four weeks. This implied an average of two weeks for development and two weeks for regression testing. Development and regression could overlap by a week to provide more development time.

The product manager, customer manager, development lead, and I analyzed more than 1,500 defects and enhancement requests in the bug tracking system. In a two-day session, these items were prioritized and assigned an effort-to-complete value (small, medium, large, and too big for an iteration).

The next task was to study the electronic distribution system. If quick turns of product releases were going to take place, this system had to run flawlessly and be able to report on the deployment penetration. The previous subject matter expert had left the company, leaving little documentation. A junior resource inherited the system, but his training request was denied. I assigned a developer to work with the junior resource to expedite his under-standing of the product. Throughout the process, the system was tuned, the junior employee was mentored, and reports (showing deployment penetration) were generated.

The core team recruited two volunteer developers and a skeptical quality assurance (QA) lead. We determined that each group could spend approximately 160 hours on each iteration. This would yield a two-week cycle for each group (two resources each). Table

11-5 shows the iteration cycle plan. This six-week process was interleaved to create a four-week release cycle.

Since this process was new to the team, I felt a slow introduction was best. During the first iteration (each iteration produced a service pack for release), only bug fixes were included. Changes to features were strongly discouraged.

I focused on reporting. Deploying a service pack would have an immediate and positive effect on the sales and order processing groups. It was imperative to quantify the benefit to show managers the immediate effect. Getting the customer's support on the speed of delivery and showing the benefits would be critical in convincing executive management of success. The customer and steering committee approved the reporting method, which was tested on the previous project's closeout.

To help the team achieve a win, I worked to build confidence by:

- Promoting the team to the customers.
- Holding individual meetings with team members.
- Removing underperformers from the team.

Table 11-5: Iteration Plan

Week	Cycle N	Cycle N + 1
1	Prioritize features to be worked on (will deliver, try to deliver). Define features in both categories.	
2	Developers start work.	
3	Developers continue work.	
4	Developers continue only if needed. QA starts testing.	
5	QA finishes testing. Developers work with QA to fix errors.	Prioritize features to be worked on (will deliver, try to deliver). Define features in both categories.
6	Deploy	Developers start work.
7		Developers continue work.
8		Developers continue only if needed, and QA starts testing.
9		QA finishes testing. Developers work with QA to fix errors.
10		Deploy

Implementing these goals and using a firm, but fair, management style improved the team's self-image and confidence. I knew a successful deployment would raise credibility and build much needed confidence.

The concept was proposed to the steering committee, which was comprised primarily of customer representatives. The reporting methods and specific success criteria were outlined to allay fears of being unprepared. Reporting was critical since the prior management had told the committee it was impossible to report on this information. Showing management actual reports greatly improved its confidence in my skills and resourcefulness. Management approved the idea, although its members were skeptical of success.

Next, I requested the steering committee prioritize the feature and defect list. For the first iteration, I started with a preprioritized list to expedite the process. The customers rated all the items as high priority. I had to remind the committee there were only 160 hours of developer and 160 hours of QA time to make the changes. Since releases would be every four weeks, the next set would be fixed in four weeks with the next service pack. Eventually this resulted in super-high, high, medium-high, and low-high rankings.

The steering committee supported my ideas in front of IT executive management, whose members had been scared into a zero-risk (noncustomer-oriented) approach and were less than supportive of a new concept.

Skepticism was very high because the team had never followed this approach and was exacerbated by the attitude of executive management. As a hedge, I undercommitted on the team's capability and worked with the team to determine the best way to deliver more than promised. To abate many of the political issues, I worked with developers to include as many zero-time fixes as possible—minor and medium items, which developers had fixed previously. Although this strained the QA group, it was felt this approach was worth the effort.

The team agreed on a new single-page feature definition document (see Appendix), which included screen mockups, behavior, and validation rules. QA could use the same document for testing, thereby removing the need for multiple documents.

Daily status was gleaned from each team member. Instead of a formal meeting, I visited each member individually. This allowed team members to better voice their concerns without feeling pressure from others on the team. Any questions or concerns were addressed promptly. The system architect held daily meetings.

The first release fixed thirty-five major and more than one hundred minor (cosmetic) and medium (nonfunctional, cumbersome) bugs.

The response from the customer and steering committee was phenomenal. The release's penetration to the sales force was approximately 80 percent in the first 24 hours. In fact, within a couple of hours, positive effects were evident in the order processing organization. The customer's attitude toward the team and the team's self-confidence took a quantum leap.

For each iteration, the development cycle was altered. These changes included:

- Allowing reprioritization and new requests, trade-offs were usually required and, with facilitation, the customer adapted and followed the process.
- Increasing the number of items to fix or add.
- Communication directly between the development team and the feature's requestor (taboo in the organization) to streamline the solution proposal.

Unexpectedly, there was significant pushback from one of the original allies—the developers. They were frustrated with the code's condition. We added refactoring to the iterations as necessary. Developers had to follow two principles:

- Hurried changes were discouraged; they needed to be changes that could be done properly in a short amount of time.
- Each iteration had a few days set aside for refactoring code. When they touched poor quality code, they were supposed to change it.

This process actually introduced a significant bug into the product. The bug was fixed, and the fix was deployed in a week. The chart in Case Study 11-3 shows this occurrence between weeks 43 and 44. To the developers' surprise, the standard reprimands were missing because of the responsiveness of the fix. The process achieved enough benefit that tolerance for little mistakes greatly increased.

This, and the trust that went with it, made pride soar.

How a Partial Implementation of Agile Can Be Achieved

The implementation described in Case Study 11-2 is only part of what agile purists call a real agile process. Nevertheless, the compromise was very successful and has the basic traits of an agile project. Any implementation of a new methodology for a recovery will be like this—a partial implementation to use the best features. To understand this better, the following sections compare that deployment to a theoretical implementation as defined in the reference, *Agile Project Management: Creating Innovative Products,* by Jim Highsmith. This gives the reader perspective on how to use other methodologies to improve a project or help in a recovery.

How the Envision Phase Was Implemented

Agile requires specific, small definition statements to guide the project, notably a product vision box, elevator statement, and product vision document. These items are applicable to new products or projects missing this definition. Because the team in Case Study 11-2 was using the existing product architecture and project data sheet, this step was skipped.

Getting the Right People: As recovery manager, I reassigned the best people inside the project to the new effort and replaced others. Developers volunteered for the new approach and felt responsible for its success. Team members were replaced quickly to minimize anxiety in the team.

Participant Identification: The people on the team were defined, but the new methodology required new roles and responsibilities. As a team, they were struggling. Identifying the real customer was an issue—the application's users (sales) and data users (order processing) both claimed equal authority. Eventually, I reached a compromise based on the corporate cost of an error—order processing had priority. In addition, customers had been providing only high-level input to the process; they needed to provide details and be more involved with the process' workings.

Customer/Developer Team Interface: Agile is ineffective without a tight customer and development team coupling. Customer and team interaction needed significant work to enable effective interaction. It took two to three iterations to make this work properly. Training the development team to perform tradeoffs with the customer instead of agreeing to adding scope was difficult. Initially, this took facilitation.

Process and Practice Tailoring: Agile processes need to be adapted to the project, and the people need to be receptive to constant changes in processes and practices. The fact that agile is an iterative implementation allows for tailoring of every iteration.

How the Speculate Phase Was Implemented

Product Feature List: For time boxing to work, the team must maintain a feature backlog list selecting the most important features to work on. The feature list was consolidated from a variety of existing lists, so I worked with the customers to prioritize and validate the requirement for the features. Many of the items were removed, and some were combined. As the process continued, the customers removed even more features realizing many requirements were insignificant.

The feature list was the bug and enhancement list. Due to the type of interaction with the customer and its dispersed nature, a spreadsheet (see Figure 11-3, pg. 154) was used to summarize and quickly sort the list. The entries were automatically color-coded based on the number of hours required for the estimated work assigned in the service pack. This facilitated presentation over a Web-based conference tool and provided immediate feedback on what lower priority feature would be excluded from the iteration.

Feature Cards: Agile uses feature cards instead of detailed functional specifications. The focus of documentation needs to be the feature set in the current iteration. Combined feature cards and performance requirement cards were developed. In this format, feature cards (see Appendix) were easily displayed over an online Web conference session.

Performance Requirements Cards: Performance card data were included in the aforementioned feature cards.

Release, Milestone, and Iteration Plan: The iteration plan was artificially generated prior to the speculate phase; a monthly cycle was arbitrarily chosen.

How the Explore Phase Was Implemented

Workload Management: Agile provides workload management by having team members divide the work among themselves. The team involved with this process was small. Initially, the architect made strong suggestions on the work assignments. As confidence grew, the team members would split the work among themselves.

Low-Cost Change: Because of organizational issues, the cost of this process was hopelessly intertwined with other work. The cost savings from the order-processing group and helpdesk was monitored. Both showed extremely favorable results in reduction of manual processing of orders from program issues. There was also a reduction in helpdesk calls for specific usability issues. Removing the scope and placing it in a subproject reduced that main project's scope, thereby decreasing the overall complexity.

Coaching and Team Development: Training was critical in many areas. To advance their skills and knowledge, developers performed work with tools or in product areas with which they were unfamiliar. This was encouraged, but monitored closely. As mentioned, the process was new, therefore coaching was intensive.

Daily Team Integration Meetings: The team met daily with the architect. I visited each team member at least twice a week.

Participatory Decision Making: This process could have improved in this application. Partly as a result of the team's inexperience with the process, I made most of the decisions.

Daily Interaction with the Customer Team: Communication with the customer was drastically changed. Before implementing this approach, the customer was always trying to get more from the developers. Therefore, for the first iteration, I handled all communication. Before opening communication to others, the following had to be tackled:

- The process had to be defined and understood.
- The customers needed training on the new methods and the philosophy of maintaining the iteration length.
- The team needed assistance in developing feature tradeoff skills.
- Success had to be demonstrated—showing the customers that this process worked was crucial in getting them to prioritize items. They had to know that what they asked for would be delivered. Hence, lower priority items were postponed rather than being lost forever.

CASE STUDY 11-3: SHOWING DELIVERY PENETRATION TO THE CUSTOMER

As mentioned in Case Study 4-7 (pg. 59), the presentation of information is critical. The graphic below of software adoption rates showed the deployment's penetration. Each shade represents a different release. The line's steepness indicates the adoption rates, and the line's height indicates the increase in product usage. (The dip is from a lack of usage over a four-day holiday.) As the areas get thinner, it indicates replacement of the program's older versions with the newer. The chart is based on the transmission of sales orders to the corporate office and, therefore, reflects actual usage versus simply downloading of the new service pack.

Figure 11-2: Software Adoption Rates

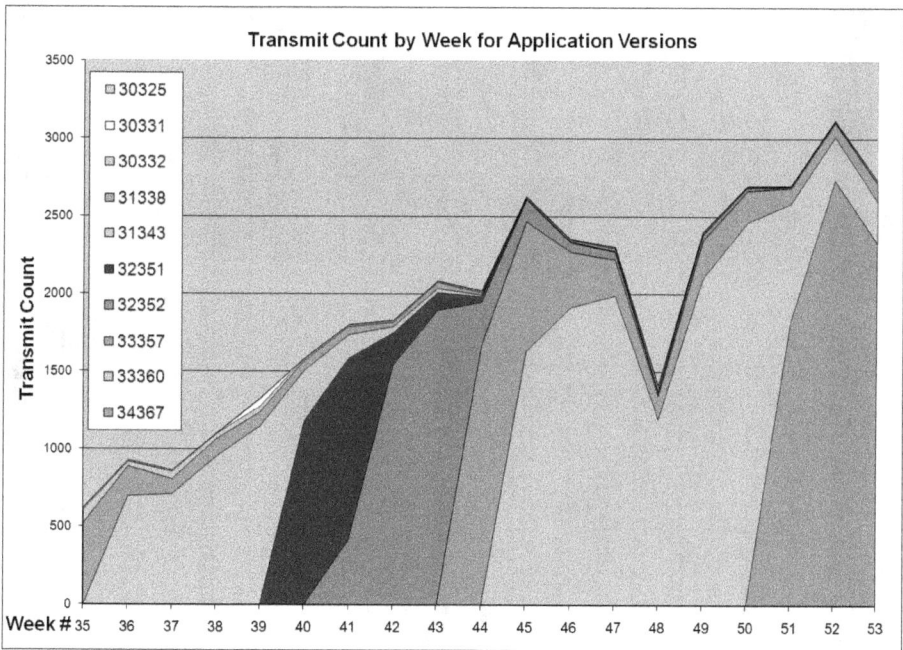

How the Adapt Phase Was Implemented

Product, Project, and Team Review Including Adaptive Action: The adapt phase was primarily applied to the process as opposed to the product. The product had a relatively stable roadmap, but the process changed in every iteration bringing it closer to an agile methodology.

Figure 11-3: Backlog List

ID	Description	Type	Target Release	CO Priority	Dev	QA	Total Dev	Total QA	Total Effort	Iteration Total	Comments
ID8297	Unable to load Background image error is reported when a document is being loaded	Bug	1.2 SP2	1-High	2	5	2	5	7	7	
ID10230	Select option: Most recent selection option should be highlighted.	Enh	1.2 SP2	1-High	2	3	4	8	5	12	
ID12449	Quote: Option descriptions are split across two pages on a printout of Apply Quote dialog	Enh	1.2 SP2	1-High	0	0	4	8	0	12	
ID12450	Quote: A blank page with just a heading row is appended to multi-page printouts of Apply Quote dialog	Bug	1.2 SP2	1-High	0	0	4	8	0	12	
ID10456	Proposal: Preview proposal will generate a users informative message	Bug	1.2 SP2	1-High	2	4	6	12	6	18	
ID10407	Deselecting orders in List of Orders shows order validation and warning dialogs again	Bug	1.2 SP2	1-High	2	3	8	15	5	23	
ID10316	Order: Sales program/Concessions warning appears if non-incentive sales program is selected	Enh	1.2 SP2	1-High	2	5	10	20	7	30	
ID12437	Concession screen permits user to insert hyphens instead of integers within the order quantities boxes.	Enh	1.2 SP2	1-High	2	5	12	25	7	37	Designed to allow negative values
TBD	Secure Internet Channel	Enh	1.2 SP2	1-High	60	60	72	85	120	157	Security issue
TBD	Provide disabling of SalesMaster login at Client	Enh	1.2 SP2	1-High	48	48	120	133	96	253	Security issue
ID11557	Rel12 Patch: Concession request transmission fails if other dealer costs/credits are negative value	Enh	1.2 SP2	1-High	24	24	144	157	48	301	
ID12125	339 Build - Rel12 Patch: Notes duplicated when an item is altered should not print on proposal reports	Bug	1.2 SP2	1-High	0	0	144	157	0	301	Assigned to Dev/Client has been assigned a task to determine if the replaced option is being approved.
ID12300	Rel12 Patch: Spec Proposal: Adjusted List Price is displayed in both the Sales Programs and Adjusted List Price fields.	Enh	1.2 SP2	1-High	24	24	168	181	48	349	
ID12143	Rel12 Patch: System generates a note revised by dealer, but there was no change to the note	Bug	1.2 SP3	1-High	36	36	204	217	72	421	
ID12417	PriceQuote: Get Error in response, but "Completed" shown as Quote Status	Bug	1.2 SP3	1-High	36	36	240	253	72	493	
TBD	Allow method to turn on Firm Order/Pre-Quote	Enh	1.2 SP3	1-High	60	60	300	313	120	613	Steering Committee request
ID12125	Rel12 Patch: Notes duplicated when an item is altered should not print on proposal reports	Bug	1.2 SP3	1-High	72	72	372	385	144	757	
ID11793	Initial concession notification via E-mail for Prod1 and Prod2 concession requests are not occurring	Enh	1.2 SP3	1-High	0	10	372	395	10	767	
ID12431	Download Sales Order: Should not include Quantity of downloaded Sales Order	Bug	1.2 SP3	1-High	12	12	384	407	24	791	
ID12398	Opening a Sales Order download spec for an obsolete model gives user a vague error message	Enh	1.2 SP3	1-High	24	24	408	431	48	839	
ID12413	With Download Sales Order, delivery information should not be imported with the spec	Enh	1.2 SP3	1-High	24	24	432	455	48	887	
ID12420	Recommended notes on recommended options do not get applied do spec	Enh	Future	1-High	24	24	456	479	48	935	
ID12445	An Altered option with no notes is transmitted in the price quote as a selected option	Enh	Future	1-High	24	24	480	503	48	983	
ID12451	SP2 Patch: Price Quote ID which appears on a printout of Apply Quote dialog is different from the ID shown on Quote Info dialog	Bug	Future	1-High	24	24	504	527	48	1031	

Chapter Takeaway

- Agile is a short cycle iterative approach to project management.
- It contains five adaptive steps:
  - Envisioning—the product's conceptual design.
  - Speculate— the project's definition.
  - Explore—development iterations.
  - Adapt—modifying the processes to achieve better results.
  - Close—a retrospective look at the project for feedback to other projects.
- An agile project strives for technical, rather than administrative, excellence.
- Agile divides work into manageable packets of highly prioritized features.
- Work packets force the customer to rate the relative importance of the feature.
- Agile's time-boxed iterations provide the opportunity to change the project's scope without letting it grow unmanageably.
- The customer's involvement in the development process helps maintain a focus on product value and inhibits developers from working on nonvalue-adding items
- Team members must have an above-average skill set, adapt well to changes in requirements, and be self-organizing and self-disciplined.
- An agile implementation can be encapsulated in a project as a separately managed subproject.
- Agile is very affective in recovering a project where the technology or the customer's concept of its product is poorly understood or small units of work can be deployed in a quick fashion.

CHAPTER

12

How Critical Chain Methodology Can Assist in a Recovery

"Nothing is so fatiguing as the eternal hanging
on of an uncompleted task"

—William James, American Psychologist and Philosopher,
The Letters of William James

Critical chain project methodology (CCPM) extends the notion of the project's critical path by accounting for resource loading and conflicts with other projects in the pipeline. In addition, it looks at how estimates are determined and defines a statistically more reliable method for generating them. This method of estimating changes the conditioned behavior of team members and management. It is the brainchild of Eliyahu Goldratt, the progenitor of the theory of constraints used in manufacturing operations. In his business novel, *Critical Chain*, he explains how the theory of constraints applies to project management. Lawrence Leach takes this a step further in his book, *Critical Chain Project Management*, with an exhaustive description of the methodology. This chapter illustrates its value in recovering projects.

Understanding the Theory of Constraints

Theory of constraints (TOC) is a manufacturing methodology that subordinates all work centers to the slowest one and focuses on improving throughput at that work-station. By iteratively executing the following five steps, analysts can identify and improve the bottleneck processes until the business' goals are achieved:

- *Identify:* Identify the system's bottleneck.
- *Exploit:* Exploit this bottleneck, making its throughput efficient by changing processes, equipment maintenance procedures, training, policies, etc.
- *Subordinate:* Subordinate the throughput of all other work centers to the slowest work center.
- *Elevate:* Invest in this work center to increase its throughput—add equipment, workers, etc.
- *Inertia:* Start the process over to determine the new bottleneck.

A bottleneck process becomes the gauge for the manufacturing line. Production start rates cannot exceed the rate at which the bottleneck can assimilate its work. Exceeding that rate would add to the work in process (WIP), wasting raw material and resources. If more throughput is needed, additional capital is invested in the bottleneck process. After elevating the bottleneck, the process of identifying the new bottleneck starts over.

This philosophy keeps the cost model (maximum throughout per work center) and throughput models (maximum line throughout with minimal investment) at odds with one another, as the subordination process necessarily decreases work center efficiency. Thus, evaluation criteria for properly managing a work center must change to reward the organization's success properly.

The use of conceptual conflicts identifies areas where theories may be proved incorrect. An axiom in TOC states if two concepts are in direct conflict, then at least one of the concepts has an incorrect assumption (see Figure 13-1, pg. 172).

Understanding the Principles of Critical Chain

When applying TOC to project management, one needs to draw parallels between manufacturing and project management terms. This makes the conceptual model of critical chain easier to understand because of the physical nature of a manufacturing line.

Picture a production line building a widget. To create a widget, raw material is processed through various work centers to transform the material into the final product. The material that proceeds through the line is analogous to time on a project, and a work center is the same as a task. Each work center on a manufacturing line has some level of material waiting to be processed; this is the prework center inventory. Slower work centers have more inventory than faster ones. The slowest work center, the bottleneck, is the constraining flow point of the line. If you start raw material faster than the bottleneck can assimilate it, inventory will build in front of the bottleneck—nothing comes out of the line faster than the bottleneck can process it.

In a project, the bottleneck is the project's critical path. Early completion of tasks off the critical path has no effect on the completion date of the project. The rate work proceeds on the critical path is the gauge of progress. If work stacks up in front of a person on the critical path (i.e., prework center inventory), the people ahead of that task are nonproductively completing work. Table 12-1 defines TOC terms in relationship to a project.

People usually pad their estimates to create a perceived high chance of success. Normal estimates promise an 80 to 90 percent chance of achieving task completion, which actually nearly guarantees failure. Critical chain uses a consistent estimation method that gives resources a 50:50 chance of completing a task.

To demonstrate the issue, conduct this simple experiment. Ask five people to flip a quarter ten times; record the results and the time it took. Repeat this five times to simulate a history. Discuss the results, along with the possible problems that can make the task time vary—variations in setup time, dropping the quarter, needing to correct results, the pen running out of ink, breaking a lead, the phone ringing, etc. Finally, ask the group to estimate of how long it will take to complete the task with these variables in mind.

Table 12-2 shows the data gathered from one such experiment, while Table 12-3 shows the estimates people gave, in that same session, for how long the task will take to complete. The average is 85 seconds. Twenty of the actual times lie under the estimate and five lie outside—exactly 80:20.

In this small sampling, many conditions reduce the risk—each person is given a quarter, a writing instrument, paper, and a watch. In reality, task setup is more difficult. In addition, the time for the flip sequence is insufficient to encounter many variations—fallen quarters rolling out of sight, phone calls, forgotten instructions, etc.—any of which would represent risk in a real repetitive task. Understanding these inevitabilities, people's estimates grow unrealistically as they unconsciously bias their answers to account for risk.

Using a 50:50 estimate says that even though one task may take more time than its estimate, another will take less—on average canceling each other. There is no

Table 12-1: Project Management Terms Mapped to Theory of Constraints

Production Term	Project Term
Work center	Task
Product	Time
Prework center inventory	Task buffer to cushion feeding tasks from the critical path
Bottleneck work center	Critical path

Table 12-2 : Quarter Flipping Experiment

Person	1	2	3	4	5
Person 1	1:25	1:15	1:15	1:20	1:40
Person 2	0:55	0:55	1:00	1:15	0:50
Person 3	1:20	1:30	1:25	1:30	1:30
Person 4	1:00	0:50	0:55	0:55	1:00
Person 5	1:10	1:00	1:10	1:30	1:05

pad in the estimate. Therefore, misuse of time, like the conditions outlined in Figure 12-1, is controlled.

Theoretical data shows estimates covering an 80 percent probability for success, nearly double the time estimate.[6] The conventional method of estimation creates task lengths with pad that allows resources to multitask on other work. As a result, resources fail to achieve the earliest completion dates for their tasks.

Since there are an infinite number of opportunities for delay, estimates should be slightly skewed (five to ten percent) to account for common cause variation. To handle special cause risk (someone stealing the quarter, etc.), a buffer must be placed at end of the project or at the end of a sequence of tasks feeding the critical path.

Critical chain also requires that management understand it is not working with absolutes. The time estimates are just that—estimates. This is essential for tracking the project plan and setting expectations.

Table 12-3: Summarized Results

Time	Count
50	2
55	4
60	4
65	1
70	2
75	3
80	2
85	2
90	4
95	0
100	1

Figure 12-1: Factors Affecting Estimates

- Requests from outsidethe project to do tasks.

- Completing work from prior tasks (i.e., documentation, testing, gold plating, etc.).

- Meetings, email, and other interruptions.

- Wasted time due to lack of pressure (student syndrome).

- Gold plating.

Differences in Doing Scheduling Estimates in Critical Chain

Critical chain theory claims that the current method of generating time estimates is the primary reason for increased expense on projects and the inability to finish on time. The commonly accepted principle is that adding pad virtually guarantees that tasks will complete on time. This theory, however, says otherwise and asserts that people give estimates for a task that give them an 80 to 90 percent chance of successful completion. The experiment in the previous section supports this. This can make the length of time for the task as much as 200 percent the time required. This excessive padding has the effect of ensuring the task will run full term or be late. As counterintuitive as this seems, it predisposes people on the project to consume the estimated time by:

- Triggering the student syndrome–resources know they have more than enough time to do the task; therefore they start the task late using up the entire pad.
- Encouraging multitasking–the padding is added knowing the resource will be unable to focus on the task and hence encouraging multitasking on other projects. This is detrimental to all projects (see Figure 12-3).
- Failing to claim early completion–behavior that conditions people to use all the time estimated to complete a task. Such behavior includes:
  - Penalizing people for early completion, as when management ridicules them for having pad in their estimates. This defeats any incentive to finish early.
  - Resources feeling that working the allotted time, even if they have completed the task early, will make the product better. This is false, because much of the time is spent on noncritical-to-quality items. Finishing early actually brings more value since the project can be completed earlier.

- Completing early will trigger upper level managers to cut time estimates. However, pad reduces the number of reprimands for being late. People want to keep the ability to pad the schedule since other activities that require time are always being inserted.

CASE STUDY 12-1: REMOVING KNOWN PAD FROM TIME ESTIMATES

Habits are very hard to break. On an overseas project that was very late, I developed a habit of cutting people's time estimates in half. Besides the late delivery, there were too many other issues to try to educate everyone on critical chain. It was much simpler to manipulate the estimates myself. Experience on the project showed that people padded their estimates to avoid missing due dates. Then, they started the task so late that they had insufficient time to complete it. Because the project was overseas, allowing me to control the external effects, it was possible to dedicate the team to the project. This worked quite well, and people finished their tasks on time.

One day a developer, who was very theoretical and enjoyed implementing new ideas, looked at the schedule and noticed the tasks times he had supplied were considerably shortened. He asked what had happened. I sheepishly admitted what I had done, but also explained critical chain theory and showed the developer that he had rarely been late and never reprimanded. The conversation was very positive, and he thanked me for the education.

A few weeks later, I needed some estimates from him for a change request. I compared them to similar tasks on the schedule, and the estimates were extremely high. I asked the developer what was going on. He grinned and replied, "Since I know you would cut them in half I doubled them." After a long conversation, the developer provided reasonable values that I could use without manipulation.

After compiling the schedule, a resource leveled critical path is determined. This is the critical chain. This path drives the project. The tasks constituting the critical chain are analyzed to determine what other paths feed them. Each feeding path has a buffer of time added to the end where it merges with the critical chain and its tasks are scheduled using an as-late-as-possible (ALAP) constraint. This creates a just-in-time (JIT) schedule—with a little buffer. The buffer cushions the critical chain from the effects of unknown issues arising in the feeding path. Figure 12-2 illustrates how buffers work. The two dummy tasks in black are the buffers.

In this illustration, the integrally numbered tasks denote the critical chain; feeding tasks are lettered. A feeding buffer is placed between the feeding tasks and critical chain "Task 4." This minimizes any impact of feeding path variation on the critical chain. After the last task, a project buffer cushions the project's completion date from accumulated late delivery on any of the critical path items. Buffers are

Figure 12-2: Critical Chain Buffers

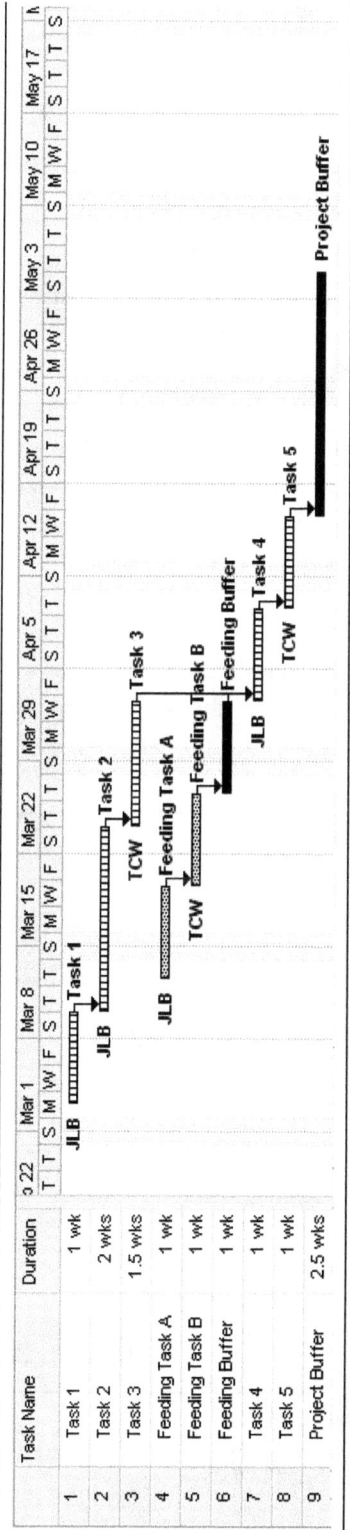

	Task Name	Duration
1	Task 1	1 wk
2	Task 2	2 wks
3	Task 3	1.5 wks
4	Feeding Task A	1 wk
5	Feeding Task B	1 wk
6	Feeding Buffer	1 wk
7	Task 4	1 wk
8	Task 5	1 wk
9	Project Buffer	2.5 wks

initially estimated at 40 to 50 percent of the duration preceding them. The result is a 20 to 30 percent reduction in total project duration.

Optimizing Resource Utilization

Last, and most difficult, the resources are dedicated to their tasks; this is in common with agile. This maintains the resources' focus, optimizing their use of time, and reducing frustration. This usually meets with the most resistance from management since other projects, using different methodologies, will not realize any of the benefits. Team members love it since they know they will work more efficiently and with less frustration.

Most organizations value multitasking and feel it improves efficiency. Critical chain and agile advocates staunchly disagree with this. They contend the start, stop, start, stop mentality wastes time and makes all tasks late. Figure 12-3 is the classic diagram to show this. This diagram shows three separate tasks, each two weeks long, being done by the same person and having the same start date. In the upper case, the person multitasks. Task A is completed two weeks late, Task B is five weeks late, and Task C is six weeks late. Multitasking will make the three projects an average of three weeks late. In the lower case, the person is dedicated to

Figure 12-3: Effects of Multitasking

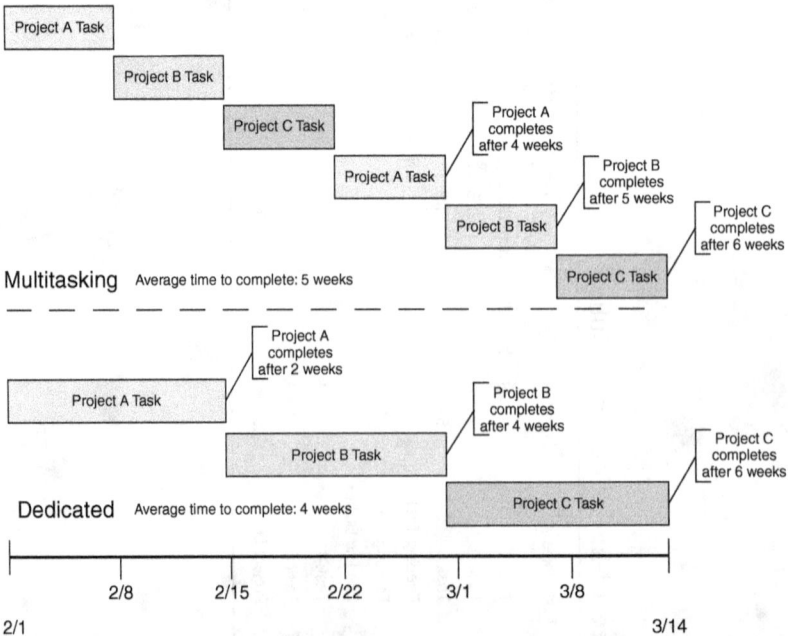

the tasks and works uninterrupted. Task A is done on time, Task B is done two weeks late, and Task C is done four weeks late (completing at the same time it would have in the multitasking scenario). Two tasks are late and the average for all three is two weeks late, while the average in the multitasking scenario is three weeks late. This simple diagram shows how multitasking is a poor concept.

To ensure that bottleneck resources on the critical chain are always busy and stay focused, use resource buffers. This is analogous to keeping work in front of a bottleneck workstation; the workstation should always have some backlog so it never goes idle. If bottlenecked resources are working on tasks other than a critical chain task, it is the same as the entire project being idle. Resource buffers help ensure constrained resources are always busy, and there is a regulated amount of pressure to ensure they stay focused.

To utilize constrained resources properly, they must be kept on task, minimizing multitasking, and ready for the next critical chain assignment, even if this means they wait idly.

Once reasonable estimates are provided and resource dedication guaranteed, the schedule is resource leveled. No resource can be booked more than 100 percent. Figure 12-4 shows the same schedule as given in Figure 12-2, but this time after resource leveling. Note "Feeding Task B" is now inserted between classical critical path tasks "Task 3" and "Task 4." This is because of the resource constraint on the resources JLB and TCW. JLB is responsible for task "Task 2" and "Feeding Task A," while TCW is responsible for task "Task 3" and "Feeding Task B." This adds about a week and a half to the schedule.

Because critical chain allows individual project tasks to be late, track project deviation by monitoring buffer reductions throughout the project. Consuming a buffer too quickly indicates it is time to take corrective action.

Because of the fact that the schedule looks longer, most project managers avoid the resource leveling function. Without this, however, the project schedule is unrealistic.

Unfortunately, many scheduling products do not have functions to identify the resource loaded critical path (the critical chain). To complicate matters, some very popular project scheduling tools create incorrect resource-level schedules.

Using Critical Chain for All Projects Sharing the Same Resources

For the maximum benefit, all projects sharing resources should use critical chain methodology. This is because almost all projects use common resources. To accommodate parallel projects and stay inside TOC precepts, projects need to be staggered to minimize resource contention. This requires developing a prioritization scheme to indicate the correct sequence of work. A centralized group, such as the PMO, should

Figure 12-4: Resource Leveled Critical Chain

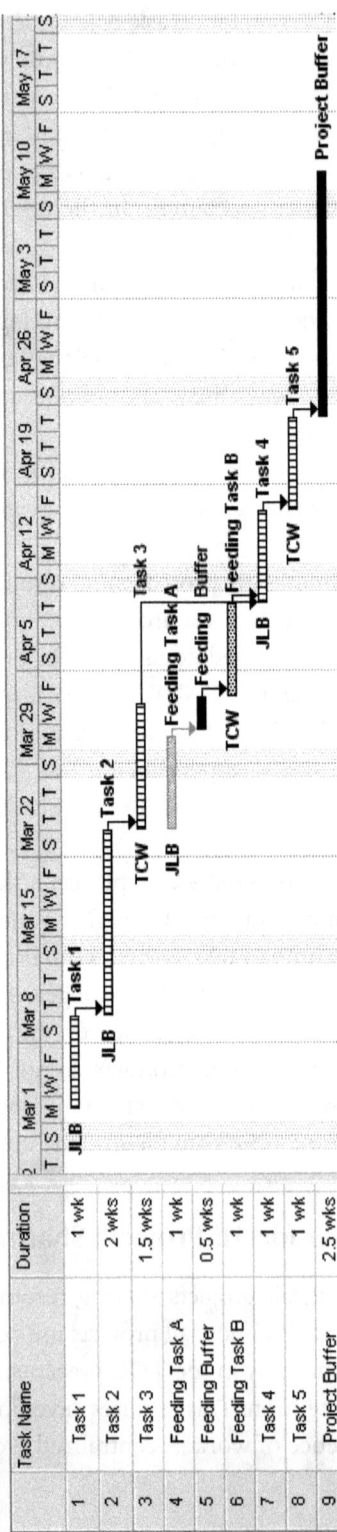

	Task Name	Duration
1	Task 1	1 wk
2	Task 2	2 wks
3	Task 3	1.5 wks
4	Feeding Task A	1 wk
5	Feeding Buffer	0.5 wks
6	Feeding Task B	1 wk
7	Task 4	1 wk
8	Task 5	1 wk
9	Project Buffer	2.5 wks

implement and maintain this. As said before, once the scheme has been implemented, resources need to be focused (prohibiting multitasking) on completing the task on or before the due date.

CASE STUDY 12-2 : STAGGERING PROJECTS TO REDUCE RESOURCE CONTENTION

Near the end of every year, one client received the following year's budget and started all its projects shortly after the first of the year. As might be predicted, the analysts were overbooked for the first few months of the year, the quality assurance group in the last half of the year, and the implementation team at year's end. I suggested that project starts be staggered to one every month and, after a year, the resources would be more naturally leveled. The biggest complaint, admittedly a major one, was that budgets would need new financial procedures to allow them to run across fiscal years. It took a year to implement, but as of this writing, resource constraint was significantly lower.

Chapter Takeaway

- Critical chain methodology is based on a reasonable estimation of the task effort and the proper resource loading.
- Time estimates are generated base on a 50:50 chance of completion.
- The critical chain is the resource leveled critical path.
- Critical chain methodology advocates eliminating multitasking and dedicating resources to one task through completion.
- Use buffers to cushion the critical chain and the project's completion date from special cause variation.
- Critical chain methodology reduces the project length by an average of 20 to 30 percent.
- Critical chain projects are more transparent because the schedule buffers are visible.
- Staggering project starts help reduce the contention.
- Critical chain is best applied:
  - Organization wide.
  - To shorten delivery cycle on longer projects.
  - When scope is well defined.

13

Comparing the Relative Value of Methodologies for Project Recovery

"Faced with the choice between changing one's mind and proving that there is no need to do so, almost everyone gets busy on the proof."

—John Kenneth Galbraith, American Economist, *Economics, Peace and Laughter*

This chapter compares the three discussed methodologies—classical, agile, and critical chain. This comparison proves valuable when determining how changes in the methodology will assist a project recovery. Mixing and matching these methodologies as a practice is unusual, but it makes sense in the context of fixing a project. Some combinations would be impossible—mixing critical chain into an agile project does not make sense, but the converse does. Removing some of the project's scope to run in an agile manner may be the best way to handle a problem with a new technology or a poorly defined scope. In general, because agile and critical chain have defined, rigorous processes, the classical form of project management can benefit by implementing the techniques of these methodologies.

In the project management community, there is significant debate about project management methodologies. These debates often have a religious fervor, as proponents of each methodology cite attributes of other methodologies they feel contribute to project failure. Each of the methodologies works, but only if implemented properly. Agile scales poorly; it would be bad methodology for designing and building the next commercial jetliner. However, there are subcomponents (both hardware and software) that would benefit greatly from the use of agile. Conversely, attempting to develop a new product that includes to-be conceived hardware and accompanying software and trying to get 50:50 estimates for task completions when the activity list is undefined make critical chain inappropriate. Misconceptions, improper implementations, and corporate abuse will cause any of these methodologies to fail.

This chapter discusses differences among the methodologies and how each can help a project, as well as noting situations in which they should be avoided. It is a neutral, high-level introspective of all three methodologies comparing ten attributes (presented alphabetically): change management; customer relationship; estimations; process; project constraints; project manager; subcontractor relations; team focus; team members; and variation. The goal is to provide enough information to determine how all or specific parts of these tools can help achieve project success.

Change Management

Scope creep is a frequent symptom of project failure. Scope balloons and projects end up over budget, late, or both. On the other hand, the user's requirements may legitimately change, and strict scope control will prevent these changes from being incorporated into the product. The result will be a deliverable with little or no value. The latter is far from scope creep; this is improper scope management. Scope changes on projects and a change management process needs to be in place and rigorously followed. Project managers need to manage change and customers need to agree to, understand, and adhere to the process.

Classical: Simply put, too many project managers fail to implement an appropriate change management process. They either allow indiscriminate change or prohibit it altogether. This drives a project toward failure. The result will be a late delivery or a product with no value. Blaming the methodology for the failure is incorrect; the improper implementation of the change management process is the real issue.

Agile: In agile, the delivery team commits to complete a set of features (as opposed to tasks) in a predefined number of hours. If something has to change, it can, but it cannot alter an iteration's theme, duration, or financial obligation. At the start of the project, the team defines the number of iterations and, in general, the members adhere to that estimate. Opponents criticize agile for allowing anything to change at any time, but this claim is far from the truth. If the customer wants to add something taking, say, 30 hours, then the customer must remove features taking the same amount of time, thereby maintaining the iteration's integrity. The engineering team and customer representatives, rather than the project manager, are responsible for controlling scope. Both need to agree on including a feature regardless of whether its source is a customer or engineer. They know what work is required, and they are responsible for delivering the iteration. If they miss the delivery, both the team and the customer representative are held accountable.

The trading process dynamically reprioritizes the features. This is a process of self-motivated negotiation addressing issues in the project. It is similar to what is discussed in the negotiation chapters (see Part IV), but it is inserted in the project prior to a failure occurring.

Agile's premise to build for future enhancements only when they are understood and defined further controls internal scope creep. It specifically frowns on engineers building in extensibility.

CCPM: Critical chain methodology preaches rigorous change management process. This is not enforced by any special features in the methodology. It addresses change through change requests and reflects their impact in the plan.

Customer Relationship

In general, customers have devolved into the project's nemesis instead of what they should be—a partner. Some conditions are:

- Fear that talking to the customer openly will expose areas where the solution is not fully understood and thereby embarrass the project team.
- Concern that the customer will try to sneak in scope. Thus, the customer is isolated from the project team.
- Assuming the project team knows more about the customer's needs than the customer.
- Limiting the team's exposure to the customer because the customer tries to make the project team responsible for the customer's scope.

Classical: Nothing in classical project management methodology causes customer relationship problems. The situations mentioned in the prior list are a result of inappropriate procedures to solve poor management technique. The project manager's inability to manage change, delineate responsibility, close open issues, and make decisions have conditioned customers to develop their own processes to drive the project.

The project manager should bring the customer closer into the project, helping to manage changes and define responsibilities. Honest discussion with the customer will resolve issues earlier in the project.

Agile: Agile goes to the greatest lengths to solve this problem by colocating the customer and the development team. Where practical, this is an excellent way to manage the problem, but this may be difficult with dispersed teams or large projects.

During an iteration, the customer validates the features being developed and can make value-added changes. This reduces confusion in translating requirements. And, when the customer and the team agree on the changes, the impact is minimized. Finally, when issues are uncovered on the project, the customer is part of the team proposing the resolution.

CCPM: Critical chain advocates approaching the problem from a different angle. Colocating teams may be a solution, but first focus them on the problem's root cause. For instance, an analysis of team communications using an evaporating cloud (see Figure 13-1) might lead to the erroneous conclusion that the team will allow the scope to change when directly talking to the customer. To minimize scope changes, an architect may be put in the middle to translate project requirements into a document that the team then interprets. This, however, can result in errors from multiple interpretations, leading to an incorrect implementation of a feature. In this case, the critical chain team looks for the incorrect assumption and works to resolve it. The solution may be educating the team on scope creep and methods to remove it.

Estimations

In general, people hate estimating. Estimates are always wrong. However, the estimates are usually correct; treating them like quotes is wrong. Management will inevitably say, "I thought you told me it would be done in twelve days. Where is it?"

Figure 13-1: Evaporating Cloud for Conflict Identification

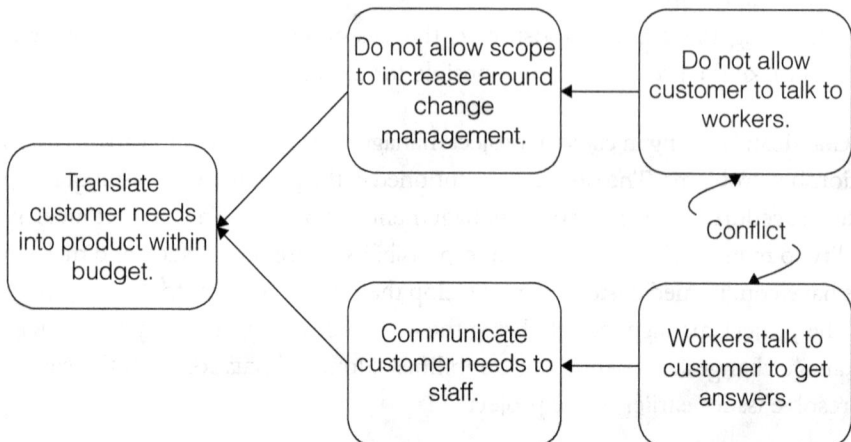

To reduce the pain, an entire culture has evolved. First, people determine an estimate they are almost certain to hit (say, an 80 percent chance). They avoid methods that use optimistic, most likely, and pessimistic estimates, since management will hold them to the optimistic numbers. If people finish early, they fear it will prompt management to trim estimates based on "current empirical data."

Essentially, once estimates are given, they are treated like quotes, and people are reprimanded anytime they are late or early on a task or over- or under budget. Management's actions mold people's behavior—in this case, it encourages people to pad their estimates.

The situation is exacerbated when management asks people to take on other responsibilities concomitantly with their project tasks. These new tasks include staff meetings; training unrelated with the project; reassignment to other tasks, and so forth. All of these actions prompt people to add significant pad to their estimates. Both agile and critical chain are empathic about addressing this issue.

Classical: Classical methods of managing projects have degenerated into the above game because managers and stakeholders fail to understand estimates, and they treat the project as if it were a deterministic system. The project manager must address this with the stakeholders and retrain them and the team.

Agile: Iterations are relatively short (30 to 60 days). The agile team provides estimates on features, rather than tasks. Therefore, at the beginning of each iteration, the team commits to provide certain functionality. Because of the short planning horizons, the accuracy of these estimates is better than in the other methods. Because the iteration's product must contain customer-ready functionality (potentially shippable), the team is required to stay focused on the deliverables and work only on the chosen tasks.

The key is accountability. The team commits to all the work to build, document, and test functionality. As opposed to creating the work plan or estimates, the project manager's responsibility is to ensure the team has the tools to do these tasks.

The project manager's responsibility in estimating is more difficult because it requires reeducating management. The team may fail to deliver on everything planned for the iteration, but this is not an issue. Reprimand is reserved for when the team violates the rules of agile as opposed to when it misses a delivery. Managers need to understand this.

CCPM: Critical chain follows the same philosophy as agile on the treatment of estimates. Tolerance of time and cost estimates means only reprimanding team members when they fail to follow the rules. The rules in critical chain, though, are different. The focus for estimates, as in classical project management, is tasks.

Estimates for costs and durations are 50:50 estimates. This means there is a 50 percent chance of completing the task within the estimated time or budget. If all tasks are estimated the same, some will take more and others will take less time or money, but on average, they will remain on the baseline.

As with the theory of constraints, the bottleneck (the resource leveled critical path, also known as the critical chain) cannot be left waiting for work. Therefore, before any branch's merge with the critical chain, a buffer of time (a feeding buffer) is inserted. This prevents statistically late branches from affecting the critical chain.

The primary rule is dedicating team members to their work. Multitasking, or working on other tasks, is strictly prohibited. Every attempt is made to focus people on the customer-valued tasks rather than on overbuilding the deliverable. Members are rewarded for early task completion. The project manager is the enabler for this behavior and must assist in prohibiting others from interrupting the team's work.

Process

The project manager or a company's project management office (PMO) generally determines the appropriate processes to run a specific project. There are few defined standard processes. This is the result, in part, of there being so many different types of projects. Organizations like PMI® have developed guidelines, but these standards focus on what to do rather than on how to do it. For a framework to apply to all projects, it must remain generic. Agile and critical chain define specific processes directed at the parts of projects that most often fail. Because of the defined process, these methodologies can only be applied to projects with the types of attributes that will benefit from the process.

Classical: Unless a project manager or an organization has a set of defined processes, most project managers only find listings of what processes they should prepare. In this case, the predefined processes are the value of seasoned project managers and consultants.

Agile: Agile is a lean methodology. Its processes are minimal, but thorough. As mentioned in the change management comparison, it has one of the most rigid change management processes. Along with being thorough, the process is also extremely efficient—and, therefore, lean. Essentially, it allows scope to include new items only after removing some number of items of equal effort and cost. Other processes and rules are also rigidly enforced, including:

- Time-boxed iterations and meetings.
- No feature additions within an iteration.
- Process adaptation to fit the application.
- Strong customer interaction.
- No multitasking.

CCPM: Critical chain follows the general outline provided by PMI®, but applies defined processes to critical areas. It further differs from PMI® in its approach to handling the human and managerial element of projects and in its categorization of common and special cause risk. This is an extremely important aspect to developing the methodology and taking corrective action. Common cause variation is normal uncontrollable variation in a process. The area where this is most evident is estimating. All estimates are established at a 50 percent probability of success. This means half of the tasks will exceed the estimate, while the others will stay within the estimate.

Processes should be in place to control special cause variation, such as pulling a resource onto another project.

Critical chain prominently enforces the following processes:

- Basing estimates on a 50:50 chance of success.
- Resource leveling all project schedules.
- Establishing feeding and project buffers at a length of 40 to 50 percent of the length of the feeding chain or the project length.
- Scheduling all feeding chain tasks as late as possible.

Project Constraints

Projects are governed by three constraints—scope, schedule, and resources. A single constraint cannot change without affecting at least one of the others. Scope cannot increase without increasing schedule or resources; schedule cannot decrease without reducing scope or increasing resources, and so forth. Most customers want more features for the same price and timeline. This, however, is simply impossible.

CASE STUDY 13-1: CONFLICTS BETWEEN GROUPS IN DEFINING THE TRIPLE CONSTRAINTS

I was creating the charter for an in-house project. When I asked the project sponsor to define the triple constraints, she replied: (1) scope, (2) budget, and (3) schedule. After she approved the charter, it was sent to executive management, whose members rejected it and said the project sponsor's boss had dictated the constraint priorities as (1) schedule, (2) budget, and (3) scope. The project team refused to accept the new triple constraints, insisting scope was the most critical. I had to ask a vice president in the development organization to redirect the team.

Classical: Nothing in the classical approach to project management inhibits enforcing project constraints. The primary reason for confusion is that the extended project team is unclear on the triple constraints for the project. When a project whose primary constraint is scope gets in trouble, the customer must understand it will cost more or take longer to complete. The change management process is the tool to control this. If the project has a poor change management process, then the project constraints are of no value.

Agile: Agile includes an additional constraint—stability. It also applies very specific rules to governing the constraints—hold the primary constraint constant, allow moderate change in the secondary constraint, and the remaining two constraints may float. After this is set, any changes in the time-boxed iteration must follow these rules. Changes in the feature list between iterations must use the same prioritization. The customer may request and prioritize new features with a full understanding that the other attributes will change. There is generally a fixed amount of time and money to implement all features; depleting either forces project completion.

Time is always constrained by the time box of an iteration. If there is a change requested to a feature during an iteration, it cannot affect the cycle's end date.

CCPM: Critical chain has very specific rules governing constraints. It is a declared step in project initiation—just like agile. The assumption with critical chain is anything worth doing is worth finishing quickly. Hence, schedule has subtle priority and is often the primary constraint. Any changes to the project must follow a strict change management process. In this light, this methodology is similar to classical project management methodology.

Project Manager

There are probably as many project management styles are there are projects and, unfortunately, the project manager title is liberally applied on too many résumés. PMI® has tried to address this through various certifications, the most popular being its Project Management Professional (PMP®) certification. Project management requires facilitating the formation of a team, motivating the members to complete their work, being the taskmaster, working with stakeholders to show progress, controlling risk, and looking for required changes in the deliverable. In addition, the project manager must be a leader, establishing a vision and ensuring functional managers meet the needs of the team. An association's accreditation cannot build these traits in people.

Classical: No rules say that a project manager must perform given tasks on a project. PMI's® PMBOK® (often cited as the antithesis of agile) enumerates processes the project manager must do, but fails to define those processes. Definition of these processes occurs in the project planning phase and is influenced by the organization or the project manager. If improperly implemented, those processes provide little value.

Agile: Project managers do not control scope, give daily assignments, or track daily progress; teams are responsible for these tasks. However, project managers remove roadblocks, report on project (rather than task or feature) status, and prevent reassignment or interruption of the team and customer representatives. They enforce the rules of agile methodology. The team reports features completed, changes between iterations, and hours needed to complete features and the project.

CCPM: Much like agile, critical chain looks to the project manager as a leader. The project manager should foster and protect the team, keep members on task, and prevent reassignment and interruptions. The project manager's key functions are coordinating with other projects, stopping multitasking of people, enforcing the rules of critical chain, and monitoring schedule and resource buffers.

Subcontractor Relations

Subcontractors introduce a significant amount of risk to a project. Unfortunately, most corporations place a purchasing department between the project team and the subcontractor. Even though the primary triple constraint on many projects is often something other than budget, the goal of purchasing is to get the best price based on a set of invariant specifications. As a result, the relationship problems between the project team and customer are replicated between the project team and subcontractor. The requirement is for a skilled responsible subcontractor that can deliver on time and according to specification.

Classical: Unfortunately, there are few defined processes for improving the subcontractor relationship. Good subcontractor management starts with developing open and honest communication.

Agile: Agile has the most stringent processes for the subcontractor. As with the customer, agile processes recognize that subcontractors are integral in creating the product and are colocated with the team. The intent is for the subcontractor to use the same methodology as the project.

The project manager and the team pick the subcontractor who will meet the same criteria as the team—self-organized, self-managed, open minded, and team oriented.

CCPM: Critical chain advocates incentives to make on-time deliveries and penalties for making late deliveries. This is simply a Just in Time (JIT) implementation. Aside from monetary leverage, critical chain relies on good communication with the subcontractor to achieve on time delivery. The intent is for the subcontractor to use the same methodology as the project team.

Team Focus

Team disruption reduces overall effectiveness. Meetings, interruptions from cohorts, and managers asking for special work draw team members off task. A general request from the team is the need for peace and quiet. Management's reaction, if any, is to provide cubicles or move the team to another area of the building. This often results in moving the staff farther away from the customer, yet management still has team members multitasking. The obvious problem with this approach is the team needs a minimum of interruptions while still interacting and communicating within the group and with the customer.

Often, in matrixed organizations, team members are located with other people within their discipline, instead of with the project team. There are two primary reasons for this. First, locating the disciplines together makes it easier on their functional manager, as they are all in one area. Second, it averts the cost of relocating people for each project. Unfortunately, the project suffers. This practice steps over dollars to pick up pennies.

Classical: The aforementioned scenario plagues classically managed projects—give the team a quiet place to work where the customer cannot introduce scope creep. This setup funnels design questions through the architect. Answers come slowly and in the form of thick documentation. This must change. Educating the team on proper communication with the customer, prohibiting management from meddling with the team, and promoting team member interaction (colocating the team close to the customer) builds stronger teams and reduces variation in the project.

Whenever possible, the project team should be colocated. All full-time resources on the project, both customer and supplier, need to be grouped together so they may easily talk to each other without using the phone. Slow, ineffective communication dwarfs the cost of relocation.

Agile: A primary goal of agile is to build a team in which the customer and supplier are fully integrated. Direct communication between the project team and the customer is a critical component. This requires team colocation, which improves efficiency, reduces interruptions, and removes unwanted distractions by management.

The project manager has the responsibility for stopping outside interference, which is defined as outside the project as a whole, not just outside the development team.

The iteration concept further focuses the team. With tight development time boxes and cleanly defined scope, the team has no room to lose focus. The customer's involvement in the iteration helps maintain concentration on the valuable features.

CCPM: One tenet of critical chain is to stop team member multitasking. The goal is to assign people to a task, let them finish it, and move to the next. Refocusing after interruptions is a huge waste of time. Removing multitasking requires thorough planning and results in a shorter start-to-finish time for all projects—some projects start later, but they finish in less time, maintaining their due dates.

Another point, much like with agile, is that task durations are devoid of any padding, keeping the pressure on people to complete their tasks. Reinforcing this is the incentive to complete early or on time. The project's atmosphere is to remain focused.

CASE STUDY 13-2: THE ADVANTAGE OF MOVING PEOPLE TO REMOTE PROJECT SITES

Running projects remotely adds a significant number of challenges. Communication, time zones, languages, and cultural issues are only a few of the trials. When a project goes red, one of the first acts is to get people together in a room talking. This action helps identify and resolve problems.

On multiple projects, where the delivery was overseas and the development team remote from the project, I have identified the critical people on the team and pulled them together at the customer site. This was a small cost in the greater scheme of getting the project back on track and completing the deliverable. Reevaluating the decisions and costs about the team's location showed that it was less expensive to incur travel and hotel expenses than to work with an uncoordinated team.

Team Members

The primary problem with team member selection is that most project managers are either given a team or allowed to pick from a limited resource pool rather than being allowed to select individuals with the best skills. The edict in organizational policy is to use internal resources first. Instead of spending $120,000 on a resource who can do the task, $80,000 is spent on a resource who will make the project four months late and cost the company an additional $800,000. Nevertheless, the individual will show up in the accounting system as productive since he or she is working on a project.

Classical: Nothing in any book, standard, or practice approves working with substandard people on a task. It just happens.

Human nature will sway even the most objective project manager into breaking this rule. Everyone has been caught in the dilemma of trying to keep good resources employed even though they are unqualified to perform the necessary tasks. These are good workers with bills to pay; why should they suffer because this project cannot currently use their skills. Being empathetic, one wants to find something for them to do on the project.

However, this is the organization's problem rather than a project manager's problem. It must develop methods to fund other work or training for good employees.

Turn bench time into productive time by using it to train the good employee on new tools, billing the time to all projects or maintaining it as a cost of doing business.

Agile: The prime directive in team selection for agile projects is to get above-average, self-managed, and self-organized members. The rebuttal is, "Of course, if you acquire better than average team members you will get better than average results." The statement should be "That makes sense, let's do it." Every agile process wants better than average, self-organized, self-managed, open-minded, team-oriented people. Team members are trained in and must adhere to agile processes.

CCPM: The requirements for critical chain are the same as for agile, but retraining is more significant since it entails changing mindsets. People are learning an entirely new culture. For instance:

- Time estimates provide for a 50:50 chance of completion rather than trying to guarantee the task will finish in the estimated time.
- Multitasking is strictly forbidden.
- Completing tasks early is more important than saving pad for the next project; never reprimand for finishing late.
- Finishing over the estimated time for a task is acceptable since there was only a 50:50 chance of achieving it.

Variation

Uncertainty is the inability to predict what is going to happen. Variation is the uncontrollable change experienced in a system. One knows there will be variation, but one is uncertain what the value will be in a given instance. Every system has natural variation, and it is fruitless to try to control it. In fact, attempting to control natural variation is normally more expensive than the projected savings. Controlling influences from outside the system (special cause variation), though, will enhance system performance.

Classical: Governing models (i.e., PMI®) do not distinguish between internal and external causes of variation nor do they discuss system theory. Hence, classical project management is often improperly equipped to handle variation. For this reason, management usually reacts inappropriately when variations are experienced. Variations from external influences can continue for long periods without being attributed to problems on the project. Small shifts in task durations or cost can be less noticeable but add up over time. At the same time, normal variations (fluctuation around estimates) may solicit overreaction.

Agile: Agile projects handle variation by continually using short time frames for project checkpoints. The common 30-day period between each planning cycle quickly highlights excessive variation and provides input for modifying plans to adjust for uncertainty. Excess variation is very visible and thus needs less explanation than in classic project management methodology.

CCPM: Critical chain methodology is built around system theory and the concept of internally and externally influenced variation. This is at the center of the estimation process. Normal variation for a system will cancel itself out since the deviation around the mean is equal in the positive and negative directions. External (special cause) variation will result in drift in one direction. The methodology relies on understanding the project as a system.

Chapter Takeaway

- The PMO needs a portfolio of processes to best accommodate a portfolio of projects.
- Critical chain and agile define processes beneficial for specifically targeted areas where projects fail. These include change management, resource allocation, task estimation, handling variation, customer relationship, and scope control.
- Classical project management methodologies state what processes should be in place, but leave them undefined.
- Use classical project management in low-risk projects where there is a history of doing a general type of project. History with projects provides a reduction in risk and less variation in the tasks. In other words, there is more predictability.
- Agile works best on smaller projects in the realm of new product development. These projects are more chaotic because they cover new areas and often use new and untested technologies. In new product development, requirements are less certain and iterative cycles accommodate change naturally. Agile loses a number of advantages when projects become larger and require coordination among numerous groups.
- Critical chain methodology benefits resource-constrained projects where scope is well defined. In addition, the estimation philosophy, although difficult for some team members and management to comprehend, is very effective in timeline reduction. Critical chain buffers provide transparency and a method for tracking schedule deviation. Learning critical chain has a longer lead-time since estimation processes and interaction with other projects is more complex.
- Agile and critical chain requires top-down organizational deployment.

IV

Negotiating a Solution

Proposing Workable Resolutions

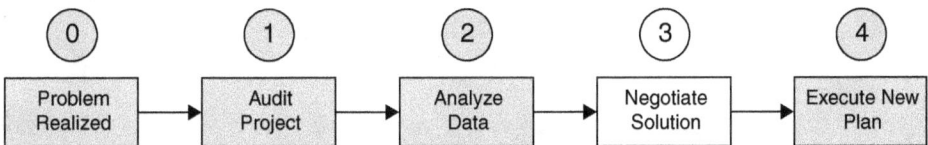

0	1	2	3	4
Problem Realized	Audit Project	Analyze Data	Negotiate Solution	Execute New Plan

The audit is complete and the data analyzed. The stakeholders' opinions and desires are known. The plan's components are ready to assemble. This section will cover packaging those plans with their options, presenting them to the stakeholders, bartering out the details, and getting their approval.

Now, more than ever, it is evident that the recovery manager is the mediator who proposes workable solutions to the supplier and the customer. The recovery manager should present plans that are reasonable and workable and provide equivalent value to all parties. The recovery manager's only stake in this negotiation is reaching a compromise amenable to all the stakeholders. Success is mediating a win-win solution. It is achieved by understanding what is valuable in the project and the consequences of failure to all of the stakeholders.

The recovery plans will include:

- The actions already taken.
- An enumeration of the deviations from the contract.
- Changes to the scope, schedule, and budget.
- Recommended resource reallocation.
- Financial considerations.
- Corrective actions to root causes.
- A formal project plan.
- High-level schedule.

14

Proposing and Getting Agreement on a Recovery Plan

"The most difficult thing in any negotiation, almost, is making sure that you strip it of the emotion and deal with the facts. And there was a considerable challenge to that here and understandably so."

—Howard Baker, U.S. Politician and Negotiator

At the core of a project recovery is change. The project is red and the schedule, budget, and scope are out of control. Without change, the project will continue to fail. Because stakeholders need to approve changes to the project, the third step in the recovery process is the negotiation to get the solution approved. Upon approval, a project manager implements the corrective action and executes the new plan.

Stakeholders will only approve the recovery plan if it provides value. Both the customer and the supplier must see reasonable value from the project. The recovery manager must understand the value targets and incorporate them in the new project. This requires selling the plan to the stakeholders; selling requires negotiation.

Few people question negotiation is an art. The way people support their viewpoint, handle their demeanor, show confidence in their beliefs, and deal with rebuttals can make or break a successful negotiation. However, it contains a lot of science. To increase the chance of attaining the desired outcome, there is a progression of steps to follow. A process ensures that valuable information will be gathered to assist in the negotiation.

The Process of Negotiation

Numerous books and Web articles detail the steps in a negotiation process. Recommended Reading lists two of great value—*Getting to Yes, Negotiating Agreement Without Giving in* and *Strategic Negotiation: A Breakthrough Four-Step Process for Effective Business Negotiation*. Most of these processes are a variation on a common set of steps—the same four used in this recovery process. When applied to a recovery, the tasks in each step support the negotiation of the solution. Let us review the steps.

1. Audit (Negotiation's Planning) – Define the problem and identify the contributing factors—drive to the root cause. Continue the investigation beyond the first problem identified. Look for all the problems, as one problem never kills a project.

2. Analysis (Negotiation's Explore) – Investigate the options available to fix the root causes and make sure that no supplemental issues are contributing to the problem. Rank the project requirements to determine which can be removed with the least effect on the stakeholder's value.

3. Negotiate (Negotiation's Propose/Barter) – Present the options and their associated rationale. Allot time to listen and reiterate the proposal. Listen to the concerns and propose alternatives. Many processes break this into two steps—propose and barter—but when proposing solutions the recovery manager must dynamically alter the plan to achieve an agreeable solution.

4. Execute (Negotiation's Close) – After reaching agreement, document the solution, implement the corrective actions, and affect the changes on the project. This is essentially a new project. Monitor the success and make adjustments as needed.

CASE STUDY 14-1:
LENGTH OF NEGOTIATION MEETINGS

Negotiation meetings take many forms and can range from a couple of hours to a few weeks. The factors controlling this are different for every project. One set of meetings became very contentious. The proposal was to:

- Return the project to the original scope. This removed a significant amount of scope that was added and unaccounted for because of a previous project manager's lack of change management process.
- Include a couple of scope items the supplier had neglected to develop.
- Phase the project.

The negotiation meetings were scheduled offsite for four consecutive days. In preparation for these meetings, I had six consecutive days of onsite group meetings with twelve different customer representatives. These people were responsible for the twelve major system components. Each meeting published minutes, and the final meeting had cumulative minutes totaling six pages. No one contested the minutes.

The offsite meetings had only two customer representatives—the customer's project manager and the production manager. The project manager had been in the six-day preparation meetings, while the production manager had not. The entire meeting's tone was different, and it appeared the project manager had forgotten the previous agreements. The meeting devolved into a shouting match between an executive manager and the production manager. On the third day, the customer walked out of the meeting.

On the fourth day, the customer returned. The meeting started with a conference call to the production manager's boss, who directed the customer to come to an agreement. Although significant time was lost, we achieved an agreement on a majority of the points. The solution to the stalemate was to have executive management escalate the issue in the customer's senior management to reset the production manager's attitude.

Project Items That Are Not Part of the Negotiation

Although both parties must face the issue of returning to the original contract scope and duties, scope creep usually makes the impact greater on the customer. Because removal of scope creep affects the customer negatively and the supplier positively, the negotiation process may frustrate the customer by seeming to be one sided. The output from the requirements traceability matrix is the key to presenting this information factually. Having a thorough comprehension of the contract, SOW, and all change orders is critical. People will try to negotiate on this, but it is the immutable baseline. Move the negotiation of these items to when options are compiled and show the net change. The contract cannot be reopened.

At the same time, the supplier must be held accountable for improperly defining or engineering components. The supplier's failure does not allow for renegotiation of the price.

The Goal of Any Negotiation

Negotiation conjures up the ideas of winners and losers, some party getting the upper hand and receiving more than the other. This view is fed by the perceived bias of returning to the baseline. This interpretation of negotiation is very shortsighted and, in this type of work, it will fail. Neither party can feel as if it has conceded an unequal share. This is a long-term relationship and must remain amenable. The plan must be the best solution, under the circumstances—one in which both customer and supplier feel the project is successful and that it will be completed as soon as possible, delivering the greatest scope at the minimal cost and maximum value. The negotiation must get the best for the common good.

To get to this point, the recovery manager needs to understand three things:

- The relative importance of the project's components for each party.
- The significance of removing a component—the consequence of failure.
- The component's features ranking—the wish list.

Failing to Deliver Functionality: The Consequence of Failure

Both the supplier and the customer suffer consequences from failure. For the supplier, it can include lost revenue, diminished reputation, demoralized teams, and layoffs. Organizations supplying a service within a company may suffer reprimands and budget cuts. Outside suppliers will see loss of margin and possible legal action.

For the customer, the consequences of failure are more complex. The project will inevitably be a compromise of components and features, with reduced market share, usability issues, missing error rate targets, and a multitude of other ramifications, each rooted in specific functions in the product.

Create a matrix of these consequences to assess their effects. Use this to determine which features can be removed easily while still providing value. These two lists, one for the supplier and one for the customer, create the baseline for the plan and negotiation. They are a guide that shows what can be negotiated, while ensuring an equal burden is borne by both parties.

Many people want to focus only on the resulting system's positive features. Although it is critical to show what each side gets out of the compromise, this is of secondary concern. Focus everyone's attention on understanding which items are removed and the impact on the final product and revenue. This actually brings clarity to the project. By discussing only what the project includes, the stakeholders will continue to ask "but does it include. . . ?" The compromises need to be clear. The project sponsor and executive management know what value was supposed to be delivered; this will tell them what it will bring and what is left out.

CASE STUDY 14-2:
WHEN CANCELLATION IS NOT AN OPTION

In trying to resolve the issues with a project that had already spent seven of its eight million dollar budget, it was evident the supplier was going to lose between two and four million dollars. In a one-on-one meeting with an executive manager, I laid the data on the table showing how bad the financials were. My recommendation was to cut the losses and immediately cancel the project. The executive disagreed, since walking away from the business would have a negative impact on his company's reputation. He gave me a new assignment to generate a plan that would minimize the loss and deliver the system as defined in the contract.

Offsetting Removed Functionality: The Wish List

The wish list, as the name implies, is a list of what each party would like to have. Most likely, these are features, but it can also include financial compensation, indemnification, or other nonproduct related items. Many of these items may have been removed when the project was returned to its contractual baseline.

Modifying the plan requires bartering. When the customer asks for additional items, it will have to pay for them or remove something of equal cost. Knowing the wish list items gives the recovery manager the ability to add value to the recovery plan and still meet the recovery's overall goal.

Table 14-1 shows general wish list categories by stakeholder group. In general, this matrix is ranked by importance. The people who are more important to please are near the top. This rule is malleable; it depends on the project. Nevertheless, since the people near the top hold the financial strings, they normally need to be the most satisfied. However, the project will continue to have trouble if the technical team is relegated to putting the system together using outdated or inappropriate tools that force them to work late into the night or on weekends.

Unmotivated resources will find other more rewarding opportunities and leave the project. Therefore, do not ignore the people at the bottom of this list.

The Goal of the Negotiation

The general goals of most recoveries are:

- Complete the project as soon as possible.
- Deliver the greatest scope at the least cost.
- Provide value to both the supplier and the customer.
- Meet the recovery guidelines.

If the recovery guidelines are too restrictive to provide enough value, then canceling the project may be the only choice. On the other hand, the recovery options may include delivering the original project's entire scope since the bounds set were loose enough to allow it.

Whatever the decision, everyone must win. The recovery manager has the responsibility to propose solutions meeting the needs of each party as closely as possible. Since there will be compromises, they should be explicitly listed in a pro-and-con format.

Table 14-1: General Wish List Points

Project Participant	Desire
Project sponsor	Earliest delivery
	Lowest cost
	Meets requirements
	High quality
Executive management	No cost or schedule overrun
	No surprises
	Happy customer
End users	Maximum features
	Easy to use
	Good performance
Maintenance team	Few, if any, defects
	Easy to maintain architecture
	Thorough documentation
Project team	Mentally challenging
	Something to learn (new technology, technique, or business)
	Reasonable work schedule

Compiling a Complete Negotiation Package

Recovery managers are a tool for gathering information and compiling it into an acceptable proposal for the two primary parties in the negotiation—executive management and the project sponsors. Recovery managers are mediators, proposing plans that will eventually be joint agreements between the supplier and customer. If they were arbitrators, they would have the authority to enforce agreements. This distinction is important. The project sponsors and executive management, rather than the recovery managers, will own the plan. Therefore, the plan is correct if it is fair and provides equitable value to all parties. During negotiation, changes should improve the plan rather than expose its flaws. Recovery managers should therefore present evenly valued, workable plans throughout the negotiation. The optimal situation is, after analysis of the options, a plan that is agreeable to both parties.

For the meeting, consolidate the information in a manner that supports the proposed options. Previous conversations should have educated key stakeholders on the recovery's approach. Therefore, the meeting should be a review rather than a proposal. Following are summaries on what to cover in the recovery plans.

Returning the Project to the Contractual Baseline

The contractually agreed upon scope is the sum of the contract's and SOW's scope and the approved change orders. If change requests are unapproved or verbal, exclude them. The only fair and equitable solution is to return the project to its contractual baseline. This is the process' most emotional part because the customer feels it is losing something, when, in fact, it was never paid for. Everyone is simply returning to the initial agreement.

A recovery manager's best defense in this portion of the negotiation is a thorough and in-depth knowledge of the contract, SOW, and change orders. Contentious issues (i.e., contractual clauses with unquantifiable terms) need a reasonable solution. Many of the items removed in this process are items for the wish list. They may be added back into the project with an accompanying offset for the other party.

Providing Three Options for the Recovery Plan

Prepare three options for the recovery. These options should be:

1. An optimal plan matching the recovery guidelines.
2. A plan well within the guidelines (i.e., lower cost, shorter timeline, etc.).
3. A plan in excess of the guidelines (i.e., more features, longer time, etc.).

These plans accommodate the decision makers' and the primary stakeholder's needs—the moderates, the minimalists, and the end-user, respectively. All plans must be equally low risk and achievable. Adding scope will require the budget to cover it and may require additional phases. Predefined plans make it easy to discuss options.

Start by presenting the plan that meets the guidelines. If the sentiment is that there is too much in the proposal, drop to the lesser option. Alternatively, if the consensus appears to be that there is insufficient value, then present the larger option.

CASE STUDY 14-3: AN EXAMPLE OF A SHORT NEGOTIATION

On a recovery for an in-house project, only the project's executive management was present at the negotiation meeting. The Chief Information Officer (CIO) took the recommendation to the business unit to present the final agreement. The meeting was a little more than an hour. Although the recovery plan was making substantial changes to the customer's approach and removed significant scope, the meeting's focus was to fix the failures in the Information Technology group. The CIO wanted internal accountability and assigned it to people in the room using words from my presentation. The proposal's acceptance was achieved two days later with no changes.

Using Wish List Items to Tune the Options

Wish list items fine tune the options. If, in principle, there is agreement on a specific option, but there is frustration about losing an item, then use wish list items to offset it. Make sure to understand each item's scope ahead of time. Explore substitution options prior to the meeting in order to make suggestions to offset changes. In pre-meetings, you can even drop hints of potential alternatives. Making the idea the stakeholder's is the best. Try to set the stage for the antagonist to say, "If we can't get the 50-character LCD panel to show errors, can we at least get a red light indicating an error condition?" The 50-character LCD panel was the feature having some consequence of failure, and the wish list item is the red light.

Highlighting Changes in the Team

The team is the project's most critical component. Without the right team, nothing happens. By the time the proposal meeting takes place, many corrective actions have affected the team. The most common is replacing the project manager. The stigma around the original project manager's role in the failure often makes it impossible for him or her to continue to work with the team and customer.

Usually, the recovery plan includes additional team changes. New people may be needed, and some people may need to leave. Reasons for team changes include:

- People moving to new responsibilities on or off the project.
- Changes in the timeline requiring different resources.
- Changes in scope and technology resulting in new skill requirements.

Concisely describe the changes, past and future, including their reasons without assigning blame. Many people are innocently moving on to other opportunities.

Make sure to enumerate all assumptions around resources, underscore the effect if resources cannot be secured for assigned tasks.

Identifying Further Process Change to the Project

By the time of the proposal meeting, numerous processes have probably been put into place. There may be more to implement. Enumerate the processes already implemented and the results of their implementation. List the reason other processes are required, including their benefit and the effort required to get them in place. Only implement justifiable processes. Regardless of the organization's policies, all processes must provide a benefit to the project. Document the reasons for excluding any organizational processes.

For example, a recovery manager closely involved with the team can remove the need for weekly status reports. Levying this on the team simply to placate another manager wastes time and frustrates the team. This unneeded work will detract from the project. The project manager should still supply status reports, but stakeholders should refrain from telling the project manager how to run the project.

Identifying Changes to the Project's Scope

There are usually two aspects of scope to cover—the reason scope was out of control and what is removed. If scope is, or is perceived to be, out of control, inform the stakeholders of the actual situation and the steps to rectify it. Doing this without levying blame may be difficult, but attempt to keep the discussion neutral. Because of prenegotiation meetings, most people should be aware of the conditions and will accept them as fact.

The big debate will center on removed scope. Leave this subject for a point in the presentation where there will be time to discuss it. If there is going to be contention, it is likely to be here. Depending on the degree of contention, the recovery manager may need to plan multiday negotiation meetings.

Build a table showing what is in and out of scope for the new project. If there is a specific contractual reason, state it. Include an indication of the impact to the plan if one of these item's status changes. This format provides a method for quickly trading items and maintaining the same workload in the plans. Make sure there is a reference to resources required for all scope items, since changing scope has a huge impact on resource planning.

CASE STUDY 14-4:
EXAMPLE OF A SCOPE CHANGE LOG

Representing scope issues requires a neutral presentation with as many facts as possible. Table 14-2, an extract from an actual matrix, shows the type of information required in a log. This shows whether the items were in or out of scope, the item's cost, and enough descriptive data to familiarize the reader with the issue. Refer to Case Study 4-7 (pg. 59), for a description of a pictographic version from a different recovery.

Table 14-2: Scope Change Log

CCR #	Scope Issue	Phase	Scope	On-going	Person Days	Amount Charged on	Actual Value of the CCR	What Motivated the Change Order Item
Audit 7	Authorization server	2	OOS = OUT OF SCOPE To be delivered in Phase 2, however 20 days of design analysis has been done to date.	Phase 2	10	$0	$16,280	An overall authorization service for the CIM system that provides authority to perform specific tasks. A requirement was noted in the SOW "Authorization and Certification." The supplier response called for the standard MES functionality for user access and privileges. This requirement appears in the requirements analysis and is out of scope, currently attempting to implement this deliverable.
Audit 8	Conceptual design	1a	IN Scope, expanded to scope expansion	Yes	45	$0	$74,250	This effort is within scope. But, it has been drastically expanded and complicated as a result of the addition of the out-of-scope items.
Audit 9	Inadequate office space	1a	IN Scope	No	10	$0	$16,500	Customer had a requirement to provide network access, office equipment, and office space to establish a work environment for the supplier at the customer site.

The Project's Timeline

Recovery guidelines often set a timeline for the recovery. To meet this constraint, scope must be removed or resources added. The timeline needs to be clearly stated, and the assumptions to meet that timeline discussed. Assumptions are often conveniently forgotten when they prove false, so make sure they are documented and understood by all participants.

The Project's Budget

Nearly everything in the project affects budget. Present the project's cost, but refrain from presenting the details. To lower project cost, someone will want to line item veto certain items. If absolutely required, save this for last. Before discussing the detail, first get the stakeholders to agree to the plan's concept. Be prepared, however, to itemize the effect of changes on the budget for each major area—resources, scope, technology, timeline. Common complaints include the need for specialized resources for implementing some part of the system, the need for a given technology, or the requirement to outsource some portion of the project. Have complete justification for these actions.

Methodologies to Be Used in the Recovered Project

Some of the processes needing implementation may be part of a different methodology than currently run in the organization. It is best to avoid mentioning the processes' source; this extraneous data obfuscates the value. For instance, if the plan is to implement an agile approach, simply say the process is iterative, leaving the name out of the conversation. In actuality, since you would only be implementing a small part of a methodology, this is a more accurate representation.

Reaching agreement to phase the project makes implementing agile easier, as the iterations will provide natural deployment points. Define the deliverables for each phase and, if they change, make sure the project sponsor is agreeable and submit a change request.

Trying to implement critical chain's resource utilization schemes will be difficult without prior education and buy in. Dedicating resources will only be agreed to in principle. When the first organizational crisis happens that requires the project's resources, people will forget their commitments. Get the agreement, and handle each request as it is encountered.

CASE STUDY 14-5: EXPLAINING SCOPE DELIVERY IN PHASED PROJECTS

When preparing for phasing the deployment, make sure there is a clear understanding of each phase's scope. Many components have scope delivered in multiple phases. Table

14-3, extracted from actual meeting minutes, shows an example of one presentation method. All stakeholders need to understand how this will affect the product's usage.

Table 14-3: Feature by Phase

Application	Function	Phase 1a	Phase 1b	Later
Business Object Reports	Reporting data extracted from production database (change of scope)	X		
Defective Material Report	Manual workaround			
Advanced Process Control	Miniadvanced process control (advanced process control corrections user interface)	X		
	Final advanced process control			X
Special Work Request	Display special work request number and hold code, set future hold in MES	X		
	Link to special work request to retrieve special work request instructions, sets hold automatically		X	

Preparing the Information for Presentation

The meeting's target audience is the decision makers. These are most likely the project sponsor, executive management, and the steering committee, or some combination. However, the meeting will have people who have been working on the recovery team throughout the process and some who have only heard about what has been happening. Therefore, the presentation has to address the varied needs of all the attendees.

The actions suggested to this point prepare the attendees for the meeting. The key to success for the recovery manager is knowledge—detailed, in-depth insight about each issue on the project. This is Lesson 4: "Objective data is your friend, providing the key out of any situation." The attendees will gain confidence in the recovery manager by knowing he or she has a complete understanding of the project and its complexities.

Plan to familiarize the audience with the contractual agreements. Enumerate what was supposed to happen. Highlight the contentious issues and their proposed solutions. Try to defer discussion of these issues until later in the meeting when presenting the options.

The recovery manager must tailor a story to show cause and effect of the failure and their relevance to the recovery steps. (Refer to Table 14-4 for a complete outline.) For instance, if the recovery suggests cutting scope, state the reason for the recommendation and the net result. Present all the data. Try to state the proposal in the format:

- People involved in the decision.
- The decision (i.e., what replaces what).
- The negative effect on the product and any mitigating factors.
- The positive effect in terms of cost, scope, and schedule.

Talk directly about the consequences of failure and the wish list. The negative items should show what is missing from the contractual agreement. Positive items should show the offset of the negative effects. For instance, "Claude's team determined that adding business rules to the client enrollment forms is of less value than other features. To mitigate its absence, a report will be generated of all exceptions in the backend systems to show analysts what needs to be addressed. This removes two weeks of definition, four weeks of coding, and six weeks of testing."

The recovery manager should have notes addressing each potential issue. This should be available on supplemental slides in the presentation deck or as a handout. Each item should have the major alternatives and objections addressed in the discussion.

Table 14-4: Presentation Format

Presentation Steps
Provide a brief project history with critical decisions made or actions resulting in a red project.
List key people involved in the audit and providing input to the solution.
Summarize the root causes discovered and the ancillary issues they manifested.
Estimate the actions taken to date and their effects.
Present cost of canceling project or doing nothing else.
Show baseline contractual obligations.
List the proposal elements in the format:
"It was determined by X, scope element B was less important than other features. To mitigate its absence, feature C is added, which only takes Q amount of work. The resulting impact is $Y and X weeks are removed from the project."
Show the pros and cons of this solution, including a table of the relative effects (+, -, or neutral) on the stakeholders in Table 14-1.
Summarize risk and mitigation plan for the proposed solution.
Acceptance of plan or action items to get acceptance.

Discuss how each stakeholder's win-points (see Table 14-1) are addressed. No solution is perfect, and there will be negative attributes needing open and honest discussion. It is common for stakeholders to agree to further compromises on a feature to show they are a team player. This is the joy of peer pressure.

After describing the solution's elements, list and fully describe the risk and the mitigation plans. Explain why this plan will catch risks and why this list is better than that of the failed project. It is doubtful this project would be in this situation if the original risk register were correct.

One risk must always be present in the risk register—missing a root cause. The audience needs to understand that most root causes have been identified. However, some may have been overlooked. If so, they must be addressed immediately. Without this disclaimer, the project manager may be unable to get the appropriate attention to affect the resolution.

Preparing the Attendees for the Meeting

Walking into the heart of the negotiation process without preparing the audience will likely lead to failure. As the plan and options start to take shape, the recovery manager needs to meet with decision makers and key stakeholders to ensure they are comfortable with the direction of the proposal (see in Chapter 8, Preparing to Negotiate with Management). Preliminary meetings familiarize the individuals with the plans and remove surprises.

So far, the stakeholders have been exposed to the recovery manager in four primary ways:

1. Interviews gleaning their impressions and suggestions.
2. Status reporting informing them what has gone right and wrong with the project.
3. Approvals on early actions to slow the bleeding.
4. Stakeholder process modifications.

These interactions have set people's view of the recovery manager and have supplied the recovery manager with some of the data needed to construct the recovery plan. Replay this data to stakeholders in a manner that enables them to see the recovery's big picture.

Just as the recovery manager had to persuade stakeholders to advocate for implementing the early fixes, he or she must now get them to accept changing the project's basic parameters and implementing corrective actions. These affect each stakeholder directly.

Prior to proposing the recovery plan, the recovery manager needs to lobby the stakeholders and convince them that the plan accommodates their best interests and provides value. It is critical to understand the prominent objections to the plans. To avert as many objections as possible, provide free and open access to the planning ideas. Address all objections by modifying the plan or having a solid rebuttal.

Decision makers may delegate meetings. The preference is to work directly with the decisions makers instead of their representatives. Ensure delegates have a complete understanding of the recovery plan and are properly representing it to their superiors. This representation must be objective and free from delegates' opinions. Just as in prior meetings, the recovery manager should meet with each decision maker and primary stakeholders in one-on-one private sessions to discuss the upcoming change. The goal is to explain the impact and obtain support. In summary, the task is to size up the stakeholders and have them agree that the plan is acceptable.

CASE STUDY 14-6: PROMOTING A SOLUTION'S ADVANTAGE

As mentioned in Case Study 5-1 (pg. 65), phasing a project has a number of good and bad points. A common objection is that multiple deployments inconvenience the users.

Marketing departments have a very negative view of disrupting the company's customers. Make sure the phasing minimizes this impact (possibly by affecting different classes of users).

On a project to upgrade a product that had not been maintained for many years, one of my selling points for the phased approach was that marketing could use the phasing to show a renewed commitment to the product, including a roadmap for the product's enhancements. This could be used to decrease the number of customers leaving to go to competitors with better products. The marketing group also underscored the gradual learning curve the customers would have, lowering their training costs. All of these points successfully sold the phasing.

Recovery managers must understand the stakeholders' expectations. They need to know how the stakeholders will receive the plan. The required information about the stakeholder is:

- Who will support or refute a plan.
- The grounds on which they will disagree.
- What will get them to agree.
- Who needs the most explanation.
- Who are the quiet nonsupporters.

This will give the recovery manager an accurate assessment of the amount of effort required to get acceptance for the proposed plan.

Selecting the Venue and Preparing the Agenda

The meeting's goal is to get the solution approved. Make sure decision makers are in the meeting. This means at least one person from executive management and the project sponsor. Determine whom else they may invite and try to control attendance. Too many people will cause unnecessary distractions. As mentioned, brief all the attendees prior to the meeting. The critical people in formulating the proposal need to be present in a supporting role to the recovery manager.

CASE STUDY 14-7:
REMOVING OUTSIDE INTERRUPTION

In a large project with significant issues to address, it may be best to move the presentation to a neutral offsite location. On one project, scope negotiation meetings were scheduled for three consecutive days, followed by one day of commercial discussions. A location was chosen requiring travel for both the customer and the supplier. All key decision makers were present in the meetings from 8:00 A.M. to 5:00 P.M. Lunch was brought in, but the team went out to dinner each night. It was an intensive team-building experience. The attendees were different for both the technical and commercial discussions, but the goal of both the customer and the supplier was to achieve closure. Out of the hundreds of items open at the meeting's onset, only one remained open at the end.

Depending on the project's size, the recovery's extent, and the number of contentious points, the meeting may be a single meeting for preselected stakeholders capable of making a decision or it may be a set of multiday offsite meetings at which numerous people debate the virtues of the plan. Both require the same degree of preparation. Select a venue appropriate for the meeting. Hold small recovery meetings in an onsite conference room and conduct larger, more contentious meetings remotely to reduce interruptions and distractions.

Culture is important. In cultures where confrontation is frowned upon or the presentation is not in the native language, allow time for people to assimilate the plan. Schedule at least two meetings, one to present the options and one to gain acceptance. Be prepared for additional clarification sessions between the two meetings. In cultures where confrontation and haggling are the norm, the recovery manager needs to be well prepared to control the meeting and prevent it from degrading into a blame-assigning shouting match. Keeping people focused and tempers under control takes an extreme amount of energy.

Be sensitive to people or groups that will be wounded. Although it can be anyone, the customer will likely be in this group since customers perceive rolling back to the contractual baseline as conceding features. Their animosity may spill over onto the project manager, the engineering team, and the recovery manager (shooting the messenger).

Have a plan for capturing and publishing detailed minutes of the salient discussion. Request the presence of a stenographer for this task. This leaves other meeting participants to focus on the discussion. This person should record finalized decisions and read them back to the group for confirmation.

The meeting should start with a recap of problems with the project. Relevant history should be included to explain the reasons for the failure. Everyone should understand the event timeline. Although no one should be alienated (surely, no blame should be assigned), be objective and enumerate the facts. These steps ensure all the people have the same general education on the issues. This also suppresses rumors. Address rumors directly by requesting that people present any data contrary to the information provided.

Describe the details of the actions already taken, including the reasons they were implemented early. Most of these items will center on cutting the burn rate, but some are to use resources efficiently. Report on their success.

Tell the attendees the cost of not implementing any changes and of canceling the project, as these are the two boundaries of the options.

List the contractual agreements and any open or contentious items. Since many of the questions will be addressed in the options, hold discussion until later in the presentation.

Present the primary proposal's outline. This will act as a roadmap of the items to be covered, reducing the number of questions. The discussion should then turn to the proposal's details. Review the data supporting each aspect of the plan before opening the floor for discussion. There will still be questions, which you should address openly and honestly. When presenting each portion of the plan, leave plenty of time for questions and suggestions from the audience and for providing detailed answers, including rebuttals or ways of incorporating the idea through a trade. Anything new or unanswerable will require an action item and a deadline. Research them after the meeting; then, answer them in a subsequent meeting or memo. Most action items will be assigned to the recovery manager. However, ensure the premise for an objection is correct. If there is doubt, assign the action item to the stakeholder to validate conditions. Refuse to take bold statements as facts—validate them.

If objections seem to be leaning toward one of the other two options, propose the alternative closest to the direction the group is leaning. This will lengthen the meeting, but it will have a positive effect on the group. If moving to a lesser option, make sure it is clear that certain items are removed from the prior plan.

Even after doing the recommended lobbying, plan for significant pushback to the proposal. Refrain from a quick rebuttal. Let people have their say, listen, and ask them to clarify their concerns to make sure they are understood. After listening, address their concerns with factual data. Knowledge is power, and the data has to support the reply. Otherwise, take an action item to get back with that person and the group. Determine if this will be a showstopper to making a decision.

Capture and publish detailed minutes of the salient discussion. The stenographer should record finalized decisions and read them back to the group for confirmation.

CASE STUDY 14-8: WHEN A COMPROMISE POSITION CANNOT BE FOUND

There are times when there really is no compromise. A new dot-com startup had an over-aggressive sales team that grossly oversold the company's product, which was still in development. Features on the five-year roadmap were sold as if they were in the product's initial release. I was asked to reconcile the issues with the angry customer. The culture was one where no one, neither supplier nor customer, could lose face. Approximately 85 percent of the proposed scope needed to be cut. To ensure the start-up got its desperately needed cash, every tactic was needed to maintain the three-year service contract at the same monetary level. Manual workarounds, development compromises, and external processing in other desktop tools, which were developed by the deployment team, allowed the project to deliver nearly 25 percent of the functionality. Delivery was only slightly behind the anticipated schedule, while successfully retaining the annual payment schedule.

Close the meeting by asking for a decision (or a conditional decision based on any open action items) to go forward with the proposal. If they cannot make a decision, ask what is needed to give them enough information to make a decision. Identify any critical action items. Clearly define which members still need to show their agreement to get approval. If a second meeting is required, schedule the meeting and identify the people whose attendance is required.

Based on the comments and concerns, handle the follow-up via meeting or memo, whichever is appropriate. Until direction is set, the recovery manager's job is incomplete.

Variations on the Meeting Goals

As mentioned in Chapter 2, "Creating the Assignment's Statement of Work," the recovery manager's engagement may have been only for an audit. The audit findings presentation (see Appendix 1) is very similar to what has been described above. However, it stops at presenting the problems uncovered and only suspected root causes. Expect that the stakeholders will ask questions on how to resolve the issues.

Chapter Takeaway

- Negotiation meetings are a step in the negotiation process.
- The recovery manager facilitates negotiation by mediating the plan between the two parties—customer and supplier.
- Return the recovered project's scope to the contractual baseline plus any change orders.
- The recovery plan value is determined by looking at:
  - The components' relative importance.
  - The significance of removing a component—the consequence of failure.
  - The component's features ranking—the wish list.
- Create three options for completing the project:
  - The optimal plan, which will meet the recovery guidelines.
  - One plan inside the guidelines (i.e., lower cost, shorter timeline, etc.).
  - One plan covering more than the guidelines (more features, longer timeline, etc.).
- The recovery plan must have value in the project for each party, as well as corrective actions for root causes of all problems.
- While formulating the recovery plan, the recovery manager should review the plan and options with both parties to ensure the plan meets their needs.
- Lead the negotiation session with the optimal plan and determine whether group consensus is leaning toward one of the other options. If so, then present that option.
- After settling on a basic direction, fine tune the option to meet the group's needs.
- Mitigate needs that are in conflict between parties or the recovery guidelines.
- The recovery meeting's primary goal is acceptance of and closure on the recovery plan.

15

Dealing with "Unprojects"

"Error is a hardy plant; it flourishes in every soil."

—Martin F. Tupper, English Writer and Poet, *Of Truth in Things False*

Occasionally, a project violates the definition of a project—usually by including nonproject work or by combining two or more conflicting projects. This is prevalent in companies that attempt to perform all work as projects. These belong to the class known as "unprojects."

Projects by definition have a distinct beginning and end. Work that does not have an end, such as maintenance work, should not be included in the project. Multiple case studies discuss this (see, for example, Case Studies 15-1 and 15-2). Mixing two styles of projects creates conflicts, particularly if they have different triple constraints. These issues need to be resolved by the customer's or supplier's senior management, whichever group is the source of conflict. Discuss these items in private, as changes will be required in the organization's strategic directions, structure, budget, or some combination of these factors. These issues can have long-range political implications that will affect the organization rather than the project team.

What to Do When Maintenance Is Part of a Project

Putting maintenance into projects is a direct result of a matrixed organizational structure in which resources are pooled to better utilize their skills over multiple projects or systems. In creating a matrix organization, people are divided into groups according to their skill sets. Some of these groups are even in different organizations. When a project is started, resources are then pulled from these groups based on job descriptions for the project. This disbands the cross-functional maintenance teams, which are no longer available for quick fixes or minor enhancement work. This spreads knowledge of the core system across multiple functional managers, and no single group has technical or budgetary responsibility for the entire system. At first, the project appears to solve this problem by bringing the correct resources together under a budgeted entity to work on the system. The project temporarily creates a new group with the resources to fix bugs and add new features. The problem is creating the correct conditions to justify forming a team to fix only bugs. The required resources may be working on other projects, and management may be reluctant to divert resources to a bug-fix project. Therefore, bugs languish and end users get frustrated waiting for a project to act as the vehicle for repair.

For the project, the bugs are just one more piece of scope to be defined by the project's parameters. Managing that scope is a simple, possibly even a trivial, task. Bug fixes are delivered at the end of the project with the rest of the project scope. Customers, however, are keen to slip in additional bug fixes throughout the project. A good project manager handles this through the change management process until the project is so close to completion that fixing bugs adds too much risk to the project. In other cases, the bugs slip into the project by lax control or covert means. Regardless, the scope increases. If the product is buggy, this can have a significant impact.

Another, less quantifiable, negative aspect of this relationship is the hostility just below the surface. The customer is generally annoyed about having to tolerate a bug in its system based on a political decision benefiting some other department or company.

Faced with this situation, the recovery manager's efforts should focus on getting maintenance removed from the project. The recovery manager has one ally in this effort—the customer. Whether the project is captive or through a third party, the customer will be excited by removing the artificial tie to a project and gaining a quick repair and deployment mechanism. The recovery manager has a number of options to address this. One is to dedicate specific resources within the project to fix bugs— such as creating a subproject inside the existing project. This is a little more difficult to manage, but can usually be done early in the project by resources not being utilized to design the project's primary product. This solution is open, transparent, and usually faster. Bug fixes are deployed prior to project development, at which time they need to be limited. It is only short term, however, since the maintenance stops as soon as the project is over. It provides a stopgap for the recovery manager and the customer to work on the bigger issue of the missing maintenance group. How the organization solves this issue is outside the scope of this book, but solutions include:

- Creating a maintenance group to support the product.
- Outsourcing the bug fixes to another group (even the customer).

- Creating small bug fix projects that periodically, say monthly, deploy service packs to one or more products.

CASE STUDY 15-1:
COVERT MAINTENANCE IN A PROJECT

Some project teams are less open about how bugs are fixed. In an organization with no maintenance group, a project was building an add-on to a sales tool to replace an older bug-laden product. The project got in trouble as the timeline doubled in the course of two weeks. The source of the scope was a drastic increase in features above the inception baseline. The problems were threefold. Having no maintenance group was the source of two of the issues. Without a maintenance group, the customer knew there would be poor support after the deployment. Therefore, the customer added both bug fixes for the old system and minor enhancements to handle new business situations. This resulted in a laundry list of features and requirements and an open-ended testing cycle, as the customer tried to create a perfect system. In addition, other bug fixes were included for ancillary systems touching the product. The effect of the missing maintenance group was that the scope had swollen the project with months of work. The recovery plan drastically reduced scope and removed most of the bug fixes. Unfortunately, I had to keep close tabs on the developers. They were sympathetic to the customer's plight, and bug fixes continued to creep into the project.

How Data Utilized by a Project Is Handled

Most projects involving technology have a data component. They must load or transform data to make it ready for the new system. This transformation is a temporary endeavor undertaken to create a unique product, service, or result, which means it is a project. Unfortunately, a methodology that is good for one set of work may be inappropriate for the next. For instance, if a project's goal is to build a new global positioning system (GPS) relying on a set of maps with a data format different from prior versions, the creation, or conversion, of the data is part of the project. Neither the product nor the data is useful without the other.

Maintaining the map information, on the other hand, is not a project; it is a maintenance effort. Some organizations try to make this a project by creating discrete units of data to maintain but it is still a maintenance effort. It never ends. Therefore, taking a region of maps, say eastern Canada, and placing that in a project to add dissimilar functionality, say a print feature, is mixing two projects into one. This resembles the original project, but is quite different because the two efforts are no longer related. Problems on one effort affect the other and cause artificial constraints. The remedy is simple on paper; separate the two activities. As with the maintenance effort above, the organization may need reorganization. This effort can be large.

This may sound like a rare occurrence, but with rapidly changing high-tech products, this has become a common phenomenon. Examples include maintaining data for geographical information systems (GIS); tax form and table updates; data interchange services among companies; virus and spam detection systems; and online vehicle configuration and purchasing systems.

CASE STUDY 15-2: ULTERIOR MOTIVES OF THE PROJECT MANAGER

At times, other motives drive a project to assume nonproject tasks. At one client, two separate groups were working with a handheld product—a hardware group building new features and a data group creating the information to run the product. Approximately one-third of the hardware project's budget was for testing the data group's work. The data group trained the hardware group's quality assurance team to test the data, but the data group would handle disposition of the bugs found by QA. Literally, the only work the data group did not do was testing.

The project to add the new hardware features was in trouble, and I determined that testing data had no relationship to the hardware changes. After some investigation, it was determined that the project's previous management was making a bid to outsource the entire project to its company. Therefore, getting as much scope as possible into the project would be beneficial to its business goals.

I was able to convince executive management to move the data quality assurance function to the data group. This required transferring budget and creating additional workspace for the testers in the building where the data group resided. In other words, this would require a significant amount of work and expense. I enlisted help to get the transfer completed.

Problems When Mixing Strategic Initiatives and Tactical Projects

In companies performing all work in projects, building infrastructure requires a customer-financed project to act as a carrier. This has the potential of creating one project with two goals—one goal for the customer and another for the strategic initiative. In turn, this creates conflicting goals. The strategic project has a long-term goal to satisfy needs not included in the funding project. Solely out of convenience, the funding project may only use or take advantage of a portion of the strategic component. There may be many other ways to provide the same functionality—potentially from an existing tool. This causes a conflict in the triple constraints—a strategic project usually has scope as its most critical issue, while a tactical project has schedule, cost, or a different set of scope as the primary constraint. If these two items are too different, the project gets in trouble. One of the two, or both, needs to be compromised.

Infrastructure rollouts often fall into this category. The organization wants to ensure there is a business case to use the infrastructure. Therefore, it waits for an appropriate customer-funded project that can use the technology and deploys the two together. This cuts down on deploying new technology that goes unused. Unfortunately, it results in a conflict of interest.

CASE STUDY 15-3: CONFLICTING CONSTRAINTS

A services company launched a large mission critical program implementing a new line of business. Numerous projects were started company-wide. Information Technology had five of these projects for setting up systems, enhancing front-end tools, and developing new infrastructure to interface existing systems. Because they were in the middle of developing a new IT infrastructure, some new technologies were included in the project. The individual project managers highlighted the risk of coupling the efforts, but senior management ignored the complaints. Throughout the program, the infrastructure implementation was significantly compromised. The tools developed as part of the funding project were also compromised due to the drain from the other work required. After the project's completion, additional work was commissioned to fix the deficiencies in the infrastructure and the tools. This required an additional year to implement.

Infrastructure deployments need to handle more than the scope of the funding project. Installation must accommodate other products on the strategic roadmap. The burden of designing for other enterprise systems is placed on the current project with little benefit to it. Delays, costs overruns, and scope creep in the infrastructure portion and make matters worse. The result usually has long-term impact. The strategic project's scope is cut or its implementation is switched to bias the tactical project; quick decisions are made to implement it to support the funding product. This usually results in a substandard implementation that needs to be reworked twice—once to fix the short cut, making it applicable in a generic sense, and then to make the tactical product fit the generic implementation. The latter two fixes prolong the project's actual recovery.

When seen in a project recovery, the first step is to determine if it really is a problem and then to address it with executive management. There are a number of options for the recovery plan, including:

- Convince management to remove the strategic implementation from the tactical project. This will require decoupling the interfaces between the two projects.
- Continue the project, and tailor the strategic tool deployment to the tactical project's needs. Later, commission two projects, one to implement the strategic

tools in a generic manner and a second to retrofit the tactical project to the strategic implementation.

- Cancel the strategic project and plan its deployment later.

For clarity, Table 15-1 presents the advantages and disadvantages of these options. In all cases, someone in the organization is going to have to admit the policy of mixing projects was a failure—openly or by quietly abandoning the idea in the future. The complete solution is to fund and execute strategic projects separately.

When fixing these situations, make sure the recovery plans include the details of the follow-up work required to correct any compromises in either implementation. Secure funding along with approval of the recovery plan. Otherwise, the plan of record should show the denial of the request.

Table 15-1: Option for Mixed Tactical and Strategic Projects

Option	Advantage	Disadvantage
Remove the strategic implementation from the tactical project, creating two projects.	Both systems are deployed. The product is delivered earlier than if waiting for the strategic piece to be deployed properly. This assumes the strategic piece is on the critical path. Follow-up work outside the project completes the interfaces as originally designed. This is attractive since it removes the dependence and minimizes the rework to the interfaces.	It assumes the workarounds for the interfaces are less work than the optimal solutions and that they will be replaced later. This could be a poor assumption and the substandard interfaces may remain.
Tailor the strategic tool to the deployment of tactical project's needs.	Gets both products deployed, building familiarity with the strategic tool.	Rework is required for both the strategic and tactical projects, instead of just one.
Cancel the strategic project and plan on its deployment later.	This decreases the work and strain on the project potentially reducing other risks.	This may be the death knell for the new technology since its deployment is considered a failure. It assumes another technology will fulfill the needs being offered by the new technology.

Chapter Takeaway

- Projects should consist of related types of work with common goals.
- Remove nonproject work from projects.
- Projects with multiple products must have the same triple constraints; otherwise, some products will need to be compromised to handle conflicting goals of other products.
- Address these types of problems outside the normal negotiation process because only the customer or the supplier is involved in the resolution.

V

Executing the New Plan

Implementing the Solutions

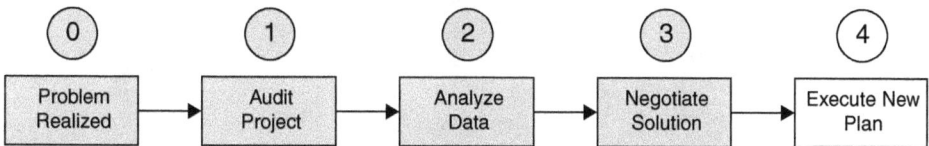

0		1		2		3		4
Problem Realized	→	Audit Project	→	Analyze Data	→	Negotiate Solution	→	Execute New Plan

This process has identified the project's problems, remedial processes have been put into place, solutions to the problems root causes are ready to implement, the extended team is on-board with the recovery plan, and the steering committee has approved the plan. It is now time to finalize the schedule with negotiated changes, implement corrective actions, and execute the plan.

16

Implementing Corrective Actions and Executing the Plan

Talk doesn't cook rice.

—Chinese Proverb

If the result of the negotiation is to continue the project, it needs to be reset to the definition phase. It now has a scope of work, tentative timeline, potential resource list, initial risk register, and project assumptions; it is ready to roll. It has the traits of a new project, and everyone should treat it as such.

Implementing Corrective Actions

Before restarting the project, implement the corrective actions. Treat their implementation as any other project's prerequisite start-up tasks. Shuffle the team, acquire new people, and make new assignments. The scope was probably altered, and the plan now has different objectives. As opposed to new projects, some areas may have significant amount of work completed—project plans, assumptions, and risks are better defined, and quality plans may be complete. Even some of the technical work may be done, needing only minor modifications. The temptation is to try to build the sections that were nearly designed, but the team must stop and properly integrate the changes. Treat a recovered project like a new project to ensure old habits are removed. The label of being a "failed project" must be removed or the team's morale will suffer.

CASE STUDY 16-1: IMPLEMENTING CORRECTIVE ACTIONS TO REDUCE PROJECT COSTS

Every project is different, but on many, implementing the corrective actions turns a very wild project into a calm and simple project. Routinely, a recovery manager or senior project manager can turn the project over to someone else to complete after the corrective actions are in place.

On a $1 million project, the audit showed that most of the problems were outside the project and could be corrected by fixing three root causes. With those corrective actions in place, the project ran very smoothly. After six weeks, I turned the project over to a junior project manager reducing the management cost. The junior project manager ran the remaining six months of the project. Reflecting on Table 2-1 (pg. 21), it is clear how this can drastically reduce expenses.

Special Problems That Exist on Recovered Projects

With corrective actions in place, the new project should run like any other successful project. A few differences may arise that are specific to a failed project:

- Some problems, especially behavioral issues, may reoccur on the new project because they are difficult to fix.
- Some problems are impossible to fix—a troubled technology may be the only option, management may remain unresponsive, or a team is still remote.
- Overlooking root causes—some may still be lurking.
- The project has a history. The team is tainted, the project has a bad reputation, or the customer feels it was treated unfairly in the final compromise.
- New problems arise and, unlike other projects, stakeholders overreact.
- As the customer's subject matter experts realize the impact of the compromise, they push to get additional features back into scope.

Old Problems Reoccurring

All recoveries have irresolvable problems. The resolution will take longer than the project, the cost is too high, or no solution can be found. The project manager must do his or her best to manage them. In some cases, workarounds can be put in place (overtly or covertly) to mitigate the issue. For instance, management's lack of response or commitment will plague a project forever. Assume a decision-making problem aris-es. When developing the recovery plan this should have been placed in the risk regis-ter, but was surely removed in the negotiation process with a tacit "That doesn't hap-pen here." The problem is, it does happen and must be addressed. Escalate it. Without escalation, the project manager can only assign action items and let the project floun-der or make the decisions for the decision-challenged manager. Use discretion; each of these options has an inherent risk.

Some problems are less political, but equally stressful to resolve. Technology issues identified in the audit may continue to plague the project. It may be infeasible to switch to a different technology. In these cases, define a solution implementing the least amount of the technology's scope. This may produce a less elegant solution, so ensure that the steering committee knows it will be a suboptimal implementation requiring correction later. The project manager will need a combination of both sell and tell with the project team to implement a substandard solution.

Another class of issues is human behavioral problems. These are never completely fixed, only mitigated. The project manager needs to pay special attention to this issue and stay involved in day-to-day activities (Lesson 3). The methods defined in Chapter 3 are the best way to detect and avert these issues. Visiting with team members, attending meetings involving interactions among different groups, and listening to the water-cooler talk are all ways to determine if old problems are returning.

Root Causes That Were Missed

Missing some of the root causes in the audit and analysis is an unfortunate, but distinct, possibility. This may be frustrating, but it is far from disastrous. This is the reason the recovery manager highlighted it as a risk in the negotiation meeting. When this hap-pens, the project manager has to address the new issue ensuring that the actual root cause has been identified and implement a solution. Address it openly as an error in the recovery. This alerts the steering committee that the project manager is following the plan and mitigating risks as needed. Escalating the problem may seem like overkill, but it serves as notice to the stakeholders that the project manager is minding the project properly and addressing issues in a prudent fashion.

Dealing with People's Perception of a Failed Project

The label of a failed project is strong and demeaning. Unlike other projects, this project has history and the team is viewed with a jaundiced eye. Continually promote the project and protect the team's morale. To help combat the stigma, the team must have its wins advertised to the greater organization.

This attitude is especially evident when the project successfully deploys. The team should have an opportunity to celebrate its success. Many people may feel it is hypocritical to celebrate a failed project, but the failed project was the old project. Even though the team had to fight a serious uphill battle, this is a newly completed successful project.

CASE STUDY 16-2: BIASES AGAINST THE PROJECT

Finding internal resources to correct a project is difficult. Biases existed long before the project failure is even recognized. Many times, they continue long after the recovery plan's approval and well into its implementation.

One organization, designing and building a flat panel display system, experienced many failures. As no one could give the CEO an objective opinion, an external audit was requested.

A month after approving the recovery plan, directors and managers were still talking in the halls about how the project was wasting resources and should be canceled. This was demoralizing and became a severe distraction for the team. I requested that the division manager talk to his direct reports and peers about stopping the criticism. He did, and it worked.

Management's Overreaction to Small Problems

Recovered projects never have small problems. Superiors address normal issues that would creep up on any project with alarm and skepticism. As a result, they make a big production of nothing. The project manager will need to handle these explosions with utter calm.

To minimize these overreactions, the project manager should be the first to raise any issue. Someone else notifying a stakeholder of an issue will place the project manager in a defensive mode. Therefore, the best tactic is an offensive drive that describes the issue, the probability of its occurrence, the impact, and a mitigation plan. Tell superiors no action is required on their part and that the message is just a cautionary comment to ensure they are aware of the situation. Update stakeholders and adjust the plan if needed.

As the project proceeds, the need for this will diminish and the project manager can quietly resolve lesser issues independently.

New Scope Creep

Although scope creep may not have been an issue for the project in the past, it can become an issue if the negotiation changes the scope. Be attentive to customer representatives and the technical team to ensure items removed from the plan stay out of scope. A customer that feels it has forfeited too much during the negotiation may put extra pressure on the guilt-ridden project team to add items back into scope and perform little favors. This is the primary reason the negotiation must be perceived as fair. As pointed out in Chapter 4, scope added by the team can increase work significantly. One needs to watch the task durations carefully to ensure scope stays constant. Tasks ending up in the almost-done category for a significant time may need the project manager's attention, as this is often a sign that features are being added. This may require micromanaging to ensure the work constituting the tasks is in scope and the team is refraining from inserting frills.

CASE STUDY 16-3: AN EXAMPLE AUDIT AND RECOVERY

Depending on a project's size, the complexity of the issues, and the receptiveness of the stakeholders, project recoveries usually take from three weeks to six months to plan and significantly longer to implement. The following information is about a $1.5 million project originally specified as six-month endeavor; the recovery analysis showed it would take sixteen months.

The recovery's original scope was only an audit. The audit took about three weeks. This includes interviews, as well as the audit report's preparation and delivery. Executive management's decision process took only a day. The problems on the project were:
- Scope creep because of a lack of clarity on project's end user.
- PMO gate process that was inhibiting the project's progress.
- No delegation of decision-making authority.
- Executive management neglected the project.
- Big bang deployment.
- The project manager ignored the project team.
- Maintenance was included in the project.
- A demoralized team.

Executive management requested that I take the place of the project manager, prepare the analysis, and propose a recovery plan. The analysis took another five weeks. The recovery plan was submitted and approved. It consisted of:
- Defining a single end user.
- Reassigning job roles to delivery-focused members.
- Changing to a four-phase delivery.
- Declaring the definition process for the first three phases complete.
- Empowering the leads to make decisions.
- Creating an early win using iterative development to show new functionality.
- Stopping background communication to senior executives.

I ran the project, implementing the corrective actions and working with executive management to set up a maintenance team. After four weeks, I stepped into a mentoring role and turned the project over to a junior project manager, who was already working as a lead on the project. The project completed ten percent under budget.

Chapter Takeaway

- Fixing root causes to problems prior to project execution will return the project to a normal status requiring less special management.
- Aggressively address overlooked root causes.
- Irresolvable items need workarounds and extra attention.
- Behavioral problems are rarely fixed and need continual monitoring.
- Monitor and abate issues such as allowing the project's history to affect the project or management's overreaction to small issues. Both will fade with time and the proper leadership of the project manager.

VI

Doing It Right the First Time

Avoiding Problems That Lead to Red Projects

Being able to fix a project is a wonderful talent, but doing it right from the beginning is the proper approach. Understanding the behaviors that cause projects to fail is a big step in preventing a project from going red. The first part of this book is a good source for understanding those problems.

Many actions can help projects avoid trouble. An experienced and detail-oriented project manager, who follows a methodology that is a match for the project and who communicates with managers, will get most projects started in the right direction. This includes creating specific procedures to correct the common challenges that will inevitably arise, such as:

- Improving the inception and proposal processes.
- Building the right team.
- Understanding uncertainty and risk.
- Managing change.

CHAPTER

17

Properly Defining
a Project's Initiation

"A new type of thinking is essential if mankind
is to survive and move toward higher levels."

—Albert Einstein, German Theoretical Physicist,
New York Times, 1946

Before an initiative becomes a project, significant work has already been completed. The customer's decision to justify its value over other initiatives indicates the initiatives have cleared a series of qualifying hurdles. The first is simply the decision to move forward with the project. This vetting process requires the resolve, passion, and determination of people in a business unit.

This process occurs long before the first phase of a project. It creates the seed for the project and provides input to the project team that will make it a reality. The first miscommunication happens here, and it can set the project on a course for disaster.

Customer Inception: When the Project and the Problems Really Start

Projects start going bad at inception—the customer's inception. From this point forward, customer expectations are set, dreams envisioned, and compromises negotiated. The initiative proposal process is usually part of an annual planning process. The individual business units gather for planning meetings with their wish lists of initiatives. Through a winnowing process, a few select projects move forward. Others are postponed or rejected. The controlling factors are budgets, resources, estimated impact for the business (value), and strategic and tactical goals.

By analyzing the characteristics of postponed projects, the supporting organization can better understand the customer's direction. Using this information helps the project team address issues with design, cost, and technology. For example, if the long-term goals of a business include allowing client visibility into the company's workflow (i.e., allowing the customer to see where a request is in the company's process), then initial systems allowing clients to update their demographic data should be very robust. The proposal might even include prototyping future technologies. On the other hand, if the long-range goals are outsourcing the entire system, a simple disposable solution is a better utilization of resources. In short, including the project staff in the customer inception process will provide clarity to the roadmap. It provides a dimension to the "what" and "when" by adding the "what after that."

Using a Guidance Team to Smooth Project Start

The problem is that these are initiatives rather than projects. Managers often fail to include the implementation professionals in these early meetings. To improve project inception, assemble a guidance team to participate in the business planning meetings and to provide oversight and monitoring throughout the project's lifecycle. This will ensure the project team stays close to the intended baseline.

As detailed in Chapters 6 and 9, people are enamored with technology—it has become the Holy Grail. They accept the limited information provided by sales material as definitive and ignore the hidden complexities in the implementation. As a result, during the inception of a project, customers use buzzwords and concepts they believe they understand and make assumptions about the idea's implementation.

Correcting this is the responsibility of the guidance team. This team consists of two or three people with architecture and project management skills, who stay with

Table 17-1: Advantages of a Guidance Team

Set expectations on the possible deliverables.

Alert the customer on the items having higher expense or risk.

Help the customer with informed decisions.

Get the customer to focus on the solution's "what" and "when," rather than "how" it will be implemented.

Provide an assessment for the business in the inception phase.

Provide project guidance throughout the project lifecycle.

Maintain a baseline intent for the project.

Assist in change request review.

the project from customer inception through deployment. Members guide the teams, set direction, and perform audits rather than working on the projects. Among other things (see Table 17-1), its members minimize speculation on the initiative's implementation details—speculation that biases the product's definition. The guidance team redirects the conversation back to *what* is needed and away from *how* to build it. By assessing the level of complexity in the product, team members help set early and realistic expectations. It removes the opportunity for the customer to conjure up an infeasible or overly expensive solution. Thus, the guidance team helps the customer that knows what it wants create the definition of what it needs.

Understanding the reasons behind the decisions also enables the team to see any incongruities in the project. This is especially helpful as the team thinks about the solution's robustness or potential workarounds. Thus, when the project reaches a point of someone saying, "I thought we were going to. . .," the guidance team will have the background and knowledge to address the question and maintain direction. Table 17-2 summarizes a number of tasks performed by the guidance team.

CASE STUDY 17-1: AN EXAMPLE OF A GUIDANCE TEAM

A new start-up company for manufacturing flat panel displays requested a bid from five different vendors for a computer integrated manufacturing system. They delivered the Request for Proposal (RFP) via email to all vendors on the same day; vendors were given four weeks to respond. The customer felt the 150-page RFP covered all the topics, and its purchasing agent was surprised at the number of questions he received on the document. He finally decided to organize a two-hour bidder's conference with all five vendors to answer questions. Bidder's conferences were uncommon for this industry and none of the vendors felt it was the proper venue or provided sufficient time for questioning. Many questions were left unasked since the feeling was that asking a question would remove a competitive advantage. After four weeks, all the proposals were submitted and were within the same price range—$25 to $30 million. The customer was shocked, as it expected the bids to be approximately $5 million. As a result, the customer had to restart the bidding process and ask the vendors how to improve the process and bring down the price. Had the customer asked any one of the vendors for help with the process initially, three months of work would have been saved. In contrast, the project was now three months late simply because the inception process had too many invalid assumptions.

Guidance Teams Supplied by Vendors

The concept of a guidance team is difficult for many companies to understand and objections will abound (see Table 17-3). For organizations considering outsourcing the project, the feeling is that using potential vendors as a guidance team will bias the proposal in favor of the supporting vendor. This may happen but reputable firms will

Table 17-2: Guidance Team Tasks

Task	Benefit
Help with the overall strategic and tactical business plans by providing capacity planning for the business and engineering resources.	The business can envision a set of work the supplier is incapable of handling. Significant time can be wasted assuming the supplier has the capacity to provide the solution.
Look at each initiative and the load it will put on existing technology. Understand the upgrades needs.	Determine if the initiative strains technology or systems already in place thereby requiring additional infrastructure.
For each initiative, look for new technology requirements.	Identify new capability requirements to support the business. This will tax resources more than simply expanding the existing known systems.
Assess the maturity of technology required to accomplish the proposal.	If the task requires new untested technology, it will be high risk and may cause delays.

note this. The liability of a biased definition is better than having a definition that does not meet project needs.

Guidance Teams Internal to a Company

Captive shops simply seem to overlook the option of including delivery personnel, possibly because of the feeling that the engineering organization should be removed from business plan development and prioritization. Rectify this perception, as early involvement in the project is invaluable.

All too often, senior management is involved in the early phases of initiative planning and, although this information is perfectly understood, it is inaccessible to the project team. Because of other responsibilities, managers are unable to attend the number of team meetings required to see if the project is adhering to its intent, but the guidance team can do this. Its members have access to the teams building the solutions and must allocate part of their time to providing steering and auditing functions.

Improvements to Project Proposals and Charters

The process for coordinating the project team and the customer is different depending on whether the project is run in-house or outsourced. When projects are outsourced, vendors submit a proposal or bid that result in a contract and SOW (hereafter referred to as simply *contract*). The contract may differ significantly from the proposal. However, the proposal is widely disseminated among members of the group, while the contract, because of commercial terms, is more restricted. Because these documents

Table 17-3: Objections to a Guidance Team

Objection	Comment
The planning stages are too early and many irrelevant proposals will be reviewed that will never see the light of day.	Seeing the rejected proposals and the reasons they are culled is valuable data for the team.
This team will sit though unneeded discussion.	This discussion and the outcome provide the plan's temper. It is valuable information.
The customer is unfamiliar with which vendor is best qualified to do the work, let alone work as the guidance team.	It can be one of many vendors. They are there to listen and provide input. Ideally, the company would make a strategic alliance with a vendor to help in this process. Often the RFP development process is bid out to make sure it contains the necessary information.
There are people in management who know the inception information and there is no reason to spend money having lower level people take part in this.	Managers cannot provide the time or technical input required to steer the customer away from getting into implementation. Managers are unable to spend time with each project team to see drift in the project.
Vendor may bias the direction to a product set it offers.	Vendors, internal engineering, and design groups have this concern alike. This bias is less than an uninformed bias from nontechnical business people. Solutions will always be biased toward the supplier's capabilities. If this concern is insurmountable, then have multiple vendors involved in the process. Select a vendor on its commitment to the customer and overall fit.

are negotiated items, this leaves room for the contract to exclude a significant number of expectations set forth in the proposal.

In contrast, in-house projects have a project charter that reflects the customer's desires. The charter often functions as both the proposal and the contract. It reflects the project team's understanding of the customer's needs and fulfills only a few of the proposal's functions. The charter also references any proposed items that were excluded based on constraints in schedule, budget, or resources. The project charter and the contract are the binding documents for the project.

The guidance team is involved in generating the proposal, contract, and charter for the project—it provides the vision and continuity. The proposal needs to have as much detail as possible, and the recommended charter must be more detailed than most standards organizations (i.e., PMI®) define. This sets the tone and anchors the business' understanding of what it is getting. Figure 17-1 outlines the charter's baseline content.

Be clear in these documents and avoid repeating deliverables; doing so will create conflicts and errors while editing. State what is being provided and refrain from listing out-of-scope items, which are, in reality, infinite. Listing nondeliverables only leads to confusion when an anticipated item is in neither the inclusion nor the exclusion list. The only items that should be on an exclusion list are items specifically requested by the customer that the supplier will not be delivering—they are no-bid items. Experience teaches that when the customer anticipates something without specifically requesting it, and it is missing from the exclusion list while other nonrequested items are included, the customer argues that the anticipated item is in scope. Review Case Study 4-1 (pg. 50) for an example of the problems this may cause.

Define the methodology, whether it is a big-bang deployment, phased, or agile. For phased or agile, reflect the projected releases in a work breakdown structure (WBS). State the reasons why the methodology is required and, if someone overrides it, document the reasons, the impact on the schedule, and risk. There must be an impact; otherwise, the suggestion had no foundation.

Proposal and project charters usually omit the WBS component; however, it is essential because it outlines the required work and responsible parties. It also sets expectations on the steps required, deliverables, mid-project approvals, and team relationships. Table 17-4 shows the minimal data required for each work breakdown

Figure 17-1: Proposal Structure

- Summary of project
- Scope
- Exclusion of no-bid items
- Development and delivery philosophy
- Estimated size of team
- Work breakdown structure:
  - Definition
  - Prototype work
  - Development areas
    - Internal work
    - Subcontracted work
  - Unit test
  - System test
  - Delivery
  - Warranty
- Estimated timeline
- Assumptions
- Risk elements
- Role and responsibilities

Table 17-4: Required WBS Fields

Field	Description
Description	A brief task description
Deliverables	Documents and products delivered and approved by the customer or supplier from this WBS task. All deliverables will be the responsibility of the task's owner.
Dependencies	Prerequisites to starting the task
Assumptions	Any assumptions made in formulating this task.
Exit Criteria	Conditions required to complete this task (i.e., deliverables' sign-off, completion of some other task)
Task's Owner	The organization responsible for completing the task (i.e., vendor customer, third party, etc.)

structure sheet (see also Appendix 1). This detail is often left for later in the project's definition phase. Although it will be refined and superseded by subsequent documents, these set the tone for the project and reduce surprises.

Since a major source of project failure is scope creep, the WBS should include concurrent approval of design and acceptance criteria, such as the functional specifications and the acceptance test scripts. This requirement is not needed in an agile projects because each iteration provides this function. There are two advantages to this:

1. Creating the acceptance documentation helps the engineers perform a sanity check on the design specification.
2. It helps provide agile's close tie of translating design information into tangible product.

Most customers have a difficult time understanding the implications of a design specification; they have a much easier time understanding the flow presented in acceptance documentation. This is the result of the acceptance documentation's step-by-step format. It creates a visualization of the product's usage, functions, and boundary conditions. This will avoid arguments about the meaning of the design specifications. Releasing them at different times leaves the project open for expensive and labor-intensive changes late in the project. It is best to handle this risk early.

The core team and stakeholders must review and the guidance team and the project sponsor must approve the charter. The core team must review and the guidance team and executive management must approve the proposal. There should be no questions or uncertainty in either. Replace unquantifiable terms with quantifiable ones.

Modifying proposals or charters after publication creates the opportunity for misalignment. Keep these documents under strict configuration control. This is especially challenging in outsourced projects, because a purchasing group is involved and can make significant changes to the proposal's intent. This can leave many stakeholders feeling they are getting something very different from what they anticipated. The guidance team helps avoid this by being the harbingers of consistency throughout the process.

Chapter Takeaway

- Project expectations are first set at inception, long before the project's supplier is aware of the pending project. From that point forward, projects are being set up for failure.
- Supplier staffed guidance teams greatly reduce misconceptions and poor definition in the customer's inception phase.
- Guidance teams provide audit and consultation services for the project throughout its lifecycle.
- Project charters and proposals:
  - Need to include information about the methodology and a work breakdown structure.
  - Should only mention excluded items if they are specifically requested in the Request for Proposal or the inception documentation and are being placed out of scope by the supplier.

CHAPTER

18

Assembling the Right Team

"Teamwork is the fuel that allows common
people to attain uncommon results."

—Andrew Carnegie, U.S. Industrialist

Teams make or break projects; they are at the crux of every success and every failure. As important as process is, if inappropriately applied or executed it provides no value, slows the project, and frustrates the team. The best processes will not compensate for a poor team. On the other hand, a team with the right attitude and drive will make up for significant deficiencies, including missing process; it will develop its own. The key is the team, not the process.

Constructing the Team

The customer visualizes the team at the same time it envisions the project—often by name, surely by skill set. The customer identifies the team by the areas crucial to product value, in other words, critical to quality items. As tools, features, and challenges are identified, the customer earmarks ideal candidates to implement them. This is further embedded into the project in the proposal and bid phase, as additional project parameters (cost and schedule) are set based on the resourcing assumptions. If, however, those resources are unavailable, alternate resources will be assigned. Groups in charge of staffing attempt to find equivalent substitutes and the guidance team, which originally identified the resource, needs to assist by developing detailed job descriptions and qualifications. To find the ideal candidate, the search should first look internally and then externally. Do not assign people to the project simply to use a resource; they must have the correct qualifications.

The Project's Management Team

Central to the project is the project manager. Without a strong project manager fostering, leading, and guiding the team, all is in vain. Poor leadership, indecisiveness, inexperience, inaction, and lack of team respect will sink a project.

Match the project to the project manager. Assign senior project managers with successful experience to difficult projects and assign junior project managers to smaller, simpler projects. Placing project managers on projects slightly over their experience level is acceptable, as long as the risk is noted and mitigation plans are in place. Otherwise, one is flirting with disaster.

The project manager should have domain experience. Building houses is different from building electronic devices. Experience with risks and mitigations, working with the different types of people, and methods of doing estimations are a few of the obvious differences. Even inside a domain, home construction is different from commercial construction and effecting a computer deployment is different from a software integration project. The project manager has to have relevant experience.

The project's management extends beyond the project manager. The second most important individual is the architect. One of this person's primary responsibilities is identifying and controlling scope creep. Anytime there is a question on the scope, the project manager and the architect need to objectively look at the contract documents or project charter and determine if a change request is required. The project manager will be unable to handle all of the scope issues since the request may be too embedded in the product. The architect needs to assess the impact to determine whether it is in or out of scope. All change requests (regardless of whether they are technical) should be approved by the architect to ensure the impact has been properly assessed.

Because of this, these two individuals need to have a perfect working relationship and hold each other's trust and respect. If either of these people have a separate agenda, animosity will build and troubles will ensue. Management needs to step in and correct the problem.

The Dangers of Reusing Teams on New Projects

In many organizations, blocks of previous teams are used to reconstitute a synergy from a previously successful project. As the investment disclaimer says, prior performance is no indication of future return. Even if this practice has worked well in the past, use it with caution. It is a mistake to think that an existing team, whose members have functioned together well in the past, will need less attention than a new team. An existing team's history can be positive or negative. The advantage to reconstituting a team is that its formation can often proceed more rapidly.

One concern is whether new people introduced to the team will feel left out, shunned, or excluded from the clique. This feeling could be well founded; the old team's culture may impede efficient assimilation of newcomers. All of the team's actions, including the day's traditions at lunch, inside jokes, technical biases, etc., influence the adoption of a new team member. These are unintentional. The team has developed a working communication pattern that is very efficient, but it may be difficult for others to adopt. Managers in this situation need to scrutinize the team's interaction, resisting acceptance of the superficial appearance of harmony.

CASE STUDY 18-1: THE NEW PERSON

An organization assigned a new technical resource to a fledgling project. A team's lead, to whom this person reported, had been working with the existing project team for more than four years and had an established rapport with its members. Within the first week, the new person asked for a meeting with me about a number of issues. She claimed the lead was:

- Failing to objectively looking at alternate options for problems.
- Providing obscure definitions for deliverables.
- Rejecting completed deliverables without explanation.
- Refusing to answer her questions.

By attending a couple meetings, I found there was strong friction between the two individuals. The lead explained he was frustrated with the new person because she did not know how to perform her job. Then, I asked him to explain a task he had assigned the newcomer and he enumerated a series of items missing from the written request. When asked why they were missing, the lead replied that she should have known to include these items, as everyone else did. He further explained that architectural decisions on the project were already made, so there was no reason to look at other options. I coached the lead on properly documenting requests to new individuals and noted the decisions he was referring to were still open and the new person had been tasked with exploring a complete set of options to provide an unbiased evaluation. It turned out that the lead was using data from the previous (failed) project to make technical decisions. Those decisions were overturned. I had to continue to stand between the lead and the resource.

Regardless of the source, address any hint of team discord with the utmost of haste. Uncooperative teams will build components that will fail to work together. Review Chapter 3 for tips on addressing this situation.

Another prominent issue occurs when teams are experienced with the product or when the customer has a preconceived bias. These issues require extra scope management effort—team members may assume that the scope or project parameters are the same as on past projects. This assumption is dangerous, as it can be a major contributor to internal scope creep (see Chapter 4). Similarly, customers who know that specific features were previously requested and were removed from prior projects, or implemented poorly, may put these items on their agenda to be addressed in this project. These actions can be either conscious or subconscious, but both require attentiveness on the part of the project manager to uncover and correct.

In his book, *The Mythical Man-Month*, Frederick Brooks refers to this phenomenon as "The Second System Effect." He recognizes that teams working on a product for the second time will want to include "frill after frill and embellishment after embellishment" that occurred to them in the first pass of working on the system, but were only noted, delaying their implementation because of the individual's newness with the product.[7]

Reusing teams for an entirely new project is another common mistake. Since blocks of people tend to leave projects at the same time, it is tempting to reutilize those individuals to create a team for the next available project. This keeps the resources billable and avoids various negative financial impacts to the organization. This practice is acceptable if the team has the qualifications to do the job. If they are not the proper fit, the deleterious effect to the bottom line will be much more significant than their idle time.

CASE STUDY 18-2:
REUSING EXISTING TEAMS

One client had attempted to build a comprehensive customer maintenance product several times. It had failed three times, although the last failure was recovered and partially deployed. In each situation, the same team designed and built the product. In the last failure, I was brought in to recover and deliver the project. I phased it, and the first two phases delivered successfully. Management canceled the last phase because of a higher priority project that needed the resources. The following year, a new project was started to complete the canceled third phase. The same team was used, and I was brought in to manage it. As in the previously failed project, the customer wanted a tactical solution. This time, though, the customer specifically asked for a minimal solution to "stop the bleeding." The goal was to avoid the expense of building a robust solution because the product's future was uncertain. It was nonsensical to invest too much money in a solution the customer might abandon in the near future.

Unfortunately, the design team adopted the prior year's much costlier solution. The members refused to look at less elegant alternative options.

Significant discord arose between the architect and me, as we were going in different directions. The architect, along with a number of members of the preexisting team, felt the executive direction was wrong and nearsighted. I had to escalate the situation and bring in upper management to help correct the direction. Management assigned a new team to the project, which followed the tactical direction.

Ensuring the Team Is Competent

To say a team needs to be competent seems obvious. However, as indicated in the previous section, teams composed using a different rationale may compromise quality for varying reasons. For example, the desired resources may be committed to other projects or a preexisting team may be available for the work when other, more qualified resources, are unavailable. But, remember that teams need to be competent to do the job at hand. To get better than average results, team members need to be above average at the tasks they are being asked to do. Superior products can only be made with superior teams. Judging from the number of books that raise this point (including every project book in the list in Recommended Reading, it is less obvious than it should be. If the resource pool is lacking the skills required for the project, use outside resources. This could have strong impact on the budget, but filling a slot with an incompetent resource could have a much larger impact.

One option is to train people in the required capabilities. However, the project will run at a lower efficiency than with pretrained and experienced resources. Organizations that cannot assemble the appropriate staff or lower the project's expectations should postpone the project.

The team members can be other than seasoned veterans; junior resources bring drive, ambition, and passion. Teams need a mix of seasoned, tested resources, as well as ambitious younger candidates. Remember that junior individuals will need more training and direction than senior members. The schedule and budget should reflect this.

CASE STUDY 18-3: TEAM INTERFACE PROBLEMS MEAN PRODUCT INTERFACE PROBLEMS

Identifying team discord helps in finding design flaws in the product. In a project building a new universal hardware adapter, the design team members had extreme difficulties getting along with each other. Personality conflicts had severely degraded communication between many individuals. Unfortunately, the people who did not get along had to design different parts of the adapter that needed to interface. My approach was to separate the specifications by author, then look at the interface specifications that needed to be paired with a specification that someone the designer did not like had written. In every case, the interfaces had at least one error. This made quick work of finding the big issues with the project's technical design and was strong and objective evidence of who was poisoning the team. It took a combination of coaching and replacement to get the team properly functioning as a unit.

Team Considerations When Using New Technology

Deploying technology that is new to an organization demands seasoned, aggressive, and ingenious personnel.

The best case is when internal staff members know the technology. If they need a refresher course, then promptly schedule training. If no internal resources are familiar with the technology, hire people to fill the void. Finally, use temporary resources, making sure their statement of work includes mentoring. The choice of direction depends on the organization's long-term desires.

The unacceptable option is to try to run the project without people experienced in the technology or in implementing new technologies. People who lack an understanding of the tool's weaknesses will cause problems that will have severe, negative effects on the project. The short-term cost savings will result in long-term budget overruns.

Chapter Takeaway

- Make sure the team meets the project's needs; the schedule and most assumptions are based on the right team.
- The project manager must be:
  - A leader.
  - At the right experience level for the project.
  - Experienced in the project's domain.
  - Thorough and detailed.
- The architect must be:
  - Aligned with the project manager—they form a management team.
  - Critical in controlling scope and minimizing internal scope creep.

- Using preexisting teams can have a number of advantages. However, there are disadvantages, including:
  - Customer or product bias.
  - Incorrect skills for the project.
  - An attitude that is closed to new members.
- If using new technology, ensure an appropriate number of team members are experienced with the technology.

19

Properly Dealing with Risk

"Fate laughs at probabilities."

—E. G. Bulwer-Lytton, Member of Parliament,
Novelist, *Eugene Aram: A Tale*

Most project managers have a poor understanding of how to quantify risk or how risk analysis can benefit the project. For that reason, they create a risk register at the beginning of a project to fulfill a PMO requirement, but then never update or review it. In fact, frustration is so high that they fail to fully identify risk items or generate reasonable mitigations. To exacerbate the problem, their managers have an equally poor understanding.

For numerous red projects, the risk register is either missing or the entries are too simplistic—omitting potential impact, probability of occurrence, or realistic mitigations. Even when a risk register exists, the project's management is amazed at the quantity of risks that become a reality. The familiar complaint is the only thing the project can do right is to execute risk. This is the result of one or both of the following:

1. The team has inadequate risk avoidance methods.
2. The number of high probability risks is so great that statistically most are going to execute.

A common problem in working with risk is that managers do not have a basic understanding of statistics, which is the cornerstone of risk management. People need to understand and trust the results of the analysis. A simple discussion of statistics can allay most fears. This chapter covers the discipline's basic concepts, so the reader can gain an understanding of how to minimize risk's effect.

How Understanding Risk Can Help Projects

There is a simple reason risk seems to be the only thing happening according to the plan—the probabilities indicate the risks will occur and proper mitigations are not in place. Think of it as having a number of people flipping quarters. If only one person flips, there is a 50:50 chance of getting a head. However, if 20 people flip quarters, approximately half the group is going to have heads turn up each time. The odds of no one getting heads are approximately one in a million (0.95 in a million, to be a more accurate). If each person represents a risk in the register, then the odds of each risk happening (flipping heads) is 50 percent. This means that approximately half of those risks will occur in each project (a project being when all people flip their quarters). Which half will turn up heads is unknown.

Now assume you will pay the people flipping the quarters $1000 for each head. Each time the group flips their quarters (symbolically, the project running), approximately $10,000 is paid out. Sometimes it is $12,000 and sometimes $8,000, but after enough times, the average will be $10,000 per project. Therefore, the budget must include $10,000 to handle the risk. The contingency is to have $10,000 dollars on hand to pay the people.

An alternative is for the project team to come up with a method that prevents some of the people from flipping heads. Determining how to prevent the event is mitigation. Mitigation for this project includes:

1. Weight the quarters to flip tails.
2. Preoccupy the people so they forget to flip.
3. Pay $500 to have people not flip their quarters.
4. Tape people's fingers together.
5. Steal the quarters.

Unlike this simple example, projects are unique and never present the same risks twice. To develop a risk register, one normally relies on history from similar projects, assessments of the project's current environment, and the assumptions for the project. It would be nice if there were empirical data to use for this, but unfortunately, projects, by definition, create a unique product. Therefore, applicable empirical data might be difficult to find. The team will have to determine the risks and their parameters from experiential data.

As the example shows, risk is an aggregate of the odds of occurrence and the impact of the event. Statistics do not predict the future. This is an essential concept everyone must understand. Assessing risk means using estimates and inductive statistics to make an educated prediction of the cumulative effects of a set of potential problems. After determining the potential outcomes, the team develops mitigation strategies based on the weighted impacts the risks will have on the project.

As opposed to the odds in an ethical casino, team members can affect the chance of problems occurring by creating mitigation plans. If the team feels a risk exists because of a lack of experience on a tool, then hiring or training resources can reduce the risk's impact and possibly remove the risk completely. If there is concern about scope creep, implementing a better change management process or switching to an agile methodology can help. The idea is to stack the deck in the project's favor, thereby influencing the odds to make the chances of winning better. Before doing this, people need to understand which risks will have the greatest impact.

In general, three factors control a project—what, who, and when. All risk fits into these areas.

- What: What is being built.
- Who: The people, money, tools, or building material to make it.
- When: The dates when tasks need to be completed.

Internal and external issues affect each of these areas.

Poor understanding of *what* is being built is the primary problem affecting scope. Scope is also affected by the customer's attitude as well as by such issues as technology. Unanticipated scope changes include market changes and governmental regulations. *Who*, or project resource, risk can be caused by inadequate effort estimates, unavailable resources, or issues at the customer site involving people, money, or materials. *When* refers to an issue with any part of the schedule, including delivery dates for equipment, subcomponents, final product, customer documentation, and the like.

The sources of risks are wide and varied. They can be beyond the project's control (common cause risk), or within its control (special cause risk). An example of common cause variation is the normal variation in time required to complete a task. Regardless of the controls put on an action, some variation will exist. Another name for common cause variation is normal variation because it follows a normal distribution curve. Trying to control the number of times a quarter spins in a single flip is an example. You can control special cause variation. Asking people to multitask on assignments causes variation in task duration. You can reduce the variation by stopping the practice of multitasking.

A Real Project Scenario

A real-life example will help clarify these terms. In the mid 1990s, a team I was on prepared a fixed-price bid for integrating manufacturing software with equipment in a new fabrication facility. At bid submission, facility construction was still months away and manufacturing equipment still needed to be identified. As the bid price was very dependent on the integration's complexity, we held a number of meetings to clarify the client's needs. The bid team felt the requested design would be expensive and a technical liability for the customer.

A requirement to provide guaranteed delivery of equipment status messages (status messaging indicates whether the machine was in running, teardown, setup, maintenance, qualification, or wait states) added to this feeling. The team assumed that replacing the requirement with the task of educating the customer on the impracticality of implementing the feature was an acceptable risk. This made the bid price lower and required the project team accept the risk that the customer would retain the requirement. If the assumption proved incorrect, the project would be responsible to provide additional software and training for the team.

Obviously, there was a risk, but this approach was successful on previous engagements. Table 19-1 shows the resulting risk items.

Using a Real Project Scenario to Understand Risk

To understand the impact of risk, basic statistics are involved. The following conceptual rules need definition:

- The additive rule.
- Independence.
- Conditional dependence.
- The multiplicative rule.

Start with the most commonsensical rule: mutually exclusive odds are additive. In other words, if two or more conditions cannot happen together (e.g., equipment arrives late or early), then their odds of occurrence are additive. If there is a 30 percent

Table 19-1: Risk Register

	Risk	Probability	Cost	Lead Time
1	A new programming tool (EquipComm) may need to be purchased to implement a given requirement.	30%	$1,500	1 wk
2	In-house developers would be unable to learn the new tool (identified in Risk 1) in the timeframe needed; may need to hire a contractor.	60%	$30,000	6 wk
3	Construction problems delaying deployment testing.	40%	$1,000 per day	N/A

chance that the equipment will arrive early and a 10 percent chance it will arrive late, the chance that one of these conditions will occur is 40 percent. Similarly, the chance the equipment will arrive on schedule is 60 percent (100% - 40% = 60%). All possible options must add up to 100 percent.

In Table 19-1, Risk 3 is unaffected by either Risk 1 or Risk 2. The odds of Risk 3 happening is 40 percent, regardless of whether Risk 1 or Risk 2 happens. Therefore, Risk 3 is independent of the other two.

In some cases, one item affects another—that is, execution of one risk will increase or decrease the chance another risk will execute. In the above example, there will only be a need for a resource with a special skill set (Risk 2) if the guaranteed delivery is needed (Risk 1). Risk 2 is conditionally dependant on Risk 1. Using the data in Table 19-1, if Risk 1 happens, there is a 60 percent chance Risk 2 will happen. If Risk 1 fails to occur, there is no chance Risk 2 will happen. So, what are the odds of Risk 2 happening?

If risks are not mutually exclusive, then the probability of both happening is the product of their probability of occurrence. To restate, if Risk 1 happens, there is a 60 percent chance of Risk 2 occurring; they are conditional. The chance of both is 30% × 60% = 18%. This is the multiplicative rule of probability.

The overall risk is determined in the risk register. First, simply look at Risk 1 and Risk 3. There is no interrelationship between Risk 1 (added requirement) and Risk 3 (the construction timeline). If only two mutually exclusive events may occur, there is a 100 percent chance both will occur, neither will occur, or one of the two will occur.

To determine the odds of each happening:

- Risk 1 has a 30 percent chance of occurring and since construction is late (Risk 3) 40 percent of the time, the odds of both happening is 30% × 40% = 12%.
- The odds of Risk 1 failing to occur is 70 percent and the odds of Risk 3 failing to happen is 60 percent, so the odds of both not happening is 70% × 60% = 42%.
- Because there is a 12 percent chance of condition 1 happening and a 42 percent chance of condition 2, there is a 46 percent chance that exactly one of the two will occur (100% - 42% - 12% = 46%).

These calculations simply require a good deal of common sense. The importance of identifying the three statements is that they are a complete set of mutually exclusive occurrences—the chance of one of the three conditions happening is 100 percent. Looking at these options in this way makes them mutually exclusive.

Table 19-2 puts all the combinations of the three risks together. This indicates there is a 42 percent chance of none of the risks (top row) firing or a 58 percent chance of at least one occurring (the sum of all the other options). The important point is that the three individual risks have relatively small odds of occurring (30, 18, and 40 percent) but when put together, there is a 58 percent chance of missing the delivery date. Casinos in Las Vegas get rich on these odds.

Extending this out to a more realistic list of risks means the project will have trouble. Bypassing the math, if the risk register has seven independent risks all with a 30 percent chance of occurring, there is a 92 percent chance one or more will occur, an 86 percent chance two or more will occur, and a 62 percent chance three or more will occur. In other words, nearly half of them will occur. No wonder it looks like risk is the only thing happening on projects.

If management fails to understand that three out of seven risks will fire on a project, then there will be a huge overreaction when it happens. Seeing three or even four risk elements firing should be of little concern unless mitigation strategies and contingencies are missing or incorrect. This is a common area for overreacting and incorrectly labeling a project red. The appropriate action is to do nothing—except train management on risk.

To generate a contingency budget requires only this basic math. Although the example is simple, the key is to understand how to derive the numbers. This makes it easier to understand how to use the answer.

Quantifying Risk in the Sample Scenario

Many projects have enough empirical data to quantify a significant number of risk elements. National or regional databases and prior projects can often provide enough information to ensure the probability and impact of risk elements are better than guesses or order of magnitude estimates.

Table 19-2: Risks Combined

Which Risks Fire			Odds			Combined Odds
1	2	3	1	2	3	
No	No	No	70%	100%	60%	42%
No	No	Yes	70%	100%	40%	28%
Yes	No	No	30%	40%	60%	7%
Yes	No	Yes	30%	40%	40%	5%
Yes	Yes	No	30%	60%	60%	11%
Yes	Yes	Yes	30%	60%	40%	7%
					Chance of all:	100%

Using the register in Table 19-1, the following example shows how to quantify risks.

Risk 1: A new programming tool may be needed to implement the requirements of a requested feature. The requirement was to track equipment status changes even when the equipment was unable to communicate with the equipment tracking system. The bid team replaced this with the task of educating the customer to accept that the function was unnecessary. This had worked successfully in the past.

To understand the chance of having to implement a solution, the team needed to understand the situations when the software would (1) be beneficial and (2) still be unable to transfer the data and require human intervention. It was determined that there were 47 conditions under which the equipment would send a status change. Of these, 14 occurred when the equipment was unable to communicate. Of these, this software might assist four. Two assumptions were made: (1) all four needed to be captured, and (2) all 47 were statistically equivalent. Therefore, the chance of occurrence was 4/14 or 39 percent.

Risk 2: Additional programming resources might be needed that were competent with the tool in Risk 1. No one in the project was familiar with the software package. The project manager asked the developers the following questions:

- Do you have any experience with the product "EquipComm"?
- How many years of experience do you have with this or similar products?
- How long would it take you to become reasonably competent with this product?
- Do you know anyone competent with this product?

The team studied a couple of scenarios requiring the software to determine if the schedule had enough slack for them to learn it. Three of the five resources could learn the tool, and their workload was only moderate at the time the work would be scheduled. They determined there was a 70 percent chance they would have the time to learn it. Therefore, the odds that an internal resource would be available and have sufficient time to learn the tool was approximately 40 percent (70 × 60). The odds an external resource would be needed would be approximately 60 percent.

Risk 3: Construction would delay deployment testing. For the construction issue, there was plenty of empirical data. One source of information was construction organizations (national and local) that could supply statistics for on-time completion. These sources were queried for late completion based on any reason—weather, client add-ons, poor performance, and so on.

The second source of information was the client. Because the integration project was a small portion of a much larger project (building and outfitting a manufacturing facility), the team asked the client's construction project manager for its risk factor. It took a lot of work to get the answer, but after some persistent questioning, the client provided a number. Lastly, the team contacted the construction company.

All sources provided risk factors that were surprisingly similar, indicating that 40 percent of construction projects of this magnitude were late. The amount of time they were late ranged from one to six months.

This calculation may appear to require a lot of work, but it is necessary to define mitigation plans and justify the findings to stakeholders. Before stakeholders will agree to added costs or delays, they need to see a complete analysis. Too many stakeholders misunderstand risk and all too often shrug it off as a way for the project manager to justify requests for additional funding. The data backs up the numbers, thereby helping defend the position and educate stakeholders.

Representing Unquantifiable Risk

Risk comes from many areas in the project and, at times, may be too general to determine a specific impact or probability. In other words, some risks are unquantifiable. Nevertheless, the team must understand their potential effect on the project.

Project conditions, such as the experience of team or project manager, the size of the project, or the use of new technology, may increase risk in unquantifiable ways. For instance, a one-month project with three people inherently has less risk than a 24-month project with 80 people on three continents speaking two languages. Unforeseen situations arise, and their chances of occurring increase as complexity increases. Handle these risks using order-of-magnitude estimates that grade them on a one-to-three or on a quintile scale for probability and impact. Various sources, such as *Identifying and Managing Project Risk: Essential Tools for Failure-Proofing Your Project* by Tom Kendrick (see Recomended Reading) provide lists of items to help guide people toward looking for failure modes.

A common presentation method is to rate unquantifiable risk on a scale of one to five for impact and probability and then plot them on a grid. Spreadsheets can use this data to generate a presentation graphic. In most cases, a scatter plot will show the density of risk in a given quadrant.

It is critical, as with all risk elements, to capture supporting information to justify the order-of-magnitude entries.

Correctly Classifying Risk for Proper Analysis

The quality of the risk items is often low because of:

- The lack of project manager's domain experience.
- The team members have an incorrect perception of the project goals.
- The identified risks are too general and need to be qualified.
- The team does not have experience with risk.

The best method for overcoming these impediments is to gather further explanation of the items. Repeatedly ask for details. Use open-ended questions to get people to explain the risk. For instance, "Why do you think construction will be late?" The answer may be that the customer has a history of asking for changes, the builder has a record of being late, it always rains in the Northwest, and so forth. These answers will help point to other risks, sources of issues, and potential mitigations. The items discovered in the drilldown may be the real issue to address in the risk register or in the task list. The goal is to determine the root cause.

For example, nearly all risk registers have an item stating key resources may leave the team. Further questioning may decompose the general risk to uncover a lack of a team atmosphere, poor management, a team member that recently left and is planning on raiding the group, no chance for advancement, low pay, a rumored layoff, and difficulty in working with the product.

This list is a mixture of issues, rumors, and other risks. The first step is to categorize the items. Table 19-3 is a summary of the types of classifications and resulting actions.

Table 19-3: Risk Analysis

Item	Type	Action
The project is experiencing poor teamwork.	Issue	Project manager: Build the team.
The project has poor management.	Issue	Project manager: Change the project management style to compensate.
A team member recently left and is planning to raid the team.	Risk	Risk: Try to work with personnel to provide incentives to stay. Remind people they are only hearing the good things about the other company.
Team members have no chance for advancement	Issue	Project manager: Look for ways to promote good individuals.
Team wages are noncompetitive.	Issue	Project manager: Talk to manager about individual pay structures. Include a project incentive.
There is a rumored layoff and people are looking for more stable positions.	Risk	Risk: Confirm rumor. If true, try to get a "contract" to exempt the project team.
The system being worked on is difficult to maintain.	Issue	Task: Add design reviews to the project.

Many of these items should be classified as something other than risk. A number of these are definite, rather than potential, items, making them issues to resolve. By making a risk an issue, it remains a problem. Add these items to the task list, while overhead items belong to the project manager.

Question all the items. For instance, classifying a product as difficult to work with is a subjective statement. Many architects and engineers simply dislike previous teams' designs and want to use their own. Instead, add a task to create design rules and reviews that provide a fixed amount of time for redesigning on an as-needed basis. Subjective items have to have some very specific targets.

For all the risk items, questions should result in acquiring enough detail to prioritize risks and generate mitigation plans.

Determining the Budgeted Cost for Risk

After understanding the risks, assess the impact. These numbers are often easier to determine than the odds of occurrence, as this is similar to building a schedule. These estimates will determine the material costs, labor rates, learning curves, and burn rates.

To turn the above example into a set of contingency values, there are a few options. If the project allows it, establish a line item contingency fund based on the estimated costs. When a risk occurs, ask for those funds. This will properly account for the contingency.

Table 19-4: Contingency Calculation

Risk			Chance of Combination	Cost			Probability Cost	Real Cost
1	2	3		1	2	3		
No	No	No	42%	-	-	-	-	-
No	No	Yes	28%	-	-	$30,000	$8,400	$30,000
Yes	No	No	7%	$1,500	-	-	$ 108	$ 1,500
Yes	No	Yes	5%	$1,500	-	$30,000	$1,512	$31,500
Yes	Yes	No	11%	$1,500	$30,000	-	$3,402	$31,500
Yes	Yes	Yes	7%	$1,500	$30,000	$30,000	$4,428	$61,500
						Risk Contingency:	$17,850	

Otherwise, use a mathematical approach to calculate the impacts' weighted average—the product of the probability and impact. Table 19-4 shows the results using data from the example risk register (Table 19-1) and the combined risk table (Table 19-2). The process takes the odds of each combination occurring and calculates the potential impact based on those numbers. The probability cost column in the table provides these numbers. This shows that the calculated contingency would be $18,000 (precision of the estimates require rounding the value).

The astute observer will note that no combinations of risks add up to $18,000. The cost of each occurrence is in the "real cost" column. The two most likely costs are nothing or $30,000. The choice of $18,000 is certainly incorrect. In addition, the worst-case scenario would result in an overrun of $61,500. This is precisely the reason people need to understand statistics.

Some schools of thought use a more conservative value, say $30,000, as it will cover risks 93 percent of the time (Table 19-5). If this value is used, management will probably trim the contingency fund since this philosophy always results in high estimates. As with critical chain estimation, avoid choosing a number achievable 90 percent of the time since this breeds lax use of money.

Other factors will also affect the decision on the proper level of contingency. For instance, in this example the unquantifiable risks were high. This could influence the decision to use the higher contingency number. If unquantifiable risks were lower, it might reinforce the $18,000 contingency.

Regardless, using a contingency less than $18,000 is incorrect. Document the contingency generation method and ensure the steering committee approves the method and the value.

Repeat this weighting process to determine the schedule impact. The project is on schedule until the expected completion date is greater than the most likely date plus the anticipated delay. This is a critical point. If managers do not understand it, they can overreact.

To determine the relative importance of risk elements, use a consistent method to relate various elements. If, for instance, two risks each having a cost impact of

Table 19-5: Odds of a Given Cost

Cost	Odds
$ 0	42%
$ 2,000	7%
~ $ 30,000	44%
$ 61,500	7%

$20,000 but one also has a 15-day schedule impact, it is easy to determine the one you should invest more time in mitigating. However, if one risk is $15,000 with a 20-day delay and another risk is $20,000 with a 10-day delay, it may be more difficult to determine on which risk to focus mitigation efforts. One common method is to convert the delay to a monetary value by multiplying it by a burn rate and using the sum of both costs to prioritize the work.

The hardest part is educating stakeholders on what these numbers mean and ensuring that the numbers are statistically as accurate as the estimates generating them.

Determining the Event's Probability

Probability of some event happening is the most subjective attribute. Unless the team has data to show a risk has executed X out of Y times while running this type of project under the similar conditions, this number could be closer to a guess. Take care in determining probabilities because small changes can have significant impact.

A common problem is to attempt to quantify all the risks. Although pressure from stakeholders is high because they want an estimation of the contingency, refuse to quantify unquantifiable risks. In technology projects, pressure to quantify risk is greater because there is a general feeling numbers can be derived for everything. To help avoid this, each risk should have a reference to how the number was generated.

In lieu of experimental data, experience from a variety of sources is the key to generating good approximations of the probability for risk execution.

The Impact if a Risk Fires

Cost and schedule impact are less subjective than probability. Regardless of the method for analyzing risk, develop a complete mitigation subplan for each risk element to estimate a reasonable cost and schedule impact. Use these numbers in a scheduling tool to determine the planned aggregate effect on the project.

Treat all mitigation plans as subcomponents to the schedule. Develop a schedule and staff it to determine the cost and effect on the project. The obvious flaw is that two risks, otherwise unrelated, may require the same resources. This is determined by comparing the various mitigation resource plans to find overloaded resources. Document any assumptions. If the probability of mutual execution is too high, mitigation plans should account for this by adjusting the resource plans. Do this by creating a secondary schedule containing those elements with conflicting resource utilization and determining the impact of mutual execution. High-end commercial risk analysis products can accommodate conditional paths and simulate random risk execution.

Tools for Calculating Risk's Impact

Most tools analyze quantifiable and unquantifiable risk. They use multiple styles of calculations to determine the likely scenarios and a window in which to forecast the risk. However, when analyzing the results of any tool, the answer is only as accurate as the input and the answers are only statistical estimates of what might happen.

Based on the estimates' genesis, classify risks as quantifiable or unquantifiable. Values for impact (cost and duration) coming from group consensus (i.e., Delphi or PERT), industry standards, prior projects, and so forth are probably quantifiable. Attributes of individual risk elements that are the intuitive feel of the project manager and the team are no more than guesses. If there is no way to make a traceable estimate, classify the risk as unquantifiable.

Document the following general factors with respect to the source of estimates:

- The team's experience and knowledge in the domain.
- The project manager's experience in estimating (or facilitating the estimation of) risk.
- The method of determining the attributes' values.

These numbers can be highly subjective and precision is far from the multiple decimal places inherent in computerized tools. Round the output from the tool—durations to the nearest day or week and financials to the nearest hundred or thousand dollars. The tools rarely do this; the user must.

Chapter Takeaway

- The project team and the stakeholders need to understand probabilities are estimates and are sometimes high or low.
- Overlooking mitigation and contingency plans is a major source of project failure.
- A risk register uses simple statistics to indicate the probable areas of failure and the impact.
- Register unquantifiable and quantifiable risks separately.
- Assess both the cost and schedule impact of all risks.
- Properly educate management on the probability of risks executing. Without this, the project will waste time with management's overreaction when an expected number of risks execute and the number appears large.

CHAPTER

20

Implementing Effective Change Management

"If you don't like something change it; if you can't change it, change the way you think about it."

—Mary Engelbreit, Children's Author and Illustrator,
Artful Words: Mary Engelbreit and the Illustrated Quotes

Improperly managing change is second only to the issues created by people in causing project failure. This is the single most important process for the project manager to implement and enforce. Improperly managing change ensures a project's demise.

Managing change, though, is more than a change management process, change control boards, and change request forms; it is the cooperative work of the project team and the customer to create a successful delivery. Although the process in this chapter is inapplicable to agile, improperly managing changes will cause an agile project to fail. On a successful project, changes have occurred in a controlled and agreed-upon manner to deliver a product that meets the customer's needs. It is unrealistic to think any project will be conceived and continue to completion without change. Allowing a project to morph in an understood and controlled manner will provide a better result than one that changes at will or one that is immutable.

Properly Handling Change During a Project

Many project managers have a poor understanding of change. They feel that giving the customer what it wants will make everyone happy and that pleasing the customer is best for the project and the organization. Unfortunately, this allows the project definition to become unclear and potentially drag on for months or years beyond its due date. The added expense can be enormous. Project managers wanting to be nice and allowing all changes are hurting the project, the product, and the customer. A common phrase from project managers who properly manage scope is, "You will like me after the project is successfully delivered."

The biggest obstacle to enforcing change management is saying no. Saying no, as hard as it may seem, is good. It is an action of accountability; it is asking for justification of the impact on the project, rather than simply asking for something in return—money, some other resource, reduction of work in another area, additional time, or some combination.

CASE STUDY 20-1:
HAVING A CHANGE MANAGEMENT
PROCESS BUT NOT USING IT

A large-scale integration project was months late. One of my first tasks was to review the change request log. Even though the project had been running for years, there were approximately 30 change orders. A properly managed project of its size should have a few hundred. I talked with the customer's project manager who told me the problem had nothing to do with change requests. Instead, the problem was that the system as conceived would not meet the customer's real requirements. I pointed out that the reason for the change request process was to make the project fit the customer's needs. The customer replied, "But that will cost us money, and these are things that should have been in the system to begin with." I added a task to build a requirements matrix from the contract to determine the project's actual scope. Although this may sound like a source of the problem, it was only one of hundreds of things wrong with the project. The good news is there was a change management process in place and occasionally it was used. The occasions were just rare.

The key is to define the change guidelines. One of the most useful tools for this is the triple constraint model. The problem with triple constraints is making sure both the customer and the project team understand the meaning and impact of defining the constraints. For instance, if the schedule is the most important constraint for the project, a change to increase scope in one area will require an offsetting reduction in scope in some other area or possibly an increase in the funds to add people to meet the deadline. Without this give and take, the team will be unable to meet the project's goal, and the project will be unsuccessful.

A simple change management process implemented at the project's initiation and strictly adhered to will set expectations early. Attempting to retrofit a strict change management process mid-project is more difficult, but much less than the problems incurred without one. Submit a change request for each deviation, whether it increases or decreases the work. The team needs to understand that any discussion of change requires approval before any work, including estimates, may proceed. For many team members, this seems overly harsh. Without this, however, resources can spend many hours investigating something out of scope without the management's knowledge or approval. Meanwhile, scheduled tasks are being delayed and resource loading is out of control.

To be sure, a change management process is just that—management instead of control. Project managers who think they must control change will be in trouble. Why? Change is inevitable. Changes in the business climate, improperly understood product requirements, realization that the product will need additional features, changes in government regulations, and competitors releasing a more competitive product are a few of the valid reasons that continuing with the current project definition will produce a product with little or no value.

Along with the customer, the project team may submit change requests. Valid reasons include technologies with performance issues, requirements that are more complex than originally estimated, and product vendors discontinuing product support. Regardless of these issues, the team must assess the impact and adjust the project plans.

It is possible for changes on the project to become excessive. The first sign of disproportionate change is the effect on team members. They will be unable to finish their scheduled tasks because evaluating the change requests is consuming too much time or implementation of the requests will modify the essence of their work. At this point, the project needs some form of management review, as it is now drifting far from its original intent. A more logical approach may be to cancel and restart it under a new premise. If this is the case, stop accepting change requests and convene a steering committee meeting to get direction on how to proceed. The project is slowing down and that is costing time and money.

CASE STUDY 20-2: BEING LATE ON A PROJECT AND ADDING SCOPE TO MAKE IT BETTER

When projects start running late, the stress and pressure makes people do strange things. The most common is the customer asking for additional functionality and the supplier agreeing to provide it free of charge. This is the result of the supplier's project manager trying to compensate for mistakes. Of course, in the calm of reading this book, this action seems absurd.

In a project delivering an automation system, the schedule had slid nearly a year. The customer wanted to get the system partially installed and demanded the ability to run the system in a nonautomated manner. Since the system's primary purpose was to automate the processes on the manufacturing floor, this required redesigning each operation to accommodate the new mode. The project manager, who was under immense pressure and felt bad about the project being late, relented and approved the change request. She did it at no cost. The project was late (hence, it experienced severe budget problems), the team was overworked, and there was now a huge amount of additional work to do at no charge.

During the recovery, I reversed the change request.

Minimizing the Impact of Change in a Project

Minimizing the effects of change is a key responsibly of the project manager and the project sponsor. The project constraints may require a zero sum effect from any change orders. Thus, to maintain the delivery date, scope cannot increase. Horse trading—the act of swapping one item for another of equivalent value—is a valuable process. It maintains the scope, timeline, and budget at relatively even values throughout the project, but it adds complexity to the change, as there really are two changes. Both the customer and the project team work to identify an equivalent amount of scope for removal, while holding the schedule and resources constant.

There is no better illustration of this than in the agile methodology. As discussed in Chapter 11, agile allows as much to be done in one iteration as possible. The team determines the features for each time-boxed iteration. If time starts to run out, the team (customer and developer) determine what to remove to achieve a deployable product in the time allotted. This is simply trading out less valuable features for those of greater value. From iteration to iteration, the customer may add different features that have become more valuable to the product based on any number of factors. Less valuable features slide down the list. At the project's completion (defined by a fixed number of iterations), the customer gets the product as it has been developed. The customer may buy more iterations if the product fails to meet the required value.

Defining and Processing a Change Request

As opposed to this book's philosophy on omitting rudimentary process definition, change management is such a significant source of project failure that a generic change request process must be mentioned. Figure 20-1 and Figure 20-2 are flow chart representations of a change request process. The process is broke into two phases:

1. Submission and Impact, and
2. Evaluate and Approve.

The logical break between the two flows is the change request's impact assessment.

Submission and Impact Assessment Review Steps

Submission and impact review determines the effect of evaluating the change request. This step captures two primary pieces of data:

1. Whether the work to evaluate the change will detract too much from the project, and
2. A high-level estimate to assess the change's feasibility.

In the initial review, the project manager and project sponsor (or other change review group) will reject change requests they determine have an excessive impact on the project without presenting an offsetting and immediate benefit. Rejecting change requests in the review phase is more predominant later in the project. By that stage of development, the product has already passed through a series of design and development commitments. Thus, the process of determining the effect of a change on the project will have, in and of itself, a significant effect on the project.

If management approves the impact assessment, the change request proceeds to the next step of the process.

Evaluation and Approval Steps

Evaluation and approval determines the change request's actual impact on the scope, schedule, and budget. The team documents the details and estimates the

Figure 20-1: Change Request: Submit and Impact Review

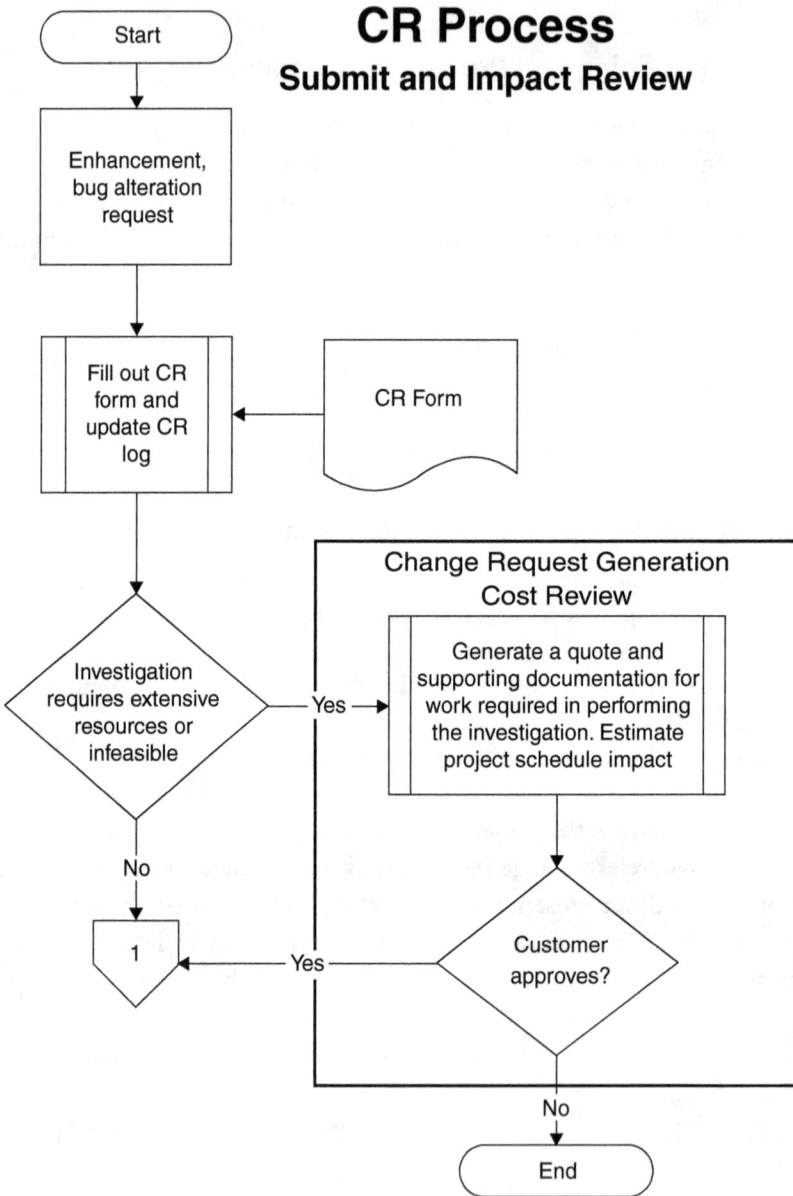

Figure 20-2: Change Request: Evaluate and Approve

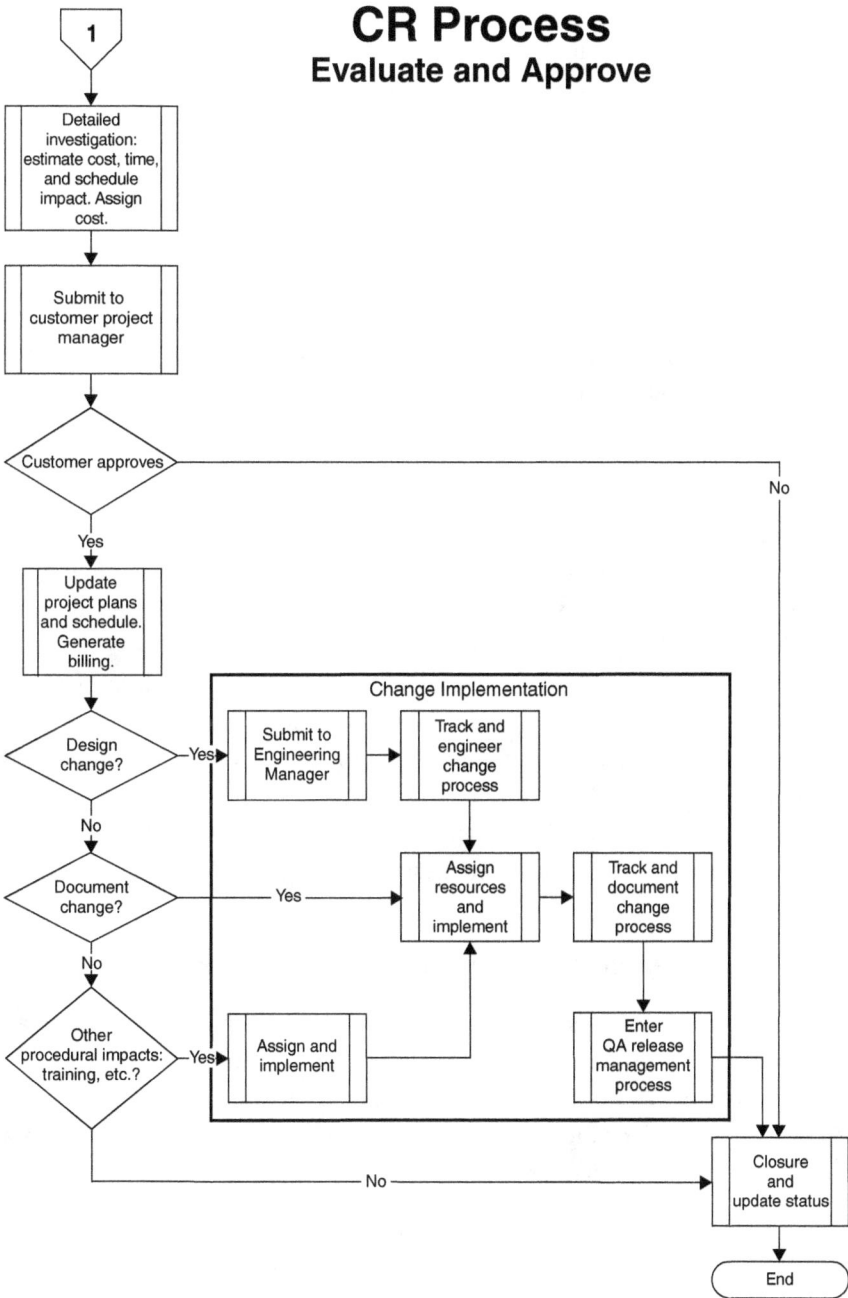

CR Process
Evaluate and Approve

1

Detailed investigation: estimate cost, time, and schedule impact. Assign cost.

Submit to customer project manager

Customer approves — No

Yes

Update project plans and schedule. Generate billing.

Change Implementation

Design change? — Yes → Submit to Engineering Manager → Track and engineer change process

No

Document change? — Yes → Assign resources and implement → Track and document change process

No

Other procedural impacts: training, etc.? — Yes → Assign and implement

Enter QA release management process

No

Closure and update status

End

change's effort for all items added and removed. All areas of the project team must evaluate the change request—architecture, engineering, quality assurance, training, and product documentation. After completion, they return it to the project manager and the project sponsor for approval. After approval, the team incorporates the change into the appropriate product specifications and project plans. Please note this process is general; it is up to the user to determine the other areas of the project affected.

The Five Sections of a Change Request Form

The request itself contains enough information to manage and implement the change. Some large projects use two forms, a change request and a change order, but in most cases, a single form will suffice. There are five sections to the form (see Appendix):

- *Initiation.* This section includes the change request's basic description. If the change requires significant information, attach on another sheet.
- *Investigation/Recommendation.* If the change request is approved for investigation, this will provide the results of the analysis from the team. It will also outline the solution for implementing the change.
- *Impact.* This section contains the change's cost and schedule impact. It will enumerate the groups affected and the documents to create or modify.
- *Approvals.* This section is the signoff section for the proper project representatives.
- *Verification.* This area will contain either the verification that the change was tested or that the test plans were modified to accommodate the change.

Tracking Change Requests in a Log

Projects can have hundreds of change requests, so track their status in a log. Spreadsheets are ideal for creating logs. Store the log in a mutually accessible area for the extended project team. This minimizes requests for status updates.

A log should list all change requests and change orders regardless of their status. It should include each request's current state and who is working on it.

Chapter Takeaway

- Failing to follow a change management process is a significant contributor to project failure.
- Lack of a change management process manifests itself in scope creep.
- Rather than controlling or stopping change, a change management process manages change so its effects are defined and disseminated properly.
- The project manager may stop all change requests in the later stages of a project since the evaluation process may have too big an impact on the project.

Appendix: Files on the *Rescue the Problem Project* Web Site

The *Rescue the Problem Project* Web site <http://www.rescuetheproblemproject.com> includes many useful items that enhance this book. In addition to templates, process descriptions, and tools, it also has a calendar of when and where lectures will be held on project recovery techniques.

Some of the items you will find there are:

- A discussion of ways to communicate effectively with management, including templates for the tools.
- A discussion on managing remote projects.
- Tools for estimating.
- An educational tool to show the effects of risk in a project.
- Change management process and templates.
- A meeting minutes template.
- The scope creep worksheet discussed in Chapter 4.
- Some project status templates.
- A document outlining the efficient use of Microsoft Word® in a project, along with a generic project document template.
- Additional case studies.
- Project audit report.

These are available free to any registered user. Please access and review the Web site to see how to make your life easier.

Endnotes

1. Project Management Institute, *A Guide to the Project Management Body of Knowledge,* 4th ed. (Newtown Square, PA: Project Management Institute, 2008), 442.
2. The Stationery Office (TSO), *Managing Successful Projects with PRINCE[2]* (Norwich, UK: The Stationery Office, 2009,) 3.
3. Frederick Brookes, *The Mythical Man-Month,* (Boston, MA: Addison-Wesley, 1995), 154.
4. Eliyahu Goldratt, *Critical Chain* (Great Barrington, MA: North River Press, 1997), 124-125.
5. Jeffery Liker, *The Toyota Way* (New York: McGraw-Hill, 2003), 239-140.
6. Eliyahu Goldratt, *Critical Chain* (Great Barrington, MA: North River Press, 1997), 43-47.
7. Frederick Brookes, *The Mythical Man-Month,* (Boston, MA: Addison-Wesley, 1995), 55.

Recommended Reading

Frederick Brooks. *The Mythical Man-Month*. Boston: Addison-Wesley, 1995.

> The *Mythical Man-Month* was originally published in 1975. It is based on Mr. Brooks' experiences in the 1960s building the IBM 360 architecture. The lessons learned are the same as we are facing today. Reading and understanding these lessons will alert the reader to address the issues early to avert their reoccurrence.

Brian Dietmeyer, Max Bazerman, and Rob Kaplan. *Strategic Negotiation: A Breakthrough Four-Step Process for Effective Business Negotiation*. Chicago: Dearborn, 2004.

> *Strategic Negotiation* discusses the negotiation process in detail in the same general order covered in this book. It explains the negotiation process in more detail in relation to sales.

Roger Fisher, William L. Ury, and Bruce Patton. *Getting to Yes, Negotiating Agreement Without Giving in*. New York: Penguin, 1991.

> *Getting to Yes* is the definitive book on successful negotiation. It focuses on the win-win strategy required for any successful negotiation and recovery.

Eliyahu Goldratt. *Critical Chain*. Great Barrington, MA: North River Press, 1997.

> *Critical Chain,* a business novel, defines the concepts of the critical chain methodology in simple terms. It is an excellent introductory book.

Jim Highsmith. *Agile Project Management: Creating Innovative Products*. Boston: Addison-Wesley, 2004.

> Highsmith is one of the pioneers of agile. This book defines the entire agile process in a generic product environment, as is used in *Rescue the Problem Project*.

Tom Kendrick. *Identifying and Managing Project Risk: Essential Tools for Failure-Proofing Your Project*. New York: AMACOM, 2003.

Identifying and Managing Project Risk is a comprehensive text that addresses risk in a holistic approach. Highly recommended for deeper understanding of addressing risk.

Lawrence Leach. *Critical Chain Project Management,* 2nd ed. Boston: Artech House, 2005.

Critical Chain Project Management takes up where Goldratt's book leaves off, providing details of critical chain methodology in the sufficient detail to implement it in an organization.

Jeffrey Liker. *The Toyota Way.* New York: McGraw-Hill, 2003.

The Toyota Way is the best selling book on the Toyota production system (TPS). It discusses numerous management techniques and methods for working with people and lean processes.

Terri Morrison and Wayne A. Conaway. *Kiss, Bow, or Shake Hands: The Bestselling Guide to Doing Business in More Than 60 Countries,* Avon, MA: Adams Media Corporation, 2006.

This is an excellent book on cultural differences and provides information on individual regions, including Latin America, Asia, and Europe

Sanjiv Purba and Joseph Zucchero. *Project Rescue: Avoiding a Project Management Disaster.* New York: Osborne/McGraw-Hill, 2004.

Project Rescue provides a solid review of the remedial processes required to execute a project properly.

Ken Schwaber. *Agile Project Management with Scrum.* Redmond, WA: Microsoft Press, 2004

Schwaber, another agile pioneer, covers agile from a software development perspective. It is complementary to Highsmith's agile project management book.

Louis Testa. *Growing Software, Proven Strategies for Managing Software Engineers.* San Francisco: No Starch Press, 2009

Testa covers the basics of managing people in a software development environment. This book is an excellent resource for people new to software development, but is applicable to nearly any discipline.

Index